OUR LADY OF T]

Shrines and visionaries are believed to be indicators of the *presence* of Mary. In the visionary perspective, she has appeared in order to reassure her followers and to warn of divine judgement. Her messages echo doctrinal Catholic Mariology with some innovations, but also express a deep dissatisfaction with the events and trends of the twentieth century, from communism to Nazism to liberalism and religious indifference. While the Marian cult evolves according to new templates for apparitions and developments in Mariology, the fundamental message of presence, consolation, and admonition remains constant.

Our Lady of the Nations is a detailed and scholarly overview of the apparitions of Mary in twentieth-century Catholic Europe. Chris Maunder discusses apparitions in general and how they are interpreted by leading figures in Catholicism, such as Karl Rahner and Benedict XVI. Maunder considers the role of women and children as visionaries, and shows how the status of visionary allows women the opportunity to contribute to Catholic theology and spirituality. He covers cases that are well known and approved by the Church (Fatima, Beauraing, Banneux, and Amsterdam), others that are well known but not approved (such as Garabandal and Medjugorje), and many that are neither well known nor approved, such as those in Belgian Flanders or Nazi Germany in the 1930s, or in France, Italy, or Germany after the Second World War. Resources include academic studies of particular apparitions, Catholic theological and devotional literature, and travel writing.

Chris Maunder is Senior Lecturer in Theology and Religious Studies at York St John University and the Chair of Trustees of the Centre for Marian Studies. His publications include *Origins of the Cult of the Virgin Mary* (Bloomsbury, 2008) and *Documents of the Christian Church* (co-edited with Henry Bettenson; OUP, 2011).

Our Lady of the Nations

Apparitions of Mary in Twentieth-Century Catholic Europe

CHRIS MAUNDER

OXFORD
UNIVERSITY PRESS

OXFORD

UNIVERSITY PRESS

Great Clarendon Street, Oxford, OX2 6DP,
United Kingdom

Oxford University Press is a department of the University of Oxford.
It furthers the University's objective of excellence in research, scholarship,
and education by publishing worldwide. Oxford is a registered trade mark of
Oxford University Press in the UK and in certain other countries

First published 2016
First published in paperback 2018

Published in the United States of America by Oxford University Press
198 Madison Avenue, New York, NY 10016, United States of America

British Library Cataloguing in Publication Data

Data available

Library of Congress Cataloging in Publication Data

Data available

ISBN 978–0–19–871838–3 (Hbk.)
ISBN 978–0–19–878864–5 (Pbk.)

*To my wonderful wife Natalie, for her love,
companionship, and shared passion for Marian shrines!*

Preface

On 2 March 1983, I visited Westminster Cathedral and quite by accident came across a low-key celebration marking the fiftieth anniversary of the apparitions of Mary in Banneux, Belgium. This was the first time that Marian apparitions caught my full attention, although I had heard of Lourdes, of course. Five years later, I was staying in a hotel at Banneux owned by the visionary Mariette Beco, by then in her sixties, while undertaking a PhD on the subject. My thesis focused on approved modern European apparitions from the Rue du Bac to Banneux as well as famous and controversial cases such as that at Medjugorje in Bosnia-Herzegovina, which was already drawing pilgrims in great numbers. However, in the years following, I became more interested in lesser-known apparition shrines in Western Europe and carried out research visits to Ireland, Belgium, Germany, France, and Italy. Discovering out-of-the-way places brings the researcher of shrines and apparitions into contact with nation, region, and locality in ways that often elude the pilgrim or tourist.

My research supervisor, the Church historian Adrian Hastings, warned me that the literature on my subject would not be abundant. In terms of insider literature written by Catholics, this was not the case; I found a whole section and several shelves of a Catholic bookshop in Paris dedicated to it. However, as far as academic literature was concerned, he was correct, with material on apparitions often limited to small sections in books on wider topics and the occasional article. Yet, as I handed in my thesis in 1991, I learned that a book on Marian apparitions, *Encountering Mary: From La Salette to Medjugorje*, had just been published by Sandra Zimdars-Swartz in Princeton. It seemed that the collective unconscious was stirring in terms of academic studies on Catholic apparitions; since then, there been several detailed academic studies on particular modern visions by scholars such as David Blackbourn, William Christian, Paolo Apolito, Ruth Harris, Eugene Hynes, and Jeffrey Bennett, and articles by researchers Peter Margry and Tine van Osselaer from the Netherlands and Belgium, respectively. So now there seems to be a need for a volume that takes the general subject forward from *Encountering Mary* by bringing together the data and theory given in those resources. However, for the task to be manageable, I have limited my research to Europe in the twentieth century.

This work concentrates on times and places where apparitions have been especially prevalent and popular, and where there is some supporting documentation. A comprehensive survey would result in an encyclopaedia, like that in French by Laurentin and Sbalchiero, whereas this volume explores and discusses a wide sample of Marian apparitions, including the famous and those of which the reader may not have heard. One learns a great deal about twentieth-century European history when researching this subject: apparitions and shrines reflect a variety of contexts from the First World War to the Internet. Of particular interest is the fact that the great majority of Marian visionaries who gain popular acceptance are women or girls.

My acknowledgements go to all those custodians of shrines, pilgrims, and priests whom I met on research visits or with whom I have corresponded; they have been very generous with their time in offering me information and hospitality. I know how much they care about the shrines in which they are involved and I hope I have represented them justly in a book that is academic rather than devotional. I also thank colleagues for their support during the writing of this book. York St John University has provided me with a fulfilling career for over twenty years and aided the writing of this book with funding for research travel. The Centre for Marian Studies has given me the inspiration of fellow researchers who share my niche subject across a variety of disciplines; my thanks go especially to its director, Sarah Jane Boss, who has always been a great encouragement. Professor Adrian Hastings, who died in 2001, was very important at the beginning of my academic career and I am indebted to him. Thank you also to Angela Volpini, for allowing me to use her photograph for the cover, and to Laura Casimo, who provided the translation of Angela's website.

Finally, I am very grateful to the two women whom the University appointed as my student research assistants in 2010–11; my thanks to Natalie Leavy and Nicola Beales for their useful resource-finding on European apparitions. Natalie's passion for the subject, including her willingness to go on shrine-hunting trips even after her studies were over, is one reason among many for our engagement and we will be married by the time this book is published. So my greatest appreciation goes to her for her constant companionship, support, and love.

Chris Maunder

31 May 2015

Note on Terminology

This book uses the pairs of terms 'apparition' and 'vision', 'visionary' and 'seer' interchangeably as synonyms.

The word 'cult', when applied to Marian apparitions, has the sense of the Latin *cultus*, i.e. all those activities surrounding a focus of faith, and should not be read as having any pejorative meaning implying deviance, as used in the media and some sections of academia.

Contents

List of Tables

List of Plates

18. Schio, Veneto, Italy. A photograph of the visionary Renate Baron next to a statue of the Madonna at the summit of the Stations of the Cross (author photo: September 2014). Renate's apparitions continued from 1985 until his death in 2004.

19. Gargallo di Carpi, Emilia-Romagna, Italy. The small shrine at the edge of vineyards bears witness to the apparitions of Gianni Varini and others between 1984 and 1993 (author photo: September 2014).

1

Introduction

Apparitions of Mary in the Twentieth Century

In certain towns, villages, and hamlets in Catholic countries or regions, individuals or groups may stir up their communities by announcing that they have seen the Virgin Mary, perhaps even that she has passed on messages through them. This frequently attracts interest and curiosity, sometimes a local or regional following, and occasionally a mass pilgrimage. Depending on the level of devotion, a small memorial may come to be erected, or a modest chapel, or a church, or even a great basilica visited by popes. The story of these shrines contains valuable information about the period, society, and Catholic culture in which they emerge. Some visionaries become celebrities; around half of all twentieth-century European Marian visionaries were children or adolescents, and about seventy per cent of these visionaries were female. This may suggest something about the expectations in modern Catholic belief about the age and gender of popular intermediaries as distinct from the adult males who make up the priesthood of the Church.

This volume offers a social and cultural history of apparitions of Mary in twentieth-century Europe and the cults and shrines that develop around them. Popular theology, prophecy, Mariology, and relationships between the Church hierarchy and Catholic networks all developed and evolved throughout the last century. Many cases of visions are discussed across a broad sweep of history in several nations, but there is coherence between these because people who believe in apparitions, who maintain or visit the shrines, regard themselves as part of a common culture. Marian apparitions display many common themes and similar experiences even though their contexts are diverse. The movements arising from them are not always in agreement and present challenges both to the societies in which they occur and to the Catholic Church of which they are a part. Yet, in general, devotees identify themselves with an international community of belief which argues that a divine initiative through Mary towards modern humanity is taking place and this community is fully aware of its own history.

The discussion in this volume neither devalues the phenomena in a reductionist analysis nor promotes them as urgent, divinely inspired messages. Rather, it explores the community and national contexts of apparitions, and shows how the reports link up to produce a global story of apparitions that is important to many millions of people and which is shared through pilgrimage, publication, and social networking. In her work on Pontmain, Cheryl Porte, a Missionary Sister of the Sacred Heart of Jesus, criticizes the reductionist approach to apparitions: 'the presence of psychological or political factors does not simply blot out the religious reality of the apparitional experience' (Porte 2005: 157). However, she is not suggesting that these contextual factors be overlooked as she is equally critical of what she calls 'a-historical studies' (Porte 2005: 154–6). By this she means publications by Catholic devotees of apparitions that concentrate on a description of the original experience in an attempt to establish theological authenticity and, in the process, ignore the social and historical background which is integral to any apparition event. The regional histories, devotions, hopes, fears, expectations, mythologies, and points of tension all play their part in the story of an apparition. For Porte, the enterprise involved in understanding this is grounded in traditional Catholic theology articulated by those such as Irenaeus and Aquinas: 'the Church has always taught that our experience of God is mediated or known through what is visible, created, and historical' (Porte 2005: 157).

Writing on Marian apparitions belongs to various categories. The polarity identified by Porte can probably be expanded into four types: first, the social scientific, which uses one or more of a range of scholarly perspectives—sociological, psychological, social historical, and anthropological. These explore the context in which an apparition occurs, individual and communal, but there is no judgement on whether there is anything 'supernatural' involved. The second is the theological, written by an insider (in the case of Catholic Marian apparitions, usually a priest–theologian); these will explore the cases critically and often to the end of distinguishing authentic visions from others. This approach certainly does assess the supernatural nature of a vision. Such works may often be examples of 'faith seeking understanding', where a theologian has accepted the value of an apparition, usually because the decision of the Church is in its favour, and wishes to explore it in depth although not without criticality. Then there is the third type, what could be called the devotional literature written by insiders, those who wish to promote particular apparitions (sometimes all apparitions) and seek interpretations that inspire and guide believers. Finally, the fourth type includes works in which authors claim to find a sensational aspect, either from a journalistic perspective, perhaps claiming that fabrication, collusion, and communal self-interest are hidden in the background to a widely accepted phenomenon, or using what could loosely be called a 'New Age' approach, for example the association of a case with UFO or psychic phenomena.

Avoiding the ahistorical approach by taking into account contextual factors establishes the uniqueness of each apparition case, a particularity that should never be overlooked. The chapters in this volume show how particular cases have their own dynamics and characteristics; nevertheless, general patterns will be identified too. While visions occur regularly, they have greater impact during periods of ideological conflict and rapid social change. Devotees will come to this conclusion just as quickly as sociologists but from the opposite direction, the former seeing the apparition as a divine answer to crisis, the latter identifying communal anxiety as the contextual trigger that gives rise to visionary cults. In the well-known statement of Victor and Edith Turner, visions 'appear at the point of major stress between contrary cultures and their major definitions of reality' (Turner and Turner 1982: 150). At these critical times, they can be co-opted by a national or international pressure movement. Lourdes was taken up in the cause of monarchical restoration in the 1870s, Beauraing by fascist nationalists in the 1930s; however, both shrines survived the demise of these movements because the original messages by children made no reference to politics. Religious people who feel alienated from social trends and priorities will seek divine sanction for alternatives, and visions (whatever the original messages did or did not state) can be readily accepted as evidence for this. Sandra Zimdars-Swartz concluded that 'the experience of a typical seer or devotee of a modern Marian apparition is ... an experience framed and defined by crisis' (Zimdars-Swartz 1991: 267). The crisis can be personal—the desire for healing, for example—or social and political. Marian apparitions have been vital supports in the Catholic Church's response to its perceived enemies of the last two centuries: republicanism, communism, moral liberalism, and religious indifference.

Much of the analysis of apparitions in this volume focuses on reactions to social change leading to prophecies of divine punishment. However, there are also more positive features of apparition messages. New shrines represent religious renewal, which is especially important during times of decline in church attendance; the apparitions of successive centuries serve to renovate the network of shrines, and those of the twentieth century have done so in their turn. There are messages of divine love as well as divine displeasure at many shrines, perhaps more of the former.

How many apparitions of Mary were there in the last century? A study can only deal with cases that have been publicized. What criteria for selection are there? This will depend on the chronicler. One approach could be to include every case that comes to one's attention, another to try and limit the list based on some principle concerning numbers of devotees, impact on the wider Church, or persistence of the cult. In this volume, all the famous twentieth-century cases in Catholic communities in Europe are explored along with many others that had some impact at the time, but these are only a subset of all the recorded apparition events. What an academic study cannot do is to examine only those cases that have been canonically approved by the Church, as then the selection would be shaped only in conformity with Catholic hierarchical criteria. Furthermore, certain times and places have enjoyed more Church approval of visions than others, another factor that would skew the data. Another complication is that apparitions are part of a wider spectrum of mysterious experiences, which include moving statues or pictures. Herbert Thurston (1934: 45–116) understood these as comparable with visions as phenomena that some people see, others do not, and those who see do not see all of the time. There are also locutions (hearing but not seeing a supernatural person). Statues are sometimes reported to bleed or weep. Nevertheless, Catholic pilgrimage is more evident at a site where visionaries have reported a mystical manifestation of a lifelike figure independent of physical objects such as statues, even if these are close by. Apparitions in this sense have priority over lesser apparitions, such as moving statues.

Trying to include every case would be an impossible task. Apparitions of Mary have been reported on battlefields before a victory: for example, during the First World War for the French on the Marne in 1914, and during the Polish–Soviet War for the Poles near Warsaw in 1920, the so-called 'Miracle on the Vistula'. These are two prominent cases among many wartime examples. In peacetime, small-scale apparitions are abundant. Recently, in Oirsbeek, a small town in the Netherlands, a couple turned their compact terraced house into a chapel (the word 'kapel' is written above the front door), with rows of chairs in the tightly packed living room. Everywhere there are statues, some of which have traces of red liquid streaking down from the eyes, as these are claimed to be bleeding statues. The wife claims to experience visions and suffer stigmata. The husband helps her promulgate the messages; there are visitors who sign a book and presumably many of these are followers of some kind. The local Catholic diocese disapproves, but the impression given is that the whole operation is on a very small scale. Can this be included? How many such cases exist around the world?

In attempts to record comprehensively the incidence of Marian apparitions through Catholic history, there are encyclopaedias of Marian apparitions in French (Laurentin and Sbalchiero 2007, also available in Italian) and German (Hierzenberger and Nedomansky 1996). There are also many lists of apparitions on the Internet. On the whole, these sources, books and websites, include anything that comes to their attention. The inclusion of so many sites discouraged or ignored by the Church hierarchy shows that there is a Catholic fascination for these phenomena that goes beyond canonical boundaries. There is a sense that the officials of the Church may have overlooked experiences and messages that may be of interest. Yet the lists cannot be regarded as exhaustive in charting the occurrence of apparitions geographically and historically, as they depend on the research methods and the availability of the data. It is not clear how the information was obtained or whether data from certain countries would have been more accessible to the researchers. Furthermore, knowledge of visionary cases would be more extensive where, in a particular period and region, written material provided lists of visions.

With these caveats in mind, some of these sources are useful nonetheless for identifying trends, particularly in Europe. Take, for example, two well-known web-based lists of apparitions of Mary in the twentieth century, those of the Catholic and Marianist University of Dayton, Ohio, and 'Miracle Hunter' (<http://campus.udayton.edu/mary/resources/aprtable.html> and <http://www.miraclehunter.com/marian_apparitions>, both accessed 31 May 2015). From them, trends can be discerned which conform to information from other sources. First, one can identify certain years in which there have been what are referred to as 'epidemics' of Marian visions. These are: Belgium 1933; Italy 1947–8; Italy 1953–4. As William A. Christian Jr (1984) demonstrated, the period 1947–54 saw a dramatic increase in the number of apparitions in Europe, especially in Italy. The multiplicity of visions in that period can be understood as a response to concerns over the emerging Cold War crisis, where Catholics were alarmed at the incursion of Soviet influence into central Europe and the possibility of communists gaining ground in post-war democratic societies. Although these anxieties did not wholly abate in 1954, Western European economies were strengthening, and it is only in Italy that the apparitions continued in any numbers. Eastern Europe did see apparitions after the war (e.g. in Yugoslavia, Alexander 1979: 64–7; Christian 1984: 252–3; web searches also reveal visions recorded in Hungary and Ukraine), but Paolo Apolito is likely to be correct when he suggests that many apparitions there remained unknown because communist regimes suppressed publications and pilgrimage (2005: 24–5).

After a quieter period in the 1960s and 1970s (with the exception of a couple of famous and controversial cases in Spain and Italy), the apparition world erupted again in the 1980s. There was a boom in the years following the Medjugorje case (from 1981 in Bosnia-Herzegovina), especially in Italy and Ireland. Reasons for this include the accession of Pope John Paul II from Poland, a country with strong Marian pilgrimage traditions; his contribution to the ideological revolution in Eastern Europe leading to the downfall of the Soviet bloc occurred while the coming millennium encouraged apocalyptic expectations. Also, the decline of traditional Marian devotions in Catholic parishes following the Second Vatican Council (Vatican II) in the 1960s may have made large-scale apparition shrines more attractive to those who wished to express their Marian spirituality and thus increased the likelihood of widespread interest in apparition claims. In the 1990s, interest in shrines continued as the Internet emerged as a major source of information: it became easier to find out about new sites of visions and cheaper air travel allowed people to visit sites from considerable distances away. Yet new cases of apparitions declined considerably in Europe in the 1990s, although not in the United States.

VISIONARY PHENOMENA, VISIONARIES, AND SHRINES

Apparitions are ancient and widespread experiences; humans in all cultures have experienced them throughout the centuries and they continue to be prevalent in the world today. In the 1980s, the Society for Psychical Research in the UK suggested that as many as ten per cent of the modern British population have seen or heard something at least once that quite clearly does not belong to the everyday world of materials and objects (Green and McCreery 1989). The vision seems realistic, but the seer knows it cannot be. How do they know that it is not real? It hovers; it disappears; it walks through walls or doors; it is surrounded by a strange oval halo of light; it is a person known or later found to have died. The interpretation of this kind of experience will depend on one's world view. Those who do not believe in the possibility of supernatural vision will conclude that it was an attempt to defraud, an illusion, or that the visionary suffered delusions. Even people who do accept the possibility might initially have the same reaction, disbelieving that a particular person could be the subject of such an experience. Many famous Catholic visionaries were disbelieved by their families when they first reported the experience, some quite forcefully. However, at least these relatives did not dismiss the possibility of a vision out of hand, even if they were suspicious of that particular one. Believing in ghosts and spirits, or being a member of a religion in which visions are regarded as a possible means of communication with the divine, leaves open the possibility of accepting the phenomenon as a genuine manifestation of the supernatural.

A believer's record of the event is very likely to conform to the expectations of the particular faith system to which they adhere. Non-Catholics do not usually see Mary, for example (as is evidenced in the records held at the Alister Hardy Religious Experience Research Centre at the University of Wales). However, if an apparition conforms to religious expectations, then there is just the small possibility that others with the same world view will be stimulated by the account of the experience and wonder if the visionary or visionaries could be a channel for some kind of communication with the supernatural. Belief that this is happening will be more likely if it is stimulated by one or more of the characteristics indicating realism, among which are: (a) the powerful charisma of the trance state of the visionary; (b) more than one visionary reporting the same experience; (c) the visionary or visionaries repeating the experience several times, during which the crowd of onlookers may increase in numbers; (d) actions that convey realism. Children are particularly expressive during apparitions and convince onlookers by displays of ordinary interaction with invisible presences: among others, photographs show Angela Volpini of Casanova Staffora in Italy (who experienced visions between 1947 and 1956, see Chapter 11) presenting a toddler for the Virgin to bless; the girls of Garabandal in Spain (1961–5, Chapter 12) holding up religious objects for the Virgin to kiss; Angela Volpini and the children at Heroldsbach in Germany (1949–52, Chapter 11) carrying the infant Jesus that, apparently, only they could see.

That such a significant percentage of the population has some kind of visionary experience means that research into Roman Catholic visions of Mary is not a study of apparitions per se. It is actually an investigation into those phenomena where a significant number of Catholics accepted the genuine status of the seer or seers and attempted to promote them as significant prophets. This brings the event into the public domain. It becomes a social phenomenon worthy of the attention of historians such as David Blackbourn (1993) who studied the apparitions at Marpingen in German Saarland in 1876. Blackbourn shows how the history of something apparently as parochial and subjective as visions can illustrate conditions in the wider society; by studying Marpingen, the reader learns a great deal about the newly unified Germany of the 1870s. This is also true of studies with twentieth-century contexts, such as Jeffrey S. Bennett (2012) on Fátima and the Portugal of the First World War period, and Christian (1996) on Ezkioga and the Second Spanish Republic (1931–9).

Apparitions are communal phenomena. As soon as visionaries are identified, they cease to be the sole participants in the encounter. Other people in the locality will now assume that the occurrence has some relevance for them, even if they cannot see or hear anything (or perhaps they do also experience visions, but far less intense and compelling ones). While only certain people have the gift of being a 'seer', it does not mean that the 'seeing' is purely a private matter. Studies in the 1980s and 1990s by Zimdars-Swartz (1989) on Melleray, Ireland, Christian (1996) on Ezkioga, Spain, and Apolito (1998) on Oliveto Citra, Italy, have shown how local priests and prominent laypeople play their part in the establishment of the visionary messages. There is a process of editing, by which some unsuitable messages from the visionaries are left out, noteworthy experiences emphasized, and an official narrative constructed. 'What has begun as an oral process within a community responding to some unusual experiences thus leads, finally, to a written account, which is usually printed and often widely distributed . . . ' (Zimdars-Swartz 1991: 15, writing about Melleray). This process is likely to present the apparitions in a doctrinally orthodox way to the wider Catholic community more robustly than the original oral reports.

Apolito shows that what took place at Oliveto Citra was a construction of an objective apparition narrative from a chaotic melange of visionary experiences, but this ultimately failed in terms of gaining a positive Church response: the sheer numbers of reported apparitions at Oliveto Citra did not help the cause of the visions (Apolito 1998: 100–16; Laurentin 1991: 95), which was also the case at Ezkioga. Apparitions have a more favourable standing in the Catholic community if particular seers can be singled out amongst multiple reports; at Lourdes and Beauraing, for example, many visions followed the initial apparitions, and so maintaining the spotlight on the original visionaries proved crucial to the success and formal approval of the apparitions in both cases. Overall, it is more correct to talk of an apparition 'event', which involves a set of relationships and selective decision-making within a community, rather than an apparition as a one-way communication process from seer to onlookers.

Blackbourn (1993: 17–57) establishes the way in which apparitions empower visionaries, a theme also explored by Michael Allen (2000) in relation to Irish visions. In the history of religions, visionaries are deemed to be mediators with the divine and/or supernatural. Once a prominent visionary has been identified, they may gain a special role as one who articulates a 'popular theology'. This helps the visionary to regain control over the development of the cult which they may have lost during the period when the believing community acted as editors shaping the content of the messages. In the nineteenth and twentieth centuries (although not necessarily before this: Nolan and Nolan 1989; Laurentin 1991: 117; Carroll 1983), women and girls dominated the world of Catholic Marian visions. In doing so, they enjoyed considerable influence and status that surpassed that of other women in the Catholic Church. For the most part, the visionary mode of knowledge has provided the major opportunity in Catholicism for women to articulate influential theological and devotional ideas. Of course, for messages to gain wide acceptance, they have to be reported as verbatim statements by the Virgin Mary and need to be expressed within the orthodoxy of traditional Catholicism. Furthermore, in the modern period, the Church has tended to prefer the messages of children as opposed to those of adult women (as attested to by Bertone and Ratzinger 2000: 37). The question as to whether children can be thrust into the role of public visionary in the changing social context of the twenty-first century is explored in Chapter 6. In the twentieth century, however, the Catholic Church responded positively in certain cases to the messages of children, which are generally simpler and less open to speculation than the often complex reports of adults, the latter more aware of social, political, and ecclesiastical factors. Nevertheless, within these constraints, and sometimes stretching them, the visionaries may develop their theology either through visions or afterwards, reflecting on apparitions. Twentieth-century examples of adult women as 'popular theologians' include

Lúcia dos Santos of Fátima (1907–2005), discussed in Chapter 3, Jeanne-Louise Ramonet of Kerizinen (1910–95) and Ida Peerdeman of Amsterdam (1905–96), both discussed in Chapter 10, and Angela Volpini of Casanova Staffora (1940–), in Chapter 11.

Apparitions and visionaries are very often rooted in a geographical location and the site should not be overlooked. It is the shrine as centre of pilgrimage that carries forward the story to new generations, and the story of an apparition can be transmitted through symbols often more powerfully than in written words. It is important for pilgrims to see the existence of a shrine as a result of divine initiative, and so a founding narrative that includes visions, healings, and miracles has an important function. It is often a narrative of transformation. Shrines may be associated with grand churches and regular pilgrimages as centres of regional interest, but the site before the apparitions may have been derelict, irrelevant, obscure, or worse. Sites of apparitions may have been spooky places associated with the spirits of the dead or devils before being transformed into places of light by the Virgin's presence: this was true of the grotto at Lourdes in the 1850s (Harris 1999: 52–4) and the castle at Oliveto Citra in the 1980s (Apolito 1998: 35).

Christian (1996: 302–15) discusses the 'sacred landscapes' of Ezkioga. There, the original site of the apparitions was vague ('up the mountain'), but then particular trees were identified: firstly apple trees and then four oaks. Trees are especially associated with the Virgin in Spain and elsewhere, and several nineteenth- and twentieth-century apparitions have been associated with them. At Fátima in Portugal, the Virgin hovered above a holm oak; the Beauraing visionaries saw her on a hawthorn; the Garabandal seers saw her among pines. The Espis children were herding geese in the woods; Marpingen's and Mettenbuch's visions took place in the woods at the edge of the villages and resulted in chapels being built there. Springs are also important; sometimes they are located after the apparitions begin, as at Lourdes, Ezkioga, and Banneux. Caves and grottoes present other natural sites where visions may occur; from Lourdes on, artificial grottoes in honour of the original became loci for visions at, for example, Beauraing (the hawthorn was next to a grotto), Onkerzele, Berg, Wigratzbad, and several sites in Ireland. Tre Fontane's visions were experienced in a cave. The hillside is important at La Salette, Ezkioga, Medjugorje, and Schio. Looking after animals has been a common reason for visionaries being out in the countryside, for example La Salette, Fátima, Espis, and Casanova Staffora; the 'herder' visionary reflects a familiar traditional motif, although such cases are no longer prevalent.

Christian remarks that places in the wild or open to the sky that represent 'otherness, otherworldliness, nonhumanness' make successful vision sites in Europe. 'Perhaps as spaces that are less domesticated, they are more appropriate for spontaneous, and less tamed, manifestations of grace' (Christian 1996: 315). Yet the emphasis on the countryside and natural features is by no means universal: visionaries' initial apparitions were in or near their own homes at Banneux, Kerizinen, and Amsterdam or occasionally in churches, as at L'Île-Bouchard. The vision site in the small town of Beauraing in the convent grounds next to a railway bridge is a good example of an urban shrine and there are many others. Overall, shrines are places which by some means— either naturally manifested or humanly constructed—have come to represent the 'liminal', the boundary between heaven and earth. Through this boundary it is believed that the Virgin and her Child, along with saints and angels, are present to the world and, at the sites of her appearances, the Virgin usually requests the building of a chapel for pilgrimage to mark the encounter. Natural sites are soon marked as sacred by buildings, crucifixes, Stations of the Cross, and statues, while pre-constructed sites are enhanced and marked as having special significance. The site itself therefore stands as a symbol of liminality, and the more its natural or constructed features suggest this, the more it will endure as a sacred place for future generations.

SEEING AND HEARING THE VIRGIN MARY

Apparitions in the Catholic tradition feature the saints (of whom Mary is one), Jesus, or angels. Yet Mary has been the central figure most frequently in well-known visions, initially from the High Middle Ages, when the Marian cult expanded and dominated over the cult of saints, then during the Counter-Reformation with the birth of Catholic 'Mariology' in opposition to the Protestant downplaying of the cult, and then again from the nineteenth century, often considered the time of the 'Marian Revival'. Many Catholic devotees of apparitions refer to the whole modern period, the nineteenth and twentieth centuries, as the 'Marian Age', a concept derived from the Mariology of St Louis-Marie Grignion de Montfort (1673–1716). De Montfort foresaw a time when the prominence of Mary would presage the second coming of Christ (de Montfort 1957). Therefore, while other figures (Jesus, Joseph, angels, and saints) appear in modern Catholic visions, with a few exceptions they are still predominantly regarded as Marian apparitions: Mary is considered the main agent of the vision and its devotional focus.

The Christian tradition has inherited the classical Greco-Roman and Hebrew patriarchal traditions in which male symbolic figures denote founders and ancestral tribal traditions, whereas female images are common symbols for the civic community and its maternal care for the individual. Athene and Roma were goddesses associated with the cities that bear their names, and Europe itself derives its name from a Greek goddess. Athene bears the shield, helmet, and trident that represent a seagoing nation, an image reproduced in her modern counterpart, Britannia. In Hebrew tradition, Jerusalem was personified as a woman, sometimes an unfaithful one: its community is the 'Daughter of Zion'. The Church was symbolized in terms of a caring mother as early as the New Testament period, and it is not surprising that the images of Mary and the Church came to be very closely associated, at least from the time of Ambrose and Augustine (Beattie 2007: 93–5). Mary is both a type of the Church and its mother, the title 'Mother of the Church' emphasized by Paul VI at the Second Vatican Council. Forces antagonistic to the Church understood the power of this symbolism, hence 'Marianne' became the female image of the French Revolution as a counter to Mary, and this anticlerical figure was reproduced in Portugal as 'Maria' in the early twentieth century. In response to this, and given that Mary had been the dominant figure in European apparitions for centuries, it is not surprising that she emerged as the pivotal figure in a Catholic revival against the revolution and its children (republicans, atheists, and 'free thinkers'). For devotees of apparitions, Mary manifested herself to assure believers that she remained the protective mother who had come to the rescue of her beleaguered children, and that she presaged the coming of a more terrible protector, God himself, who would punish the world for its disbelief. Yet, unlike Protestant promoters of 'rapture', the Catholic community in Europe has not understood itself as immune to the divine judgement. Faithful Catholics would expect to be justified beyond death and taken to Heaven like wheat separated from chaff, it is true, but in earthly life they expect to undergo the punishment that would be meted out to the whole community. They have understood themselves as an integral part of France, Italy, Spain, and the human race and, in being so, subject to the chastisements (often expected imminently) that humanity deserves.

Psychoanalysts such as Carl Jung (1954: 165) have asked whether Mary is an example of the powerful need for a supernatural mother figure expressed in various religious traditions including Catholicism which, being Christian, understands divinity primarily through male images and metaphors. While Mary in Catholic doctrine is not divine, in this psychoanalytical view she functions as a type of mother goddess. At times of crisis, she comes to console and heal but also to warn. There is a Catholic tradition in which the merciful Mary resists the just punishment to be wrought on humankind by her divine Son, and so she has also been seen (e.g. Michael P. Carroll 1986) as a stereotype of European mothers who are more central to their children's lives than fathers, consoling rather than punishing, warning of the father's judgement. However, this should probably be regarded as a generalization of motherhood and indeed of Marian devotion (note that Carroll's psychological approach to apparitions is critiqued by Apolito (1998: 22–5) for its 'relentless psychological reductionism' and scant documentation).

In some cases, such as the most famous modern apparition at Lourdes in the nineteenth century, visionaries have not immediately identified the figure as the Virgin Mary. There are other possibilities: Bernadette of Lourdes was encouraged to throw holy water at the vision to ensure that it was not demonic (an act repeated at Medjugorje), and it was also suggested that it might be the ghost of a recently dead woman attempting to communicate through her (Harris 1999: 58). Marian visions have often occurred against the backdrop of folk traditions, including belief in fairies, spirits, demons, and ghosts (Harris 1999: 23–54). At Fátima in 1917, there was the suggestion that the apparition was the Devil; at Banneux in 1933, the visionary's mother thought that her daughter was seeing a witch. The process that occurs to establish the identity of the figure is a communal one; people in the locality prompt the visionaries to ask the key question: 'who are you?'. Whether or not seers believe that they are encountering Mary on the first occasion, this question is nevertheless important. One aspect that has led to doubt that an apparition could be identified as the Virgin Mary is the familiarity with which the figure communicates to the visionaries, particularly if they are children (examples include Marpingen, as described in Blackbourn 1993: 132–4, and Garabandal, for which see Zimdars-Swartz 1991: 129). After all, Mary is the 'Queen of Heaven' and 'Mother of God' in Catholic doctrine. However, in apparitions that gain the acceptance of leaders in the Church, the answers to the question of identity establish the seriousness of the encounter above and beyond all the more trivial details: 'I am the Immaculate Conception' at Lourdes, 'Our Lady of the Rosary' at Fátima, 'the Lady of all Nations' at Amsterdam, 'the Queen of Peace' at Medjugorje, amongst many other examples. These titles root the vision in Catholic Marian doctrine and reassure priests and educated laypeople that the case is worthy of their attention.

Jan Art (2012: 74–6) provides some figures and examples showing how Mary could be seen to have had priority over Christ in the period from the ultramontane movement in the mid-nineteenth century until Vatican II (1962–5), in part due to Italian influence. The growth of the cult of Mary both fuelled and drew upon Vatican support in the defining of two Mariological dogmas: the Immaculate Conception (1854, by Pius IX in the document *Ineffabilis Deus*) for which there was strong support in France; and the Assumption (1950, by Pius XII in *Munificentissimus Deus*) in the twentieth century. These doctrines had been important for centuries; the history of their canonicity in Catholicism can be tracked by the acceptance of the respective feast days. For the Immaculate Conception, there had been a feast of the Conception since the twelfth century, but the doctrine remained controversial throughout the Middle Ages and so the feast was not universally established until the eighteenth century (Boss 2007: 207–35). The Assumption, on the other hand, was celebrated with general agreement from the sixth century onwards (Shoemaker 2007: 130–45). Yet only in the last two hundred years were these doctrines about Mary formally declared to be Catholic dogma.

The Mariology of Vatican II (see Chapter 12 within this volume), while expressed in traditional terms, presented a new emphasis on Mary to forestall the tendency to prioritize her (for the Vatican II text *Lumen Gentium* 8, see Flannery 1996: 80–92). She was to be seen rather as forerunner, type, and member of the Church, a theological approach which has been restated in papal encyclicals since (Paul VI, *Marialis Cultus*, 1974; John Paul II, *Redemptoris Mater*, 1987). This is what is known as an 'ecclesiotypical' Mariology (see Laurentin 1965, published at the end of Vatican II). It was reinforced by placing the chapter on Mary within the document on the Church, *Lumen Gentium*, as opposed to creating a document specifically on Mary, although this decision was reached only after the closest of the Council votes. Discouraging as it did Marian exaggeration, with ecumenism in mind, Vatican II had the unintended effect of reducing the importance of Marian doctrine and practice in Catholicism (as lamented by Marian devotees, both conservatives suspicious of the Council and also liberals such as Charlene Spretnak 2004). The opposite and pre-conciliar tendency is known as 'Christotypical', in which Mary's privileges—based on her closeness to Christ and participation in his mission—are highlighted. The four Marian doctrines (Mother of God; Ever Virgin; Immaculate Conception; Assumption) all stress the difference between Mary and the rest of the human race, although post-conciliar theologians (e.g. Rahner 1974) reconcile these dogmas with the ecclesiotypical theology of Mary as the first Christian.

Apparition messages clearly reflect the 'Christotypical' tradition: Mary's Immaculate Heart and Immaculate Conception are at the centre of the modern apparitions, paralleling Christ's Sacred Heart and his being 'without sin' (Hebrews 4:15). At Amsterdam in the 1950s, the visionary asked for a fifth dogma in which Mary would be defined as 'Coredemptrix, Mediatrix, and Advocate' (Margry 2009a; 2009b). None of these titles was without precedent in Catholicism, but it was not the right time for the further development of Marian doctrine after the proclamation of the Assumption of Mary as dogma by Pope Pius XII in 1950, and in the years immediately preceding Vatican II and its overtures to other denominations. Nor was it fertile ground for new canonical apparition cults. After the approval of Beauraing and Banneux in the 1940s, no case in Europe gained full approval until Amsterdam, in 2002. René Laurentin refers to 1950–80 as a period during which the Vatican was opposed in principle to new cases being authenticated (Laurentin 1991: 18, 22–3, 26), while Apolito (2005: 26, 47–8) thought that the lack of approval was due to a general Catholic unease about the possible embarrassment of believing in such phenomena in the 1960s and 1970s, which abated in the 1980s. Post-conciliar apparitions continued to portray a 'high' Mariology that went against the trend of Vatican II, and some of the interpretations of visionary messages expressed direct opposition to the Vatican Council. Nevertheless, it is possible to see the influence of the developments of the council in apparitions in the 1980s and afterwards: Medjugorje is an example. The regular deference of the Mary of these visions to her Son (whereas in visions in the nineteenth and

early twentieth centuries this was not so evident) indicated that the ecclesiotypical understanding of Mary had influenced the way in which the visionaries
expressed their encounter.

THE PRESENCE OF MARY IN
AN ALTERNATIVE HISTORY

Apparitions could be regarded as belonging in a medieval world, a superstitious society long gone. Modern people educated into a scientific world view
might dispute the notion that there is some supernatural space from which a
holy figure can emerge into the mundane world, perceived by only one or a
few individuals. Developments in psychology might rather suggest to them
that the vision is a product of the subconscious mind, sustained by an
emotional need to see and hear the transcendent realities about which religions teach and for which blind faith is normally required. It might surprise
the sceptic that *normally* the Roman Catholic Church in its official, hierarchical capacity (pope, cardinals, bishops, theologians) would agree with these
misgivings about visionary experiences: yes, they *are* subjective, imagined,
constructed, contrived. Yet, despite this critical interpretation, the Church
does accept that an actual apparition of the Virgin Mary—in other words,
the perception of this 'heavenly' person by visual and audial means—*is
possible*, even if, in most cases, unlikely or not provable. What is more, if
this possibility is shown to be worthy of belief by the standards of Catholic
discernment, the visionary along with the site of the apparition can gain a
special, sanctified place in the Catholic history of pilgrimage and devotion. It is
this context in which millions of Catholics (and some non-Catholics) in the
world today believe in apparitions of Mary, often very many more apparitions
than Catholic bishops would like. These believers are 'modern': they live in
today's world and enjoy the benefits of technology, drive cars, fly planes, watch
TV documentaries, use mobile phones and computers. Modern people accept
apparitions as literal experiences as much as and, given the increase in the
world's population, in far greater numbers than they ever did. To predict some
future great decline in such beliefs because of the ascendancy of rationalist
understanding of the universe is pure speculation for which there is no strong
evidence yet.

   Therefore, belief in apparitions is well established in communities that are
as 'modern' as any other. Robert A. Orsi describes apparitions of Mary as
'alternative modernity' (Orsi 2009). That is, while these beliefs are too easily
disregarded as anomalies in the development of European culture and its
scientific and moral norms, in fact they are some modern people's way of

making sense of the world and its vicissitudes. They belong within a Catholic world view with a strong emphasis on the active role of Mary shared with other Christians, for example the Orthodox Church and the Copts. Apolito suggests that apparitions are 'an inextricable blend of archaic elements with elements of late modernity, practically a Catholic postmodernism' (Apolito 2005: 2); yet at its roots, most human activity is a combination of the archaic with the modern. Orsi presents a more positive definition: Marian apparitions are 'instances of relationship between human beings going about the course of their days and the powerful supernatural figure of the Blessed Mother who is present to them' (Orsi 2009: 221). This defies claims about the inevitability of secularization, a process that Weber famously called 'disenchantment'. It signifies the continuation of centuries-old beliefs in 'enchantment' or the 'presence' of the divine in the world. Ruth Harris shows how the shrine at Lourdes, arising as it did in the second half of the nineteenth century, is the prime example of the modern apparition: 'the shrine's massive appeal alone indicates how much religion remained a crucial part of "modernity", itself a notion that requires reconsideration' (Harris 1999: 12). She recovers 'the mythological and imaginative universe that the Pyreneans created in their encounter with the Virgin Mary' and shows how their beliefs influenced urban and educated Catholics, thus influencing decisively the cult of Mary in the modern world (Harris 1999: 13).

Believers in apparitions interpret historical causes and interactions in ways that go beyond a straight analysis of social forces and influential personalities, and instead view them from what is understood to be God's perspective on individual, communal, national, or international events. Extending the concept of 'alternative modernity', this could be said to be 'alternative history'. While historical events are the same realities for a Catholic apparition devotee as another person, and many common-sense interpretations will be held in common, the alternative history of the apparition shrine is centred on the firm belief in the presence of the Virgin Mary as the heavenly mouthpiece of God through which humans learn the divine view of history. This fosters hope and expectation in a world in which many Catholics feel ill at ease. Apparitions are the focus for many ideas: like novels or art works, they gather a complex range of emotions, hopes, memories, and social and historical observations, and within a single story make them memorable and accessible. Apparitions are highly complex because of their intricate relationship with society, culture, and history, but underlying all the diverse stories that result from manifold apparitions is a simple belief in the power, authority, and presence of Mary, a human being of history who has risen to glory, a benign, maternal, supernatural person. 'Presence requires a history of its own, and experiences and practices of presence suggest the lineaments of that history' (Orsi 2009: 225). One such experience is an apparition, and the practices that follow include pilgrimage, devotion, and adherence to a set of messages. Many apparitions have a strong base among the Catholic laity in ways that are not always comfortable for the hierarchical Church, whose favoured approach is to single out only a very few cases and promote these as channels for Marian devotion.

Apolito (1998: 133–202) refers to the content of the visions at Oliveto Citra as 'cosmic drama', displaying the traditional Catholic imagery of the war between God—who has chosen Mary as the instrument of his Incarnation and ultimate victory—and the Devil, who is also the beast in Revelation 12. This dragon-like creature threatens the Woman clothed with the sun and crowned with stars who, because she gives birth to the Messiah, is understood to be Mary. Apolito gives many examples of how seers and pilgrims understand Oliveto Citra (and other sites, such as Medjugorje) as a place where that divine drama is being played out and exemplified. Thus the figurative language of scripture is understood as being played out in historical events, i.e. 'matters of great collective import (from ecology to war, famine to quality of life), as well as private matters (from jobs to love, from health to future prospects)' (Apolito 1998: 142). The alternative history of Marian apparition beliefs, therefore, has clear outlines based in biblical and Catholic tradition, and also works at various levels, from the global to the personal. Nor is it only social history that is viewed through the lens of God's omnipotence but also nature and human nature: apparition shrines are locations where the pilgrim encounters natural prodigies and unusual human insight (examples are given in Apolito 1998: 192–8).

STRUCTURE OF THIS WORK

Chapter 2 begins with a brief summary of nineteenth-century Marian apparition themes, as these are important precursors to the twentieth-century cases. The modern history of visions is understood as all of a piece by devotees. This culminates in a consideration of how dominant templates for apparitions arising from particular cases have been superseded by successors, a 'paradigm shift' of visionary phenomena. The chapter then moves on to the visions at Fátima in Portugal in 1917, which provided the second of these templates. This was the first major case in the twentieth century and probably the most famous and influential of all that century's Marian cases. Chapter 3 looks at the later development of the Fátima movement. The recounting of the Fátima story will give the reader a familiarity with an archetypal apparition event with which to understand more general topics: Catholic interpretations of visionary events (Chapter 4), the status of women as visionaries (Chapter 5), and of children (Chapter 6).

After these general topics, the chronological structure of the book resumes with 1930s Spain (Chapter 7), Belgium (Chapter 8), and Germany (Chapter 9).

Chapter 10 develops the concept of women as popular theologians introduced in Chapter 5 with two prominent examples: Jeanne-Louise Ramonet and Ida Peerdeman, who were active from the 1940s until Vatican II. Chapter 11 covers the spate of apparitions in the immediate post-war period, the beginning of the Cold War, focusing on France, Italy, and Germany. Chapter 12 asks whether certain apparitions in the 1960s expressed opposition to the changes brought about by Vatican II. Chapter 13 on Medjugorje, Bosnia-Herzegovina, Chapter 14 on Ireland, and Chapter 15 on various other countries discuss the period after the council and into the 1980s with the emergence of new contexts and concerns for apparition movements. While no new shrines of note emerged in Europe in the 1990s, many of the existing cults continued in intensity and popularity up to the end of that century and beyond.

2

Immaculate and Sorrowful Mary

Apparitions 1830–1917

CATHOLIC MARIAN APPARITIONS IN
THE NINETEENTH CENTURY

The alternative history of Marian apparitions has a clearly identified modern
era, the 'Marian Age' of the priest–theologian Louis-Marie Grignion de Montfort, which began in France in 1830 according to Catholic devotional histories. In the nineteenth century, mass pilgrimages to new Marian apparition
shrines gathered the faithful and signalled the resilience of the Catholic
community under pressure. The strengthening of the Marian cult represented
a Catholic response to the rationalist, egalitarian ideals of the French Revolution that continued to be persuasive in Europe, especially France. The Marian
dimension of Catholicism became the vanguard of the symbolic struggle
against republicanism, placing doctrinal certainty in opposition to the open-
ended truths of rationalism (Pope 1985). Bouritius (1979: 122–3) points out
that there was no year between 1802 and 1898 inclusive that a new religious
order was not dedicated to Mary, and a great many of these were French. The
Lourdes apparitions in 1858 occurred at a time when the intelligentsia of the
French nation was split between Catholicism and free thinking often tanta-
mount to atheism; Flaubert's novel *Madame Bovary*, published in 1856, includes
characters who articulate the contemporary arguments about religion.

As this volume focuses on the twentieth century, only a brief summary of
nineteenth-century European apparitions will be provided with source references.
The apparition community particularly remembers those that were approved by
the Church. Among these, the initial visions of the period occurred in a Vincentian convent in the Rue du Bac, Paris, in 1830. The visionary was Catherine
Labouré, a nun who remained anonymous in her lifetime; she recounted a vision
in which she saw the Miraculous Medal (also known as the Medal of the
Immaculate Conception), which became a popular talisman. The Church canonized her in 1947 (Laurentin 1983). The Rue du Bac visions inspired similar

visions among French Vincentian nuns in the 1840s, and in 1842 to Alphonse Ratisbonne, a Jewish banker in Rome who subsequently converted to Catholicism. Further famous nineteenth-century apparitions followed and were approved in France: La Salette, 1846 (Stern 1980, 1984, 1991); Lourdes, 1858 (Harris 1999; Taylor 2003); Pontmain, 1871 (Laurentin and Durand 1970; Porte 2005); Pellevoisin, 1876, where the healing rather than the apparition was approved much later in 1983 (Vernet 1988; Laurentin and Sbalchiero 2007: 713–15). However, after the final victory of the Third Republic in the 1870s over Church-supported moves towards restoration of the monarchy, no new French visions were fully approved (although one visionary, Marie Martel, at Tilly-sur-Seulles during 1896–9, was given qualified recognition).

There are a few other places in nineteenth-century Europe where apparitions gave rise to cults and shrines approved by the Catholic Church: Licheń, Poland, 1850–52 (Laurentin and Sbalchiero 2007: 524–5); Philippsdorf, Bohemia, now the Czech Republic, 1866 (Laurentin and Sbalchiero 2007: 726–9; Blackbourn 1993: 28); Gietrzwald, East Prussia, now Poland, 1877 (Blackbourn 1993: 155, 256–7); Knock in County Mayo, Ireland, 1879 (Hynes 2008); Pompeii, Italy, 1872 (a locution followed by apparitions in 1876 and 1884: Laurentin and Sbalchiero 2007: 744–5); and Castelpetroso, Italy, 1888 (Laurentin and Sbalchiero 2007: 171–2). Yet these approved cases of visions are only the tip of the iceberg in relation to the great many unapproved apparitions of Mary in the nineteenth century.

Taken together, the narratives of these apparition cases suggest several major themes in the nineteenth-century Marian apparition cult. First, the doctrine of the Immaculate Conception of Mary was integral to the European apparition cult, encapsulated by the wording on the Miraculous Medal and the self-identification of the vision at Lourdes. The title 'Our Lady of Sorrows' was also highly significant, as at La Salette, Licheń, and Castelpetroso; visionaries reinforced the belief that Mary's sorrow at the Crucifixion persisted through time because of the sins and disbelief of a modern world under divine judgement. The prayers of the rosary were important, emphasized at Lourdes and Pompeii. Several other devotions, particularly the Miraculous Medal and Our Lady of Lourdes with her imitation grottoes, were globalized and images duplicated across the Catholic world. At the apparition shrines, mass pilgrimage took place reinforcing national, regional, or political identity, especially at Lourdes, Gietrzwald, Knock, and also at the unapproved shrines at Marpingen and Mettenbuch in the newly united Germany during the 1870s. There was widespread belief in Marian protection assured through visions in times of warfare, revolution, and social unrest, as at Rue du Bac, Pontmain, and Knock. Healings were regarded as evidence for the veracity of an apparition, especially those thought to be due to the Miraculous Medal, or at La Salette, Lourdes, and Knock. Some visionaries claimed healing as an immediate consequence of their encounter with the Virgin, as at Philippsdorf, Pellevoisin, and Pompeii (or conversion, as in the case of Ratisbonne).

Church approval was not always decisive. Popular movements ensured that shrines survived long periods despite the lack of official approval, and some eventually achieved it, as at Pellevoisin (the healing approved in 1983), Knock (after the establishment of the Irish Republic in the 1920s), Castelpetroso (finally in 1973), and Gietrzwald, 1977 (but here the shrine was de facto approved since 1878, being promoted by the local bishop). Marpingen and Mettenbuch remain modest centres of pilgrimage despite the long period of refusal of the local dioceses to support them. In some cases, apparitions may hinder the Church's attempt to maintain its reputation and credibility rather than sustain it; embarrassment may be caused by further revelations after apparitions have been approved, as at La Salette, where the messages castigated the priesthood and announced divine punishment in apocalyptic terms (see Griffiths 1966). Nevertheless, despite the Church's disapproval, many Catholics continued to promote these revelations. This raises the vexed question of 'secrets' known only to seers and kept aside by them for a future unveiling, which can be seen to challenge the authority of the hierarchy, a tradition that continued into the twentieth century.

CATHOLIC MARIAN APPARITIONS IN THE NINETEENTH AND TWENTIETH CENTURIES: THREE TEMPLATES

These nineteenth-century themes provide a foundation for an understanding of the Marian apparition tradition as it continued into the next century. While each apparition event can be explored individually and has its own unique socio-historical and cultural context, the tradition develops and evolves in an international network of information and so many of the trends are global. The question of borrowing is always contentious in apparitions: supporters claim that the visionaries knew nothing of previous cases but that similarities prove divine consistency, while opponents suggest that seers draw on the literature available in Catholic circles in constructing experiences, consciously or unconsciously.

Nevertheless, some novel elements are important for an apparition to catch the popular imagination. Just as in the world of art and literature, the most prized qualities in Catholic Marian apparitions are originality, symbolic power, aesthetic harmony, and resonance with the zeitgeist. In the second half of the nineteenth century, Lourdes, with its grotto and Mary as Immaculate Conception, fulfilled these criteria and so created the first modern template for apparitions, reworking traditional themes to suit modern contexts. The Lourdes template continued to have a major influence well into the twentieth century. Arising in 1917 during the First World War, Fátima (explored in more detail later) also continued centuries-old themes, such as the focus on a natural landmark (a holm oak), the call to prayer, and the foundation of a place of pilgrimage. However, the so-called 'miracle of the sun', in which pilgrims and some sceptical observers alike reported the apparent spinning and falling of the sun, gave Fátima a new and unique characteristic. Some years later, its surviving visionary, Lúcia dos Santos, like Mélanie Calvat of La Salette before her, revealed new secrets after the approval of the apparitions (Santos 1973); while these were more warmly received by the hierarchy than those at La Salette, they were nevertheless controversial. Through them, Lúcia created a second modern template which, added to the solar prodigy, integrated ideas reflecting twentieth-century concerns about global conflict, the conversion of Soviet Russia, the eventual triumph of Mary's Immaculate Heart, and the need for reparation for sin (Zimdars-Swartz 1991: 190–219). In the post-Second World War era, Fátima's reputation increased dramatically in a period when Catholics feared the spread of communism and the coming of nuclear war (see e.g. Scheer 2006: 79–108, 410–11, referring to Germany). This process was helped by the carrying of the Fátima statue around the world (Morgan 2009).

Fátima's prophecies refer to the reconciliation of global conflicts brought about by prayer and reparation; later in the twentieth century, this paradigm evolved into a third modern template based on pure apocalyptic, with statements about future 'chastisements' and miracles at a cosmic level. These were popularized in particular by the apparitions at San Sebastián de Garabandal (Chapter 12 within this volume) and Medjugorje (Chapter 13), although present beforehand in the secrets of La Salette, at Ezkioga in the early 1930s (Chapter 7), and various locations in the 1940s and 1950s (Chapters 10 and 11). It is difficult to see how the Church could approve such messages without the very great risk of appearing foolish like any prophet of apocalyptic doom. Karl Rahner (1963) suggested that these gloomy messages resonate with a Christian hope in Christ and renunciation of a trust in earthly progress without God, but most apparition devotees would not understand these prophecies symbolically as he did, but literally. Yet they would agree with the Vatican statement that a turbulent future can be avoided with prayer (Bertone and Ratzinger 2000: 40), as this is what the messages often affirm.

THE APPARITIONS AT FÁTIMA

Fátima is probably the best-known twentieth-century pilgrimage site and it provided the most popular template for twentieth-century Marian apparitions worldwide. It was the first notable visionary event of the century in Europe and its repercussions have been felt until and beyond the year 2000. The villages that make up the rural district of Fátima lie in central Portugal, and the name bears witness to an Islamic Moorish distant past; the legend of an Islamic princess named Fátima who converted to Catholicism has been handed down to explain the retention of the name (Bennett 2012: 70). Fátima's visions became famous in Portugal while they were taking place between 13 May and 13 October 1917, and they became a crucial feature of the Catholic revival in the years of the anticlerical Portuguese Republic, 1910–26. The republic was eventually overthrown and Portugal entered a long period of pro-Catholic dictatorship under President António Oliveira de Salazar (1933–74).

The visionaries, Lúcia (dos) Santos and her cousins, Francisco and Jacinta Marto, were aged ten, eight, and seven respectively when the Marian apparitions began on 13 May 1917 (note that Lúcia claimed later that there had also been a vision of an angel to the children in 1916, at the time known only to them). Amongst the very many Catholic devotional accounts, Martindale's book (1950) is one of the most helpful for a reconstruction of the story, as it picks up on linguistic details and attempts to identify those testimonies that were recorded at the time of the events, as opposed to those that emerged later. Therefore Martindale will be used here for the chronological details while bearing in mind Bennett's warning (2012: 87) that there are difficulties in reconstructing the original accounts. Fátima is an example of the time-honoured rural vision to animal herders: in this case, very young ones. As the children watched sheep for their families, they thought they saw lightning and then a girl in white appeared, bathed in light, standing on a young holm oak tree; she seemed to be between fifteen and eighteen years old (for the first apparition, Martindale 1950: 31–3). She told them not to be frightened and then responded to a series of questions from Lúcia. She had come from heaven and she pointed to the sky. She wanted them to return to the site for each of six months on the thirteenth day at the same time, about noon. Lúcia then asked whether she would go to heaven: yes; whether Jacinta would: yes; Francisco: yes, but only after saying many rosaries; whether Maria, a recently deceased child, was in heaven: yes; Amelia, another: in Purgatory until the end of the world. This is Martindale's narrative of the events. However, Bennett (2012: 92) quotes the local priest's original transcription, in which Lúcia initiated the conversation with the vision, and in which there was no mention of the deceased girls. There was also a question as to how long the war would continue to which the vision would not answer. It is clear that Lúcia, the eldest and mentor of the younger children, was the only child who spoke to the apparition figure. Jacinta saw and heard the vision, and Francisco only saw (although he did not in the beginning and suggested throwing a stone at whatever Lúcia was seeing).

The fame of the apparitions spread quickly, perhaps unintentionally from the children's point of view. The children returned to the site at the times given by the visionary lady and adults followed them: fifty visitors in June; one to two thousand in July; five to six thousand in August (despite the absence of the children who had been arrested by the local Republican administrator, Artur Santos, to prevent the apparition); 20,000 in September; and 70,000–100,000 in October (Bennett 2012: 125). Portugal was undergoing a disastrous period of political and economic instability, with forty-five governments and thirty attempts at revolution between 1910 and 1926; in 1917, it suffered many casualties at the Western Front (Wheeler 1978; Bennett 2012: 217–18 n 9). These crises heightened the sense of importance of the visions. This, added to the fact that Catholics were fully aware of the impact of the nineteenth-century apparitions in France, created an atmosphere in which people from all over Portugal were expectant of divine intervention.

The devotees of Fátima were asserting their 'alternative history', their own narrative of the historical events that affected their lives in 1917. They were living through extremely trying circumstances, but the Virgin Mary, patroness of Portugal (see e.g. Martindale 1950: 11–14; Bennett 2012: 71–2), had come to reassure them. She was present to them and the apparitions were a reminder of this reality. It was an ancient motif, yet it was being expressed in a modern context and was no less relevant than it had been in earlier times. The French visions in the nineteenth century and Marian apparitions in Portugal through the centuries (for which, see Laurentin and Sbalchiero 2007, using the index; Fernandes and d'Armada 2007: 34–40) provided Portuguese Catholics with a template for special moments when the presence of Mary became manifest: apparitions, miracles, and pilgrimage. For the Portuguese pilgrim, the narrative of Marian intervention did not preclude other ways of understanding events—social, historical, and political interpretations still played their part—but it was the one that required simple faith in the beneficence of divine beings, and Portugal in 1917 had a high level of illiteracy for both genders (Bennett 2012: 75). The drama in which Mary prevails over unpredictable social forces is one in which good wins out and suffering has meaning. Zimdars-Swartz argues that 'the motif of suffering is pervasive in most modern Marian apparitions' and the visionary experience is 'a passage from a meaningless to a meaningful suffering' (Zimdars-Swartz 1991: 266). Fátima's theology includes popular themes of suffering that are rooted in the Cross and Resurrection: suffering borne on behalf of others. According to the adult Lúcia remembering her childhood visions, voluntary suffering effects 'reparation' for sins that offend God, and so it will lead to victory—for Lúcia, the triumph of the Immaculate Heart.

One local devotee who had experienced acute suffering, Maria dos Santos Carreira, emerges from the accounts as an influential instigator of devotion at Fátima (Zimdars-Swartz 1991: 79–80; Bennett 2012: 97, 151). She was in poor health and had a disabled son, and came to witness the children experiencing their vision as a hopeful pilgrim on 13 June. She was one of the first to attest that, although she could not see the young lady of the vision or hear her words, she did hear something like the buzzing of a bee and the bending of the branches of the holm oak. Her work in building and maintaining the shrine caused her to earn the title 'Maria da Capelinha' ('Maria of the Chapel'). She, and other rural women like her, were instrumental in the growth of Fátima as a major shrine, as she and they believed the children where others did not; the clergy, for example, were generally sceptical (Martindale 1950: 83). The creation of a shrine was a focal point in attracting pilgrims and establishing the significance of Fátima. Another important supporter was Manuel (Ti) Marto, the father of Francisco and Jacinta, who attended for the first time on 13 July (Zimdars-Swartz 1991: 80). He thought that he could see a small cloud on the tree and heard the buzzing described by Maria. These adult testimonies supplemented the descriptions of the children in the attempt to establish that the experiences were genuine. The months went by with the exponential growth of pilgrimage and considerable interest in the national newspapers, both positive and negative (Bennett 2012: 147). The apparitions continued as follows (Martindale 1950: 38–9, 42–3, 57–9, 60–2, 73–86):

13 June: Lúcia told to learn to read by the vision; a 'secret' mentioned but the children would not reveal it (these are the only originally recorded contents, according to Bennett's reading of the priest's transcript taken at the time, 2012: 95–6); a new prayer was to be added to the rosary, which is now famous in the Catholic world (Alonso 1973: 80 argues that this was documented in 1917); reassurances that a sick person would be healed if she was converted; prophecies that Francisco and Jacinta would soon be taken to heaven (they died from influenza in 1919 and 1920, respectively).

13 July: continued exhortation to say the rosary for the end of the war; Lúcia asked for a miracle that would convince people and the vision replied that this would occur in October with St Joseph and Jesus in attendance; other petitions, some of which would and some would not be answered; a moment of terror for Lúcia for then unknown reasons; another secret.

19 August (not the 13th because the children had been arrested on that day): a repeat of the assurance that a miracle would happen in October, but one of reduced scale because of the arrest of the children; the vision asked for portable stands at the site which could be carried in procession.

13 September: more details and reassurances about the October miracle; petitions; Lúcia asked whether a chapel could be built and the vision agreed.

13 October: the vision requested a chapel; she identified herself as Our Lady of the Rosary; the war would soon end (originally, the children claimed that it would end that day, according to Martindale 1950: 95–7); petitions; the

need for repentance as the Lord was offended; this was followed by the so-called 'miracle of the sun'. As this occurred, a tableau of figures appeared to Lúcia, as had been foretold: the presence of St Joseph with the Child Jesus and the adult Jesus blessing the crowd; Mary was also seen dressed as Our Lady of Sorrows and Our Lady of Carmel. However, Jacinta and Francisco did not see all these figures, only the original vision and St Joseph and the Child (Martindale 1950: 98–9).

The 'miracle of the sun' confirmed the apparitions for many people in Portugal; it was reported widely in the media, even by Republican newspapers such as *O Seculo*, which printed a dramatic account on the 15 October. Lúcia shouted to people to look at the sun, although she confirmed later that this was simply because figures were appearing there, not because she was seeing the miracle. However, many people present reported that they saw the sun spinning or oscillating (this is usually referred to as 'dancing') and then falling to the earth; many thought that the apocalypse had come. When the sun resumed its normal position, those who had seen the sun dance perceived that they were now dry despite the torrential rain that had preceded the vision. Not everyone saw the phenomenon but some reported viewing it from as much as forty kilometres away. There was no meteorological report of anything unusual, according to the Church statement of 1930 (Martins 1984: 128), although the *New Humanist* magazine many years later claimed that the 'miracle' might have been caused by a cloud of dust, without noting the irony that its being foretold by the children would have made the appearance of an unusual atmospheric phenomenon at this exact time remarkable in itself (Campbell 1989: 22–3).

That was Martindale's account in 1950, and one finds similar versions amongst other Catholic writers. Martindale's bibliography includes the earliest: that of Formigão, the priest who was sent to interview the children and their families in 1917, published under the pseudonym Viscount de Montelo in 1921; however, Alonso, a Fátima supporter, accepts that it was not critical and aimed to convey the spiritual meaning of the apparitions rather than historical accuracy (Alonso 1967: 14). Martindale also lists the work of another priest, de Marchi, who interviewed families and villagers in the 1940s (de Marchi 1986a, 1986b). He also used the recently published memoirs of Lúcia Santos herself.

FÁTIMA AND POLITICAL CHANGE IN PORTUGAL

While the spiritual astuteness, personality, and charisma of the visionary may play a part in her fame and popularity, there is no doubt that the social and political context is instrumental in this popularity. This context is usually replete with ideological conflict in which Catholicism is under pressure; the particular circumstances of a divided France undergoing modernization during the nineteenth century created a favourable matrix for the fame of visionaries. It is not difficult to relate famous Marian apparitions in Latin Western Europe before the Second World War as the reaction to secularizing republicanism. In the Iberian nations, Portugal and Spain, fascist and pro-Catholic authoritarianism won the day, but the famous apparition cults in each, Fátima and Ezkioga respectively, emerged forcibly into public view during the republican periods when political change in favour of the Church was some distance from realization.

Republican Portugal, created in 1910 with the overthrow of the monarch, regarded republican France as its model (Wheeler 1978: 67). It followed the French Revolution in its attack on the Church, which was perceived as an institution of regression blocking progress towards democracy and liberty. It separated Church and state and used a female symbol of the secular republic, 'Maria', just as France had used 'Marianne', a deliberate contrast with the Virgin Mary. This was an attempt to divest the Church of its power and influence, and therefore constituted the most severe attack on the Catholic Church since the French Revolution. The initial years of the revolution, 1910–13, saw the most direct assault on the Church's position with, for example, the banning of religious orders, church property confiscated, religious education outlawed, and religious practices circumscribed (Bennett 2012: 47). After this, the Portuguese Republic had to compromise with the Church due to the continuing faithfulness to Catholicism amongst the majority of Portuguese (Wheeler 1978: 170–1, 192, 204, 259). There was also a short respite because of the temporary pro-Catholic government of Sidónio Pais (December 1917–December 1918). Generally, the conflict was tempered by the fact that the situation was not black and white: many republican supporters remained Catholic and, consequently, Catholics did not uniformly support a return to monarchy (Wheeler 1978: 198).

Bennett (2012: 23–42) shows how the two sides of Portugal's ideological battle yearned for the same end by very different means. Their goal was to re-establish Portugal as the European power that had emerged in the fifteenth century after victories over the Moors and the Spanish, which led to independence from both, overseas discovery, and colonial expansion. Yet economic struggle and political marginalization had replaced the age of prestige: Portugal during the late nineteenth and early twentieth centuries suffered from a European inferiority complex. The myths of the past were used in different ways by republicans and Catholics. However, far from realizing a utopian return to former glories, the First Republic was torn apart by political insecurity and a disastrous economy leading to bread riots, bombings, and attempted coups. Portugal's involvement in the First World War and its troops going to the Western Front in 1916 only exacerbated the crisis (Wheeler 1978; Manuel 2003; Bennett 2012).

Bennett also demonstrates how Fátima became a symbolic focus for the restoration of a pro-Catholic government after 1926. He agrees with Barthas and da Fonseca (1947), Catholic priests who argued that the *Estado Novo*— the Second Republic of 1933–74 which was, in reality, a dictatorship under the pious Catholic Salazar—would not have been possible without Fátima. He adds:

> To be clear, I am not arguing that a direct or monocausal relationship existed between the Fátima apparitions and the birth of Portuguese authoritarianism. I am arguing that the apparition events transformed the fractured social and symbolic terrain on which political struggle and realignment took place in Portugal. They spoke to the causes and effects of crisis in Portugal in powerful, paradigmatic ways. (Bennett 2012: 22)

This analysis demonstrates how the apparitions arose in a specific context and cannot be understood except in the historical circumstances of their origin. It also shows why they were politically and culturally important as a nucleus around which people asserted their Catholic traditions. Yet the Church was characteristically cautious and aware of political repercussions as well as the threat to its own reputation. There were reports that Cardinal Belo, archbishop of Lisbon, had ridiculed Fátima in 1918 and threatened any priest speaking in its favour with excommunication, because of his concern for the delicate Church–state relationship (Martindale 1950: 128). Nevertheless, by the 1920s, he had changed his view and the shrine was de facto approved by the Church several years before the authentication of the visions in 1930 (the process had started in 1922). With a restored diocese of Leiria (later Leiria-Fátima) under the energetic promoter of Fátima, Bishop José Correia da Silva, annual mass pilgrimages were instigated in the early 1920s, despite a municipal guard attack on pilgrims at the annual pilgrimage in 1920 and the bombing of the chapel in 1922 (Bennett 2012: 169–78). Voluntary organizations were set up to help sick pilgrims and a hospital was built in 1929 (Barthas and da Fonseca 1947: 61–3). The shrine was at the centre of a religious revival based on the inherited instinct that Portugal was fundamentally, above all else, a Catholic nation.

Paul Christopher Manuel (2003) charts the progress of Fátima in Portugal after 1930. He shows that the *Estado Novo* and the Church in Portugal were not indivisible. The Church supported Salazar, who was piously Catholic, but the Church gained no great influence in politics during his time in power; from the 1950s with the growth of the Vatican II movement, the Church opposed human rights abuses in Portugal and its colonies. Paul VI used his visit to Fátima in 1967 to criticize the regime. In the non-violent 'Carnation' revolution of 1974, which marked the end of the Salazar era and the beginning of the modern democratic Third Republic, Fátima was again important, with many of its devotees supporting change to democratic socialism while opposing any possibility of a communist victory. Therefore, the shrine and its cult transcended political change. Throughout these phases and until today, Fátima has been an important icon of Portuguese national identity and pride. This has been greatly enhanced with the international fame of Fátima from the 1930s and 1940s, which will be explored later.

3

Sister Lúcia's Narrative of War and Peace

THE REVELATIONS OF SISTER LÚCIA

The task of reconstructing the history of the Fátima apparitions grew in complexity because Lúcia wrote down further details about the apparitions in the 1930s and 1940s, including material not known before. As the only survivor amongst the visionaries, she remained the sole witness to their experiences. Despite the publicity that came after the 'miracle of the sun', Fátima was not well known outside Portugal and Spain until at least the 1930s and, for many Catholics, the 1940s (Scheer 2006: 79–108, 410–11). However, with the publication of Lúcia's memoirs and new books on Fátima in different languages in the 1940s, Fátima became famous across the Catholic world (in Britain, one of the first churches of many dedicated to Our Lady of Fatima was established in Bala, Wales, in 1947). Fátima's greatest appeal rested on the fact that Lúcia's messages assured believers of the eventual demise of Soviet communism.

The anti-communist emphasis of Fátima had been initiated in Portugal in the 1930s when Spain was in turmoil; the Portuguese bishops organized a pilgrimage with this agenda at the shrine in 1938 (Barthas and da Fonseca 1947: 68, 199–201). This understanding of Fátima was easily translatable elsewhere. The possibility that communism would take hold in Western Europe through the ballot box, as it had in Eastern Europe through the military defeat of Nazism, was very real in the years immediately following 1945. Catholics in North America were also interested in Fátima's anti-communist message. In 1946, the 'Blue Army of Our Lady of Fatima' (also known as the 'World Apostolate of Fatima') was founded by priests in the USA and quickly spread elsewhere; the movement followed the Fátima devotions and tried to recruit one member for each member of the 'Red Army', i.e. the Soviet military, using prayer as a weapon (while also supporting the military deterrent of nuclear weapons). Lúcia stated that the Virgin Mary wanted Russia (shorthand for the Soviet Union) consecrated to her Immaculate

Heart and Pius XII responded to this by consecrating the world to the Immaculate Heart on 31 October 1942—although this did not satisfy Lúcia, as Russia had not been mentioned specifically (Laurentin and Sbalchiero 2007: 323, 332). The final great act of Fátima's story was Pope John Paul II's announcement in 2000 that he believed its prophecies to refer to the attempt on his life, as this had occurred on the sixty-fourth anniversary of the first apparition in Fátima in 1981 (explained in Bertone and Ratzinger 2000). John Paul II's own struggle against communism, commencing in his native Poland, underlies his receptivity to the messages of Fátima.

Therefore, Fátima is strongly associated with the belief that Catholicism would triumph over communism. The ideological battle between the Church and the Communist Party had been bitter across Catholic Europe. Communism gained many supporters in Portugal, Spain, Italy, France, and Germany, and the Church had to struggle to protect its practices and structures in Catholic countries taken into the Soviet bloc (Poland, Lithuania, Czechoslovakia, Hungary, as well as regions of other countries with Catholic minorities). Catholics were also acutely aware of the suppression of the Orthodox Church in the Soviet Union. However, the confrontation with communism was not included in the original message of Fátima—which concerned rather the need to pray the rosary for peace during the First World War—nor is it the whole of the message that emerged. The Portuguese theologian and Fátima specialist Joaquin Alonso (1967: 34) argued that the Fátima message is not anti-communist, but centres on penitence, prayer, and recourse to the Immaculate Heart of Mary. Furthermore, the story of Fátima is not complete without reference to the falling or spinning sun, its greatest miracle, which devotees have looked for elsewhere in many locations where Marian apparitions take place.

The idea of consecration to the Immaculate Heart predates Fátima, but it came to global prominence because of these apparitions. Devotion to the Heart of Mary (along with the Sacred Heart of Jesus) can be traced back to St Jean Eudes in the seventeenth century, while the concept of consecration to Mary was inspired by St Louis Grignion de Montfort in the eighteenth century (Boss 2007: 411–23). These ideas had come together by 1836, when the Abbé Desgenettes in the church of Notre-Dame des Victoires in Paris heard a voice telling him to consecrate his parish to the Immaculate Heart. In the twentieth century, the Belgian mystic, prophetess, and Franciscan tertiary, Berthe Petit (1870–1943), experienced locutions and apparitions of Jesus and Mary, and saw their hearts united and pierced by a single sword. In 1910, she received a mission to ask that the world be consecrated to the 'Sorrowful and Immaculate Heart of Mary' (Duffner 2003: 23–4). As a consequence, Cardinal Bourne (archbishop of Westminster, 1903–35) consecrated England in this way in the midst of the First World War in 1915, ordering that the act of consecration be read out in all English Roman Catholic churches (Duffner 2003: 37).

Lúcia had entered a convent as a young adult, as the Church was anxious to protect her from public scrutiny in the same way as Bernadette of Lourdes. In 1925, now aged eighteen, Lúcia reported a new apparition in her convent in Pontevedra, Spain, near the Galician coast; there Mary referred to her heart, pierced by sins, for which reparation was necessary. Those who, on the first Saturday of five consecutive months, attended Confession, Mass, and recited five decades of the rosary would be assisted at the hour of their death (Santos 1973: 401). This revelation echoes the message of St Margaret Mary Alacoque in seventeenth-century France (as noted by Martindale 1950: 141), except that the original involved the Sacred Heart of Jesus and first Fridays. In 1927, Lúcia asked her mother to practise the devotion in a letter in 1927 and then wrote down the details on the instruction of her confessor (Santos 1973: 401–3; Zimdars-Swartz 1991: 194–7). Then, in 1930, Lúcia wrote to her confessor to record that, in 1929, she had experienced a vision of the Trinity and the Virgin Mary in which God had asked for the consecration of Russia to the Sacred Hearts of Jesus and Mary by the pope in communion with all the bishops of the world (Santos 1973: 405). This would lead to Russia's 'conversion'. Thus Lúcia began to suggest that there was more to be said about the message of Fátima. It is likely that Lúcia's letter of 1930 was not communicated to the pope as she had requested, but nevertheless the Bishop of Leiria and Lúcia's confessors wondered whether she might be willing to reveal further details about the 1917 apparitions. Therefore, Lúcia was encouraged to write her memoirs, and she did so in four parts in 1935, 1937, and 1941 (in English translation, Santos 1973; see a summary in Zimdars-Swartz 1991: 198–201).

In the first of the memoirs (Santos 1973: 1–81), Lúcia (now Sister Maria Lúcia das Dores; from 1948, Sister Maria Lúcia de Jesus e do Coração Imaculado) told the Bishop of Leiria about the holiness and sacrifices of Jacinta, who died in 1920 aged nine and who had already been acclaimed in Portugal as a child saint (Bennett 2012: 40–2). The second memoir (Santos 1973: 87–213) recounted Lúcia's life, including more information about the apparitions. Here for the first time Lúcia spoke of an apparition of an angel in 1916, who gave the three children communion from a mystical chalice. There were also details about 13 June 1917, until now kept secret: the children had been asked to accept suffering for the reparation of sins and the conversion of sinners, but the Immaculate Heart would be their refuge. Lúcia wrote about the sacrifices that the children made and their self-mortification, including self-imposed fasting and wearing tight ropes around their waists hidden under their clothes. It is interesting, therefore, that the priest interviewer Formigão identified them as looking frail during 1917, although this might have been due in part to the stress of holding to their testimonies under pressure amid the constant attention and questions (Bennett 2012: 110).

In the third memoir of 1941 (Santos 1973: 217–39), Lúcia finally wrote down the details of the secrets that had been the topic of conversation since

1917. In this, she followed Mélanie Calvat of La Salette, whose secrets were written down in the 1860s, around twenty years after the events (Bernadette Soubirous of Lourdes spoke of a secret, but never revealed it because she said that the Virgin Mary had forbidden her to do so: Taylor 2003: 141). Lúcia stated that these secrets derived from 13 July 1917. The first, explaining her terror during that apparition, was a vision of hell. This was not so much a revelation as a confirmation of Catholic belief. The second was the importance of devotion to the Immaculate Heart, as might have been expected after Lúcia's concerns of the late 1920s. Consecration of Russia to the Immaculate Heart by the pope and all the bishops of the world simultaneously would convert that nation, preventing the spread of its 'errors', and bringing a time of peace. However, if offences against God did not stop, there would be another world war presaged by a strange light (there was a striking Aurora Borealis in January 1938). Lúcia also wrote a letter to this effect to the pope in 1940, although of course, she was writing when the Second World War had already begun. There was a third secret, which Lúcia decided not to reveal. This gave rise to greater curiosity and concern than before.

In the fourth memoir (Santos 1973: 243–397), Lúcia added 'other facts about the events of Fátima'. After her hagiographical description of Jacinta in the first memoir, Lúcia now wanted to write something about Francisco and his heroic devotion. She also wanted to provide more details about the apparitions in order to fill in the gaps. Again she alluded to a final section of the secrets from 13 July that she 'must not reveal now', but she hinted at its first words: 'In Portugal the dogma of the faith will always be kept, etc.' (Santos 1973: 317, 341). This 'third secret' was finally written down in 1944 and passed to the Bishop of Leiria to be sent to the pope (which he did in 1957); Lúcia asked for it to be revealed publicly in 1960 (Bertone and Ratzinger 2000: 3–4). However, while this had happened in the pontificate of Pius XII, by 1960 a new pope, John XXIII, had been elected, who decided not to reveal the secret. Nor did his successors reveal it until 2000, provoking a great deal of anxiety and speculation as to what it might be, including rumours that it might be nuclear war or the apocalypse.

While the events of 2000 will be covered later, what this detail illustrates is that the story of the visions emerged in two parts: that known in 1917, and that which Lúcia revealed later. Catholic devotees rarely separate them, as it is logical to suppose that if Lúcia could be identified as a genuine visionary, then her memoirs would be true. On 13 October 1930, the Portuguese Church declared the apparitions of Fátima 'worthy of belief' and decided 'to permit officially the cult of Our Lady of Fátima' (Martins 1984: 131). The pastoral letter pointed out that the children had concurred in their testimony and that they had foreseen the great 'solar phenomenon'. The Church denied that priests had manipulated the apparitions, as they had been prohibited from taking part (although the document judiciously omits to say that many turned up out of curiosity or even to obstruct the pilgrimages: Martindale 1950: 74; de Marchi 1986a: 132; Bennett 2012: 152). Thus Lúcia as the surviving visionary, now in the convent, had considerable public prestige and reliability as a seer.

'FÁTIMA I' AND 'FÁTIMA II'

Some Catholic theologians, in the wake of the global expansion of the Fátima cult, began to question whether the later revelations of Lúcia were acceptable to Church orthodoxy in the same way as the 1917 apparitions. In theory, the original visions could be authentic but the later messages might have been based on a false memory, exaggerated, or simply made up to suit the changing times. The context for the period of the memoirs, and therefore a reason for concern about Russia, included the increased suppression of Russian Orthodoxy by Stalin from 1929, the Spanish Second Republic, 1930–6, and the Spanish Civil War, 1936–9 (Lúcia was in a convent at Tuy, Spain, from 1925 to 1946). Apart from finding a rationale for the new details of the apparitions, there were several other arguments that cast doubt on them: first, the precedent set by Mélanie Calvat of La Salette, whose vision of 1846 had been approved in 1851 but whose later revelations were regarded as inappropriate and suppressed by the Church. Second, as Lúcia had written the memoirs *after* Church approval, they had not been included in the investigation. Third, her foretelling of a second world war was only known after the event and could not be proved to be a genuine prophecy. Fourth, the ideas expressed by the adult Lúcia are unlikely to have been understood by a child. And finally, while as a child Lúcia would not have known about the coincidence in date between the Russian Bolshevik Revolution of 1917 and the apparitions, she might have found this worth developing later. This potential separation of Fátima's original apparition event in 1917 from Lúcia's memoirs in the 1930s and 1940s became known as 'Fátima I' and 'Fátima II' or 'the old history of Fátima' and 'the new history of Fátima'. Its first proponent was the Belgian Jesuit, E. Dhanis (1944, 1952) and the more famous German Jesuit theologian, Karl Rahner (1963), also alludes to it. It is summarized (but also rejected) by Laurentin and Sbalchiero (2007: 327).

The Fátima theologian Joaquin Alonso (1967) attempted to retain the integrity of the whole Fátima story by reviewing the literature and rejecting the attempt to separate the different stages of the unfolding of Fátima, refuting Dhanis. Alonso first of all seems to yield a point to the critics by admitting that no thorough historical treatment of the apparitions yet existed; the devotional literature thus far had failed to undertake this task and had swept historical problems under the carpet. Alonso will have been aware of the critical but supportive research on the nineteenth-century French apparitions by René

Laurentin, an exemplar which was lacking at Fátima. On the other hand, the critics, according to Alonso, were equally driven by theological presuppositions (1967: 49–51). Their attempts to criticize had also failed to establish a historical, critical method that fully appreciates the complexity of the phenomenon. Therefore Alonso argues that 'there is nothing in the literature that leads us to doubt the real treasure of the living water hidden in Fátima' (1967: 20, my translation); in other words, given the devotional fruits of Fátima and the absence of conclusive proof against Lúcia's narrative of the events, Catholics might as well believe in the story in its entirety. In later publications (1973, 1979), Alonso attempted to establish with evidence that some of the themes in the memoirs—notably, the apparitions of the angel—were already in Lúcia's mind in 1917 (Alonso 1973: 80).

Martindale (writing the introduction to Sandhurst's *We Saw Her*) mentions an attitude in Catholicism whereby the fruits of a phenomenon are more important than its historical foundations (Sandhurst 1953: xvi). Years later, Joseph Ratzinger, then a cardinal, suggested that ancient pilgrimages were often fruitful, but based on very unscientific traditions. The important thing is the 'vitality' and 'orthodoxy' developing in those places (Ratzinger and Messori 1985: 112). So in the Catholic tradition, one can conceive of a situation where the strength of the cult—shrine, pilgrimage, devotion, spiritual well-being—outweighs uncertainties about the origins; it is the cult that Alonso is referring to when he writes about 'the real treasure of the living water' of Fátima. However, neither Martindale nor Alonso thinks that the history should be discounted. Establishing the facts helps the believer to gain a full understanding of the phenomenon and the resulting shrine and, just as importantly, it guards against the embarrassment of a third party discovering questionable aspects of the origins. Yet Martindale and Alonso are not in total agreement about the evolution of Fátima: Martindale believes in the apparitions but accepts some separation of 'Fatima I' and 'Fatima II' by saying that he would not be disconcerted if Lúcia had expanded her childish and undeveloped perceptions of the visions into a more adult version (Martindale 1950: 166, 179). Alonso challenges Martindale in this; he wants to preserve the literal understanding of Lúcia's narrative and feels that the documented evidence does not undermine it (1979: 95–6).

CATHOLIC CONTROVERSY OVER FÁTIMA

The more recent history of Fátima is marked by secrecy, controversy, and strong emotions. The arguments have become rather technical within relatively limited circles, so here they will be summarized in order to indicate the powerful impact that Fátima has had on the Catholic world. The consecrations of the world to the Immaculate Heart that were made by Pius XII on 31 October 1942, 8 December 1942, and 7 July 1952 did not conform to the instructions given by Lúcia: the first two did not mention Russia, the third did so, but none was repeated by every bishop around the world simultaneously (Laurentin and Sbalchiero 2007: 322–7). After John Paul II was shot on 13 May 1981, he noticed the coincidence that this date was the sixty-fourth anniversary of the first apparition. While in hospital, he asked to read the remaining ('third') secret and from then on Fátima became very important for him. The bullet surgically removed from his body was placed in the crown of the statue at the shrine. He repeated the consecration to the Immaculate Heart on 13 May 1982, but again, neither was Russia mentioned explicitly nor were all the Catholic bishops involved, and so Lúcia again refused to give her approval. Finally, on 24 March 1984, John Paul II repeated the consecration, finally to the satisfaction of Lúcia, despite the fact that Russia was not mentioned but only implied (Bertone and de Carli 2008: 82; this lack of an overt naming of Russia was for 'diplomatic reasons', according to Laurentin and Sbalchiero 2007: 326, i.e. diplomacy with the Russian Orthodox Church). The bishops did not enact the consecration publicly as she had previously asked, but had simply been informed in advance. Nevertheless, the fact that Gorbachev's succession and *perestroika* followed one year later convinced many Catholics that the consecration had been efficacious.

However, a particular group of Fátima devotees led by priests, most notably the publishers of *The Fatima Crusader*, noted the discrepancy between Lúcia's previous instructions and the circumstances of the 1984 consecration. They started a campaign for the consecration to be enacted fully, and so came into conflict with the Vatican, accusing the cardinals of overruling the pope and silencing Sister Lúcia (e.g. Leonard 1990). Yet the wholesale changes in the territories of the Soviet Union in 1991 were persuasive arguments against the view that the consecration had not been performed, as well as endorsing Lúcia's prophecies.

On 13 May 2000, John Paul II visited Fátima to carry out the formal beatification of Fátima's deceased visionaries Jacinta and Francisco in Lúcia's presence, and there finally the pope revealed the remaining 'third secret' (Bertone and Ratzinger 2000). The paper on which Lúcia had written in 1944 was shown to the public. The secret was not a message from the visionary lady but a symbolic scene that opened with an angel bearing a flaming sword crying for penance; then a bishop in white—'we had the impression it was the Holy Father' wrote Lúcia (Bertone and Ratzinger 2000: 21)—was shot dead by soldiers at a cross on a mountain along with many bishops, priests, religious brothers and sisters, and laypeople. The blood of these martyrs was collected by angels; they sprinkled it on souls who had died in the ruined city below and 'were making their way to God'. Thus John Paul II saw his own attempted assassination in the scene (seeing it as symbolic because the details were very different from the attack on him in

St Peter's Square in 1981). He believed that an intervention by the Virgin Mary caused him to survive, unlike the prelate in the vision.

Thus began another fringe Catholic campaign directed against the Vatican. For several reasons, commentators regarded the 2000 publication as not consisting of the original secret in its entirety (e.g. Socci 2009). These complaints—answered by Bertone (Bertone and de Carli 2008, with foreword by Pope Benedict XVI)—are too detailed to be reproduced here. In summary, they concern hints made by popes or cardinals before 2000 that do not seem to tally with the published secret; the argument that the length of the secret does not conform to what is known about the original; the words, 'In Portugal, the dogma of the faith will always be preserved', do not seem to introduce this vision as was expected from the fourth memoir. This phrase had invited speculation that the third secret concerned wholesale apostasy from the Church, perhaps even amongst the hierarchy, and so it was presumed that the Vatican had decided that this was too sensitive to reveal. It is not possible here to make any judgements about the consecration of Russia, or the third secret, and the actions of the Vatican. This is the stuff of sensationalism and conspiracy theories and it has spawned many publications, some by genuinely concerned Fátima devotees, others by people seeking gain by mass publication. However, what the whole matter demonstrates is the seriousness with which Catholics took the revelations of an enclosed nun remembering visions she had experienced at the age of ten. This indicates the importance of the visionary medium in modern Catholicism, and the role that children and women have played in this. It also shows how difficult a task it is for the hierarchy to manage and channel this popular movement, despite critics who believe that they manipulate and orchestrate it. Brettell (1990) shows how often the Portuguese priesthood—and this is duplicated in other Catholic nations—is conscripted into the service of popular religion, even where it is unorthodox, and heavily criticized if they refuse. What happens at village level is also true of global Catholicism. It is crucial for the Fátima devotee of any nationality to know whether or not the hierarchy has responded fully to the requests of the Virgin Mary in her communication to humanity. The idea that the messages might be vaguely remembered, or have been embellished, or that the general meaning is more important than the details, are possibilities accepted by the Vatican but not by most members of the apparition movement.

ASSESSING FÁTIMA

How to evaluate Fátima? The reaction which the fear of communism evoked in Catholic countries with authoritarian regimes—notably Portugal, Spain, most Latin American nations, the Philippines—led to many human rights abuses. Fátima was integral to that campaign and so it will have a negative association for many who suffered. There is little in the devotional literature to suggest a genuine concern for the victims of anti-communist pogroms, many of whom were not revolutionaries or even politically motivated. It is ironic that the person who is the best match for the bishop in Sister Lúcia's 'third secret' is not Pope John Paul II, but Archbishop Oscar Romero, shot and killed in San Salvador while celebrating Mass, one of very many Catholics, priests, religious, and laypeople, murdered by military regimes in Latin America during the 1960s, 1970s, and 1980s. Those who were killed paid the price for connecting biblical theology with the demand for human rights and social justice. The liberation theology that Romero represents did adopt some aspects of Marxist political thought and was condemned for so doing by John Paul II and Cardinal Ratzinger during the 1980s (Romero was not beatified until the papacy of Francis). The Vatican did not sanction brutality, but it could have done more to prevent it; John Paul II was concerned about the spread of communism and so seemed to tolerate the excesses of dictatorships in developing countries. For Catholics with sympathy for the liberation theology movement, there will be concerns as to why the Fátima cult, if divinely inspired, did not contain messages that might have condemned government assassins. However, from Lúcia's point of view, communism threatened the Catholic way of life and her national traditions; the messages simply stated that communism represented 'errors'. Her response to this threat was consecration to the Immaculate Heart and not the terror of the secret police, and so responsibility lies with those who used Fátima as an icon for hatred and bigotry.

On the more positive side, to understand and appreciate Fátima is to understand and appreciate Portuguese Catholicism. Pilgrims still approach the shrine on their knees as they did from the very beginnings of pilgrimage in 1917: they bring all manner of anxieties, illnesses, and yearnings to the statue of the Madonna in the little chapel that stands in the middle of the great square with its extensive basilica and side buildings. Portuguese Catholics, young and old, wave to the statue with traditional white handkerchiefs when it is processed around the square at festivals and on anniversaries of the apparitions.

As part of the global movement to reinforce Catholicism after the Second World War, the statue of Fátima began to be taken round the world. The 'Pilgrim Statue' of Fátima, created in 1946, has been transported abroad for the purposes of informing Catholics about the Fátima apparition and its messages. It is 101 cm (40 in) high, not far from the reported size of the apparition itself, and is a copy of the statue in the chapel at Fátima. The Marian devotee Pope Pius XII commended the journeys of the statue and saw it as an important element in the battle against communism (Morgan 2009: 54). David Morgan sees this as an 'inversion of pilgrimage', i.e. whereas the pilgrim normally travels to the holy site, in this case the representation of the sacred travels to the believer (Morgan 2009). Copies of the statue were made to increase the number of visits possible and these have included countries all over the globe. In Portugal itself, the dictator Salazar—who had always recognized the political capital of Fátima—encouraged a tour of the image in the 1950s (Brettell 1990: 73). Anna-Karina Hermkens (2009) shows how a Fátima statue made in Bougainville (off the east coast of Papua New Guinea) was taken around the islands in a call for peace in a war-torn region. This effort represents a local version of the global travels of the Pilgrim Statue.

Another interesting element of the shrine at Fátima is its attraction to Muslims who visit regularly (Bertone and de Carli 2008: 77–8). This is primarily due to the name of the village. De Carli, in speaking with Cardinal Bertone, points out that Fatima, daughter of Mohammed and wife of Ali, plays a role for Shi'ite Muslims that is rather similar to that of Mary in Catholicism. He goes on to say that Shi'ites believe that the message of Fátima is for Muslims. Bertone, in his reply, dismisses this as irrelevant to the case and argues that Fátima is for Catholics alone. However, the clear demarcations of the Church hierarchy do not always correspond with the sentiments of popular religion: Albera and Couroucli (2012) show how many shrines in the Mediterranean region attract Muslims, Christians, and Jews together, including jointly erected Marian apparition shrines in Egypt and Palestine.

Fátima's most constant message is the yearning for peace during a troubled century. Pope Benedict XV referred to the Virgin Mary as 'Our Lady, Queen of Peace' and added this title to the Loreto Litany in 1915; his initiative advocating prayer for peace was echoed in the Fátima apparitions. A desire for peace amongst rural people suffering the loss of loved ones in a distant war as well as economic catastrophe is certainly a reasonable one. Perhaps one could also argue, in a Cold War age, it was reasonable to think that peace would come with the 'conversion of Russia'. Lúcia originally thought that this conversion would be to Catholicism (Alonso 1979: 83–4), but most interpreters are content with the idea that it means simply the end of an anti-religious government. However, it should be noted that the Western European fear of Russia is perennial: ironically, Benedict XV had an 'obsession' with the threat of tsarist Russia before the Bolshevik revolution (Rhodes 1989: 249) and, in more recent times, there has been the Ukrainian crisis. Fear of Russian military strength is not confined to the communist period. The 'Queen of Peace' and yearning for peace in a time of conflict is a theme that has been repeated elsewhere, notably Medjugorje. There is clearly a counterargument in both cases that asks whether the desire for peace can justify the killing of one's enemy, either in the anti-communist crusade in which Fátima played its part, or in the pursuit of Croat nationalism that cannot be separated from the story of Medjugorje.

It now remains to be seen whether the message of Fátima will be regarded as having come to a conclusion. The shrine will survive as a centre for healing, devotion, and prayer, and it is now the major Portuguese Marian pilgrimage centre, but there are good reasons to think that the drama of secrets has no further purpose:

- Communism is regarded as outdated and no longer a threat in Europe.
- The Vatican has revealed the 'third secret' and interprets it within a Cold War context.
- For many devotees, the prophecy of the triumph of the Immaculate Heart has been fulfilled. The surviving visionary, Lúcia Santos, died in 2005.
- Other apparitions with a narrative of secrets, particularly Garabandal and Medjugorje (see Chapters 12 and 13 within this volume) are in the ascendancy.

Nevertheless, there are still some devotees who favour a conspiracy theory in which the Vatican has not yet revealed the secrets in full. These people promote an apocalyptic view in which the papacy of John Paul II did not bring a conclusion to the story of Fátima. For them, the as-yet-unrevealed secret tells of a coming apostasy from the Church, even at its higher levels, which will bring about an end-times scenario. And, as will be seen in later chapters, there have been many twentieth-century apparitions in the tradition of Fátima, foreseeing coming chastisements and miracles that have fuelled this apocalyptic expectation.

4

Catholic Interpretations

CATHOLIC DISCERNMENT OF APPARITIONS

Marian apparitions such as those at Fátima take place in a Catholic culture in which there is an expectation that the Church will make a ruling, using a process that has existed for several centuries and which often leads to argument and controversy as Catholics take sides on whether an apparition is genuine or not. What began as a private experience becomes public knowledge through report, observation, then ardent support and promotion, so there might be a need to instigate the formal discernment process. This was originally set up in the sixteenth century at the Council of Trent (Session 25), which sought greater order and structure within the Catholic Church. The judgement process as established at Trent is governed by the diocesan bishop of the area who has the authority to set up a commission. He may choose priests, theologians, and professional laypeople such as psychologists and doctors to help him in the task. The commission will interview the visionaries and check the consistency of their statements, interrogate people who were witnesses or who claim to have experienced miraculous healing or conversion, look at the facts of the case and its reception in the wider Catholic community, and examine the theology of the messages that are promulgated. This process can take a few months or several years and may involve consultation with higher authorities—archbishop or Vatican—if difficulties are encountered.

Shortly before being elected pope in 1740 as Benedict XIV, Cardinal Prospero Lambertini, the archbishop of Bologna, wrote a document on the discernment of sainthood entitled *De Servorum Dei Beatificatione et Canonizatione* ('On the Beatification and Canonization of the Servants of God'). A decision on whether a deceased Catholic can be regarded as a saint rests on the assessment of claimed miracles both before and after death, and so the third volume of this treatise discusses the discernment of visionary phenomena. Lambertini's treatment of apparitions, locutions, ecstasies, and miracles was largely based on previous Catholic writing but, as a new and compact collection of the wisdom of the Church on the subject, it became the standard text used by Church officials to make decisions about visionaries. It included some classic statements of discernment often referred to by nineteenth- and twentieth-century bishops ruling on apparitions. They embrace the four pillars of the authentication process: consideration of natural causes; the character of the visionaries; outcomes ('fruits') of the visions; orthodoxy of the messages.

- Visions could be natural, diabolical, or divine in origin; natural causes included privation, illness, old age, and melancholy.
- Positive signs in visionaries were humility, not promoting oneself as a visionary, seeking self-mortification and solitude rather than fame, not desiring to receive visions, not being curious about them (something from which Augustine had suffered before his conversion), an experience in which fear gave way to peace and joy rather than the other way round (which would be the sign of a diabolical vision).
- Authentic divine visions should lead to good fruits and charitable works (but not works that prevented a greater good, another sign of the diabolical).
- Agreement with scriptural, apostolic, traditional doctrine and accepted Christian morality was required (Lambertini 1852 III: 320–406).

Lambertini also gave guidance on the correct approach to visions when they had been approved by a bishop, including those experienced by canonized saints. This confirmed that the official Catholic understanding of visions remained within clear boundaries; it was no more than a permission to believe, rather than a binding endorsement:

- Catholics should only believe in visions with 'human faith' (as opposed to divinely revealed Catholic faith) as they are only 'probable' at best.
- Catholics could disagree with the decision, as long as this was done with modesty, on the basis of good reason, and without contempt.

Could Lambertini have foreseen the importance of his guidelines over a hundred years later in the nineteenth century? His reservation about the importance of visions and deference to scientific explanations reflects the century of the Enlightenment in which he lived (Boss 2004: 337), and he could not have anticipated the Catholic reaction against 'rationalism' in the nineteenth century. He wrote before the Industrial Revolution, French Revolution, and Napoleonic Wars, all of which changed Europe. Apparitions in the nineteenth century took on a new vitality as bulwarks of a Catholic way of life under threat. How they were investigated and used would be ever more crucial. The unopposed and speedy agreement on Pontmain in 1871–2 provides a good example (although see Laurentin and Sbalchiero 2007: 750–5 for further developments in the twentieth century) as the case met various ideal criteria:

- The message was devotional and orthodox in content and not political.
- The message contained a prophecy, using the language of prayer and God's mercy, which could be understood as having been fulfilled.
- The child visionaries were witnessed during the apparition by a priest and nuns as well as other adults, and local Catholics believed in it.
- The apparition coincided with an ecclesiastical initiative: local prelate Bishop Wicart led four thousand people to the church of Notre-Dame d'Avenières in Laval and vowed to restore the tower and steeple if the 'Immaculate Virgin' protected the town, and this occurred three days after the visions at Pontmain at which time Wicart was still unaware of them (Laurentin and Durand 1970 I: 54; Kselman 1983: 115).
- The apparition and its message were complete, without the prospect of secret revelations, and so there was nothing else to come, thus no danger of future embarrassment for the Church.

In the late twentieth-century climate of globally famous and sometimes controversial apparitions, the Sacred Congregation for the Doctrine of the Faith updated the criteria of discernment in 1978, following traditional lines (Šeper and Hamer 1978). Yet *The Message of Fatima* (2000) is the most recent definitive statement on Marian visions from the Vatican, co-authored by Cardinals Tarcisio Bertone and Joseph Ratzinger (later Pope Benedict XVI). While this booklet presents strong support for approved apparitions, there are numerous caveats. The hierarchical Church accepts that apparitions may have a message for the whole Church, but they have been traditionally regarded as 'private revelations', subordinate to 'public Revelation'—the Gospel of Jesus Christ passed down through the apostolic tradition and formulated in the Nicene Creed—and only useful in so far as they refer back to this central doctrine and help to inculturate it in new circumstances (Bertone and Ratzinger 2000: 32–6). The vision always includes a subjective element: 'Such visions are therefore never simple "photographs" of the other world, but are influenced by the potentialities and limitations of the perceiving subject' (Bertone and Ratzinger 2000: 37–8). The Vatican document follows the Jesuit theologian Karl Rahner's *Visions and Prophecies* (1963) in arguing that, for authentic visions, the one objective supernatural reality is an encounter with the divine of which visions represent only a subjective articulation. For Rahner, visions 'are relatively unimportant compared with the infused contemplation from which they derive' (Rahner 1963: 79–80). Therefore the Catholic Church recognizes the subjectivity of apparitions but also asserts that, in particular cases, they arise from a real encounter with *something*, a supernatural being (hence the occasional concern that it could be a demonic one). So the official Catholic model for visionary phenomena worthy of belief stands somewhere between credulity (the visionary is quoting verbatim a conversation with a heavenly visitor) and scepticism (that it is all fabrication). Canonical approval moves the Church towards the former of these poles, as the messages become part of the accepted narrative, while rejection takes it towards the latter.

Rahner's analysis draws on the fact that the Catholic tradition, as represented by the doctors of the Church, Saints Thomas Aquinas and John of the Cross, devalues the act of 'seeing' as opposed to that of inner contemplation. Using the taxonomy of Augustine, in which visions could be categorized as corporeal (of material objects), imaginative (in the mind's eye), or intellectual (understood by intuition without an image) (Bourke 1945: 242–7), Aquinas concluded that 'the prophecy whereby a supernatural truth is seen by intellectual vision, is more excellent than that in which a supernatural truth is manifested by means of the similitudes of corporeal things in the vision of the imagination' (Aquinas 1922: 49). In the sixteenth century, John of the Cross used these distinctions to downplay the great number of apparitions in Spain at that time (John of the Cross 1994: 2. XIX). This shows how the Catholic tradition gives 'popular religion' a lower priority than official doctrine or the mystical insights of a saint. Visionaries emerging from the mass of the laity, often poor and uneducated, create new power bases for the right to speak on behalf of the divine which present an alternative to the authority of the Church hierarchy and the Church's promotion of what it deems appropriate systematic and philosophically based theology. Only by expressing their loyalty and obedience and by subordinating their claims to the oversight of the Church can the visionaries hope to become established as officially approved Catholic seers.

In Catholic doctrine, it has been possible for apparitions to be both miraculous *and* material. The Jesuit Auguste Poulain's classic *The Graces of Interior Prayer* (originally written in 1901) draws on tradition and lists four possibilities for a supernatural object that is seen physically by the eye (1950: 314–5). It may be objective, as in Jesus' post-resurrection body (this is also possible for the Virgin Mary); objective but borrowed (by angels or demons); semi-objective (a body of light); or subjective (image imprinted by angels on the retina). However, Rahner (1963: 31–47) brings the Catholic interpretation of apparitions into line with the modern view of such phenomena; the subjective, imaginative vision and not the corporeal is the normal case. This is true even when apparitions are seen collectively; an encounter with God may stimulate the imagination of several people who have sensitivity. The vision 'must largely conform to the psychic laws determined by the intrinsic structure of the seer's spiritual faculties' and if authentic, 'must be caused by God' (Rahner 1963: 41). This is not a suspension of natural laws, as was thought in tradition, because the psychic dimension is natural in itself. Thus Rahner, as was his mission, restates Thomist theology in ways that accord with modern thinking and uses language familiar to twentieth-century Catholics. It is better to regard God as working through nature than effecting grand miracles. The belief that Catholic apparitions are natural phenomena, along with precognition and telepathic knowledge, is explored more recently by Lisa Schwebel (2004). She argues that the mere existence of strange phenomena does not prove a divine origin; like Rahner, she looks for evidence of the divine in transformation of people and communities, not in the impact of the phenomenon itself.

A classic statement of Roman Catholic reserve about apparitions was made by another Jesuit, Herbert Thurston (1934), writing in the wake of a multiplicity of apparitions in Belgium. Thurston agreed with psychological studies of visions, which classed them as subjective phenomena based in personal or collective 'auto-suggestion' that was merely drawing on well-known religious ideas (Thurston 1934: 44). He compared them to the evangelical Protestant revivals in Britain and the USA, in which visions, conversions, and moral improvement were seen as evidence for divine action (Thurston 1934: 20). Nevertheless, he rejected any idea that the majority of apparitions were hoaxes fabricated by the visionaries; normally, they were sincere and genuinely believed in the objectivity of their experience. To support his view that visual phenomena caused by auto-suggestion or collective hallucination were common in religious devotion, he cited several cases of moving and weeping statues, many of which were observed by respected Catholics, including bishops and priests. The interesting features of these were: firstly, not everyone saw; secondly, not everyone seeing was a believer; thirdly, different witnesses had varying experiences; fourthly, the local context (e.g. a history of mystical phenomena in the area) may have played its part (Thurston 1934: 133–4). These elements suggest a psychological provenance and they describe the more influential apparitions as well as moving statues. Therefore, while Thurston agrees that the visionary experience is often profound and edifying, he argues that it is not necessarily to be taken as an indication of special divine action. He is even suspicious of apparitions approved by the Church, such as those at La Salette. Yet there are certain cases that he regards as supernatural experiences beyond reasonable doubt, in particular, the visions of Bernadette Soubirous at Lourdes (Thurston 1934: 119). Thurston does not really convince the reader as to why Lourdes can be regarded in a separate category; his argument relies on its general acceptance in the international Catholic community.

The science of the paranormal or parapsychology, developed since the late nineteenth century, has had an impact on Catholic thought and in published Catholic analyses of visionary phenomena a line can be traced from Thurston through Rahner to Schwebel. This thinking downplays popular emphasis on the miraculous and sensational nature of apparitions. It regards them as natural even if unusual, although without automatically reducing them to the level of hallucinations caused by mental illness or neurotic reactions to social upheaval. This leaves the case open to being understood as divine inspiration as, in Thomist theology, everything except sin is the work of God (Rahner 1963: 42–3). An apparition that is not manifestly tainted by questionable social or political agendas has the potential to strengthen faith, bring peace and healing, and restore community life. Following the logic of this line of thinking, this could happen through a charismatic teacher, a community initiative, or an inspired publication—these are also works of God—and while the apparition is a particular type of phenomenon, it is of the same order as these others despite the sensationalism that surrounds it.

CHURCH JUDGEMENTS ON APPARITIONS

Many apparitions are taken very seriously by the Church hierarchy, despite its reservations. If bishops do decide to investigate a case formally (and in many cases they do not), the commission they instigate can determine whether an apparition is 'true' or 'false' (see the studies by Alonso et al. 1973). Commissions come to one of three conclusions:

(i) The supernatural nature of the apparition is established (*constat de supernaturalitate*).

In the absence of alternative explanations or heretical or implausible statements, and due to the observation of strongly positive signs such as edifying messages, claimed healings, and increased devotions, the Church in its official capacity has accepted that a communication with supernatural beings (holy and not demonic) is the most likely cause. Following Lambertini, Roman Catholics are not constrained to believe in this nor required to express any devotion at the shrine concerned (although it would be regarded as disloyal if they were to publicly disparage or disavow the case). In twentieth-century Europe, apparitions that have been formally approved in this way number only four: Fátima (Portugal, 1917); Beauraing (Belgium, 1932–3); Banneux (Belgium, 1933); Amsterdam (1945–59, approved in 2002, overturning a previous negative decision in 1956). The culmination of Church authentication is recognition by the Vatican and a papal visit, which has occurred at Fátima, Beauraing, and Banneux, but the decision at Amsterdam was a diocesan one that has yet to be affirmed at Vatican level. International approval can be reinforced by the inclusion of a shrine in the 'European Marian Network', in which each country is represented by a major shrine: of the modern European apparition sites Lourdes (France 1858), Knock (Ireland 1879), Fátima (Portugal 1917), and Banneux (Belgium 1933) are listed as national shrines.

(ii) The supernatural nature of the event has not been established (*non constat de supernaturalitate*).

There is not enough evidence for the Church to accept the apparition as genuine, although the indications are not wholly negative. This decision leaves open the possibility of further examination and so pilgrims may be allowed to visit the site, although often they are discouraged from doing so and from promoting the apparitions as if they were genuine. The 1991 decision of the Yugoslav Episcopal Conference on Medjugorje is the most famous decision of this type, and devotees await a final statement from the Vatican.

(iii) The non-supernatural nature of the event has been established (*constat de non supernaturalitate*).

In this case, clear alternative explanations have been found or the apparition report has not been found worthy to be accredited with the claims that are made on its behalf. There may be evidence that one or more of the following can be ascribed to the visionaries or their followers: mental illness; illusion; contrivance to gain through pilgrimage and devotion; self-aggrandizement; desire to cause agitation; statements that are in obvious discord with Roman Catholic doctrine; the likelihood that the visionary messages will lead to discord amongst believers, embarrassment, ridicule, or loss of confidence in the Catholic faith. In these cases, pilgrimages will be prohibited with ecclesiastically imposed penalties for those who disregard the Church's ruling.

The Church's decision to make a formal judgement on certain cases leads to a *canon* of apparitions, those that have been accepted into the devotional life of Roman Catholics. In some cases, the apparitions are approved and there is no barrier to the resulting shrine—built at the place where the apparitions normally occurred—becoming a large-scale pilgrim destination. Many millions go to Lourdes and Fátima and a majority of the pilgrimages to these places are organized by Catholic dioceses across Europe and beyond. Before the apparitions of Mary at Lourdes and Fátima, they were not known as shrines at all. Now they have taken their place at the centre of Catholic Marian geography and to some extent replaced older shrines. There are replicas constructed around the world, holy pictures distributed, and films made. There are other modern apparition shrines, such as Beauraing and Banneux, where pilgrim numbers will not be as great as at Lourdes and Fátima but there is still a steady flow of pilgrims. Dioceses in the same nation and neighbouring countries will organize visits to these places on a regular basis. Beauraing has formed a network of local pilgrimages, which allow people to walk to the shrine from relatively short distances (around eight to fifteen kilometres), passing wayside shrines en route. This is a traditional Catholic practice in Europe; not far from Beauraing is the seventeenth-century shrine at Foy

Notre-Dame with a similar but older network of pilgrimages. Church-led pilgrimages have been joined in recent years by the growth of shrine tours, where pilgrims can visit the Internet to book a journey that takes in several holy places, ancient, medieval, and modern.

However, the canon of apparition shrines does not only include cases that have been formally approved through a commission of enquiry. There are other possibilities:

- The apparitions occurred in a period before rigorous examination was either required or feasible (usually before the Council of Trent, but later dates are possible). They were accepted informally by the Church, both hierarchical and lay, and have become traditional places of pilgrimage.

- The process by which the apparitions were examined was inconclusive or unfinished, but the apparitions were accepted nevertheless and the shrine made official. In the nineteenth century, the Rue du Bac and Knock are the most famous examples. In the twentieth century, Heede (Germany, 1937–40) was the subject of an episcopal commission in wartime that never came to a decision, but the site was finally accepted as a diocesan shrine in 2000, although the apparitions themselves have not been given ecclesiastical approval in the same way as at the Rue du Bac or Knock.

- There was no attempt to mount a full-scale commission into the apparitions, but the visionaries satisfied the Church to the extent that episcopal blessing has been given to either (i) organized pilgrimages, as at L'Ile-Bouchard (France 1947) or (ii) the building of a chapel, in some cases leading to a larger-scale shrine, of which there are several twentieth-century examples: Wigratzbad (Germany 1936); La Codosera (Spain 1945); Tre Fontane (Rome 1947); and Cefalà Diana (Sicily 1967). Pilgrims may be reminded that the apparitions themselves are not approved as genuine supernatural manifestations.

- In certain cases, even though the Church originally came to the decision that the supernatural was unproven or even that the non-supernatural was established, the passage of time and the persistence of pilgrimage mean that the Church, while giving clear indications that the apparitions are not approved and should not be promoted as such, accepts the shrine as a proper place of Catholic pilgrimage. Two examples of this in Germany are Marienfried (1946) and Heroldsbach (1949–52), which are now diocesan shrines.

The status of an apparition can change with time and this may depend on the *sensus fidelium*, the 'opinion of the faithful'. Peter Jan Margry shows how the Amsterdam cult, originally discouraged but now approved by the diocese, is an example of successful popular pressure that eventually convinces the Catholic Church to accept apparition cults (Margry 2009a; 2009b). Other examples of Western European cases where episcopal displeasure in the earlier

stages was replaced by a more lenient policy that allowed pilgrimage and
devotion include shrines in Germany, San Sebastián de Garabandal in Spain
(1961–5), San Damiano in Italy (1964–81), and Medjugorje in Bosnia-
Herzegovina (1981–present), although none of these apparitions has yet
been approved by local bishops. There is very often disagreement amongst
the clergy and members of the religious orders over apparitions. When
diocesan bishops declare that a case is not approved and that pilgrimage,
devotion, and promotion should cease, they often do so in the face of a
number of priests or members of religious orders who frequent the shrine,
and with these most in mind. Indeed, most shrines would not survive without
the backing of clergy; for example, support for apparitions such as Amsterdam, Garabandal, San Damiano, and Medjugorje has been based on mass
movements, including priests, members of religious orders, and the laity. To
speak of popular movements or the *sensus fidelium* does not imply that these
are based purely on the laity. Dissident clergy were responsible for the schism
at Palmar de Troya (from 1975). The Franciscans promoted Medjugorje
against the wishes of the diocesan bishop. It can be the other way round; in
the case of Beauraing, the Carmelites led opposition to the apparitions despite
the bishop's support for them.

During the pontificate of John Paul II, there were greater efforts by diocesan
bishops to reach compromises with persistent non-canonical apparition cults.
From the late 1980s, there has been some measure of liberalization at sites
previously under strong censure or diocesan recognition where calls for
official status had until then been ignored. This coincided with a call from
the Mariologian and apparition historian René Laurentin for a more balanced
and sympathetic pastoral approach, neither blindly supporting nor repressing
phenomena (1991: 209–11). It seemed to Laurentin that the acceptance of
apparitions from Rue du Bac to Banneux resulting in globally known sanctuaries such as Lourdes had caused Catholics to lose a sense of perspective; a
shrine does not need to be the latest version of Lourdes but can act as a local
source of grace. This requires neither solemn approval nor strict suppression
but pastoral support. In this way, shrines neither claim an inappropriate
proportion of Catholic attention nor become sites of schism and unhealthy
devotion. Yet, at the same time as his publication, the Internet was being
developed. Paolo Apolito (2005) demonstrates that Marian devotion on the
web can be subversive, providing a sphere of individual authentication and
popular interpretation that can undercut the process of canonical approval.
This does not help Laurentin's suggested strategy, as there is a tendency for
people to seek the most up-to-date global sensation as well as use websites to
promote their own version, rather than work on faith and renewal on a more
modest and limited scale.

In summary, the Catholic tradition from Trent proclaims consistent
themes: the strong possibility of an explanation that makes unnecessary belief

in a supernatural cause of an apparition; the need for the local bishop to seek a canonical decision where apparition cults become influential; the insistence on obedience to episcopal prohibitions where an apparition is not deemed suitable for devotion; and the non-binding nature of a decision on Catholics where the apparition is approved, as it is not part of doctrine. All of this suggests caution and provisionality about apparitions in the teaching of the Catholic hierarchy. So a statement of authentication is often couched in language such as that an apparition is 'worthy of human faith'. However, there was a tendency for the Catholic hierarchy in the nineteenth century to venture beyond this boundary and to make statements, such as Bishop Laurence declaring his decision on Lourdes in 1862, that Mary 'actually appeared to Bernadette Soubirous...eighteen times...this apparition assumes all the character of truth, and the faithful are justified in believing it certain' (Cros 126 III: 42–53). At this time, apparitions were regarded as crucial weapons in the ideological battle against secular humanism in its various forms. In this way, Lourdes and other major cases such as Fátima have inserted themselves into Catholic culture in a way that seems to suggest that they are central to the belief structure; visits by popes to shrines reinforce this common understanding. Not surprisingly, then, the latest apparition is put in a position of all or nothing: it is either the new Lourdes or Fátima, or a non-event. Laurentin's call for a more nuanced approach in which there may be local benefits arising from an apparition that may never come to international attention, and Ratzinger's statement of the subjective nature of visions in *The Message of Fatima* (2000), are recent attempts to remind Catholics that apparitions are limited in import, epiphenomena of Catholic life rather than central and focal elements. However, there are a great many Catholics who do not seem to be responding to this advice.

5

Women as Visionaries

THE PREDOMINANCE OF WOMEN
AND CHILD VISIONARIES

Although Cardinal Lambertini's work on discernment is so often referred to in diocesan commissions investigating apparitions, he does not seem to have anticipated the influence of women and children in the new era. He writes, drawing on the work of the seventeenth-century Cardinal Bona:

> The same author adds, that age must also be considered, for old men, their strength being exhausted, frequently dote; and children, whose brain is more moist, are easily moved, and receive false impressions instead of the true. Sex, too, is to be regarded, for women are naturally of a more moist constitution, and by reason of the vehemence of their thoughts and affections, think they see what they desire; and what results from their perturbation of mind, which in them is most violent, they believe to proceed from truth . . . (Lambertini 1852 III: 322–3).

Lambertini is arguing that age and gender can be regarded as factors that provide alternative explanations which tell against a supernatural origin, although he adds that visions experienced by women could not be wholly discounted, as many female saints had received visions 'beyond the power of nature'. Nevertheless, despite the doubts about women and child visionaries held by Bona and Lambertini, the most important apparition shrines erected in France in the sixteenth and seventeenth centuries were Garaison and Le Laus, where the visionaries were girl shepherdesses aged twelve and sixteen respectively. Therefore the importance of the young female visionary predates Lambertini; after all, it is the category of visionary that most resembles the Virgin during the time of the annunciation and birth of Christ. It is also difficult to correlate his analysis with the honour paid to the women and child seers of the nineteenth and twentieth centuries, especially those who were both female and either child or adolescent. It is true that visionaries at Rue du Bac, Lourdes, and Fátima were canonized or beatified in time, and so moved into the category of saints to whom Lambertini conceded genuine visions, but there were a greater number of others who did not.

How do the seers of the modern era divide along gender and age lines? Carroll (1983: 209) uses William Walsh's data (in *The Apparitions and Shrines of Heaven's Bright Queen*, 1904) to point out that, between 1100 and 1896, women had not been more prominent than men as visionaries; indeed Walsh's list of Marian visionaries for that period includes only 42 per cent females. Nevertheless, in Europe in the nineteenth century, females were clearly more favoured than males in the eyes of the Church. In the approved or part-approved European cases of the nineteenth century (see those listed in Chapter 2 within this volume), the identified seers number nineteen, seven of whom are women (six unmarried) and ten children or adolescents under eighteen years of age, seven girls, three boys (see Table 5.1, first row). This gender bias continues in twentieth-century Europe; when apparitions have been approved to some level (Fátima; Beauraing; Banneux; Wigratzbad; Amsterdam; Tre Fontane, but not including Bruno Cornacchiola's children, who were of secondary importance; L'Île-Bouchard), these figures result: sixteen seers, of whom two are women (both unmarried) and thirteen children or adolescents, eleven girls and two boys (Table 5.1, second row). Taking this further, if now the twentieth-century cases mentioned in this book are totalled where there was some reserve or no decision about apparitions, but the shrines or their cult became official, in some cases quite smoothly, in others involving a substantial volte-face from the Church (Orto Nova; Bad Lippspringe; Heede; Marienfried; Montichiari; Casanova Staffora; Balestrino; Heroldsbach; Cefalà Diana; Belpasso; Crosia; El Escorial), this results in twenty-six visionaries, five of whom are women (three unmarried) and twenty-one children or adolescents, fourteen girls and seven boys (Table 5.1, third row). Amongst the original instigators of all of these officially sanctioned shrines, there is only one adult male visionary: Bruno Cornacchiola of Tre Fontane, and even he fell out of favour eventually (see Chapter 11 within this volume).

An interesting shift results if the table now includes all other twentieth-century European apparitions mentioned in this book where definite seers can be identified (therefore not Ezkioga, La Codosera, and Oliveto Citra, for example), the Church has not approved the case, and the shrines have either fallen into abeyance or continue to cause controversy, such as Medjugorje (Table 5.1, fourth row). In this category, there are ninety-eight seers, of whom thirty-three are women (seven unmarried) and forty-three children or adolescents: thirty-six girls and seven boys; there are twenty-two adult males (although of these, fourteen are accounted for by Belgium in 1933 and the Palmar de Troya movement). This suggests that, while single women and children or adolescents are the visionaries most likely to be approved by the Church, other categories of visionary (married women and adult men) are also popular in cases that deviate from the clerical canon. Nevertheless, while the percentage of adults increases substantially in unapproved cases compared to those approved in the twentieth century (but not the nineteenth), the

Table 5.1. The gender and age of seers in Europe in the nineteenth and twentieth centuries

	Girls (under 18*)	Single women	Married women	Boys (under 18*)	Men
Approved nineteenth-century cases	7 (1 healed)	6 (3 nuns, 2 healed)	1 (1 healed)	3	2
Approved twentieth-century cases	11 (1 became a 'victim soul')	2 (1 healed)	0	2	1
Part-approved twentieth-century cases	14 (1 became a 'victim soul')	3 (1 healed)	2	7	0
Non-approved twentieth-century cases**	36 (1 became a 'victim soul')	7 (2 involve women suffering illness, 1'victim soul')	26 (2 healed, 1 'victim soul')	7	22

* The age is given for the time of the first vision: some visionaries pass into adulthood during the period of the visions, notably at Medjugorje.

** The sample comprises the cases mentioned in this book for which specific seers can be identified.

percentage of males, even when boys are included, does not exceed 30 per cent in any category (see Table 5.2, first four rows). Of the females, the unmarried and young are clearly the most prominent. Badone notes how it was in Jeanne-Louise Ramonet of Kerizinen's favour that she, being unmarried, 'remained in the social category of pure, virginal women' (Badone 2007: 466), although this was not enough for Church approval.

These figures can be checked by comparing them to the long and comprehensive lists given by the University of Dayton and Miracle Hunter websites, where almost everything is included that has come to the attention of the list compilers. The lists do not specify age and gender in every case and marital status is rarely given; nevertheless figures for the proportions of female/male and adult/child can be drawn from all those where this is identified (Table 5.2, fifth and sixth rows). What we can now conclude is that, in twentieth-century Europe, seers are generally female, at least in the proportion 70/30, even in unapproved cases. While this may not be the case before the twentieth century, the prominence given to women and girls during the nineteenth century may have had the effect of creating greater expectation when female visionaries emerged, thus leading to reports, the visits of pilgrims, records, narratives, and ensuing cults.

Ezkioga in Basque Spain (1931–6) is not included in these figures because of the proliferation of visionaries there. Christian's analysis of the apparitions of Ezkioga records the distrust of adult married females as seers; they gained prominence only after the apparitions were condemned by the Church (Christian 1996: 245–50). Adult males were more acceptable to the Catholic

Table 5.2. The age and gender weighting across the categories in Table 5.1, by percentage, checked by website lists

	Female	Male	Child under 18	Adult
Approved nineteenth-century	74% (5% married)	26%	53%	47%
Approved twentieth-century	81% (0 married)	19%	81%	19%
Implicit approval twentieth-century	73% (8% married)	27%	81%	19%
Not approved twentieth-century	70% (27% married)	30%	43%	57%
University of Dayton list for Europe	73% (of sample 223 where gender specified)	27%	52% (of sample 345 where child/adult status specified)	48%
Miracle Hunter list for Europe	71% (of sample 390)	29%	46% (of sample 497)	54%

press recording the visions, but they were not regarded as likely initiators of visions. At Ezkioga and elsewhere in Spain in the early 1930s (see also Chapter 2, the section on Fátima in Portugal), children and adolescents were afforded special and sacred status as visionaries because of their 'alleged lack of guile and their supposed ignorance of the wider world' (Christian 1996: 248), and also because 'adolescent girls stood ultimately for the Virgin herself' (Christian 1996: 246). Furthermore, there is evidence to suggest that the concentration on specific females identified as genuine seers renders an apparition more likely to receive Church approval. Failure to identify central seers is a negative criterion because the apparitions were then deemed out of control. Thus, in addition to Ezkioga, some of the most closely studied non-approved apparitions—in Belgium in the 1930s (van Osselaer 2012) and at Oliveto Citra in the 1980s (Apolito 1998)—included many adult or late-teenage males amongst a host of visionaries. Tilman Côme at Beauraing is an example of an adult male seer becoming prominent but eventually being discarded.

In Belgium in 1933, the popularity of some adult male visionaries challenged the apparent dominance of female visionaries in modern Roman Catholicism. Tine van Osselaer (2012) writes about the masculinity of visionaries at Herzele; Lokeren; Olsene; Etikhove, as well as Tilman Côme at Beauraing. These male visionaries managed to combine the emotion and expressive piety associated with seers in general with the calm rationality that was expected of men. More important than gender was the simplicity of the seer. Just as the Beauraing and Banneux visionaries, like others before them, impressed people because their experience could not have been contrived from theological learning, this was also true for the working-class male seers in Belgium; a factory background was an argument in favour. This was a period when the ideal of the Christian worker was being promulgated in Catholic Europe, with a special emphasis on those converted from anarchism or socialism (van Osselaer 2012: 154–8). However, none of these males was recognized as a visionary with a long-lasting legacy because of decisions made by the Church in Belgium (see Chapter 8 on Belgium within this volume).

Overall, the predominance of teenage women and children as visionaries in nineteenth- and twentieth-century Europe is best regarded as a result of cultural expectations and choices made by Catholic leaders, both clerical and lay, rather than a natural phenomenon. The popular theory that Christianity was 'feminized' in the nineteenth century can be debated; church-going figures show a majority of women, but just what this implies is unclear. Pasture (2012) critiques the 'feminization' theory and asks whether feminization actually means female presence in contrast to masculine power in the Church (Pasture 2012: 17–18, citing Ann Braude). Van Osselaer (2013) shows how 'masculinity' and 'femininity' were constructed in European Catholicism over the nineteenth and early twentieth centuries; Catholic men were considered to be members of a 'pious sex' too, and examples of devotions that attracted males include the Sacred Heart. While the Church has been concerned to increase the involvement of men in parish life and to combat interest in socialist politics, the belief that women are naturally more religious than men is a cultural construct and often the result of either (i) rhetoric around the importance of women as mothers in keeping the faith alive for new generations, or (ii) slurs about the effeminate nature of religion (especially Catholicism), which became normalized. In the same way, a theory that women (especially young unmarried ones) and children make more naturally suitable seers than adult males needs to be subject to an analysis that recognizes the socio-political historical contexts and ideologies behind this assumption.

VICTIM SOULS AND WISE WOMEN

The substantial number of women seers who suffer or who are healed from what appear to be serious or terminal diseases merits attention. There are several instances of illness amongst female visionaries, which comes under two kinds: first, where an apparition brings healing to a seriously ill woman. Examples include, in the nineteenth century, Magdalena Kade of Philippsdorf, Estelle Faguette of Pellevoisin, and Fortuna Agrelli of Pompeii; in the twentieth century, Antonie Rädler of Wigratzbad, Odilia Knoll of Marmagen, and 'Mama' Rosa Quattrini of San Damiano. Harris (1999: 306–9) notes that the majority of healed people (*miraculées*) at Lourdes in the late nineteenth century were women and the greatest number of these were single; Kaufman (2005: 137–9) shows that being healed at Lourdes enabled some women to assume spiritual authority and to write about their experiences.

The second type is where a visionary seeks the vocation of suffering. The figures in Table 5.1 do not include three famous female mystics who experienced apparitions (including those of Mary) and whose work has achieved some measure of recognition by the Church: the Belgian Franciscan tertiary Berthe Petit, who experienced visions between 1909 and 1938; the French Augustinian nun Yvonne-Aimée Beauvais of Malestroit, between 1927 and 1947; the Polish Sister of Our Lady of Mercy, Faustina Kowalska, in Warsaw and Vilnius, between 1910 and 1938 (Laurentin and Sbalchiero 2007: 149, 577–81). All three were known for their vocation of suffering, a tradition in female religious orders that goes back through centuries. However, there are also examples of women not in religious orders who sought this life. Grete Ganseforth, visionary of Heede in north-western Germany from 1937, first experienced stigmata in 1939 as a very young teenager, then offered herself to God as a 'victim soul' on 28 June 1940, experiencing the suffering of Jesus. She is then reported to have become completely paralysed from 1947 until her death in 1996; Brinkmann (1999: 16–18) states that she had undulant fever, but admits to not being sure as to how much the health problems can be attributed to the disease and how much to the spiritual vocation of suffering. As a bedridden victim soul, she was popular, contributing prayer and advice.

Richard Burton's book (2004) shows how Catholic women took on voluntary suffering in reparation for sin during the many social and political changes in France during the nineteenth and twentieth centuries; an exemplar is Marthe Robin (1902–81), who began experiencing ill health aged sixteen (Burton 2004: 106–15). Burton shows how these women and the associated phenomena, such as stigmata and consuming only the Eucharist, are rejected by the male Church hierarchy mostly because of their perceived spiritual power (Burton 2004: 115). Science, too, is sceptical; drawing on the work of Ruth Harris, Burton argues that the nineteenth-century medical ascription of 'hysteria' to this phenomenon is no more scientifically convincing than assuming that they are supernaturally inspired (Burton 2004: 188–9; Harris 1999: 356). Yet, while the hierarchical Church is generally nervous about encouraging these kinds of female charismatic vocations, the women concerned usually depend on support from the laity, priesthood, religious orders, and occasionally the episcopate, without which they would not achieve fame and influence. Such victim souls participate in the suffering of Christ for the redemption of sin. Burton, writing about Mélanie Calvat, who lost the support of the Church, says that Mélanie offered herself as a sacrificial victim for the faults of France; she followed the female martyrs of the Revolution in taking on the vocation of expiatory victim. 'In the postrevolutionary French Catholic imagination, the spiritual function of woman is to weep, bleed, and starve for the salvation of others, to offer herself up as a holocaust to appease a revengeful male deity' (Burton 2004: 19).

The concept of redemptive suffering is also found in other countries in Europe and the status of a Marian visionary can be associated with it. The young Mary of the Annunciation and Birth of Christ can be represented only by young unmarried women, but it is the older woman sufferer who is in the image of the Our Lady of Sorrows, the Pietà of the Crucifixion. In this tradition, one of the most famous women of the twentieth century has been the Bavarian lay stigmatic Therese Neumann (1898–1962); a Catholic analysis of her spiritual gifts is given in Graef (1950) and a devotional biography in Schimberg (1947). She suffered from paralysis and it was alleged that she ate and drank nothing but the bread and wine of the Eucharist. Her spiritual powers were well known, although she was never recognized by the Church; her home in Konnersreuth is still preserved as a shrine and visitors are invited to sign the petition for her beatification. She was famous for her strained relationship with the Nazi government, which was suspicious of the strength of her following and her friendships with Fritz Gerlich, editor of the Catholic journal *The Right Way*, and Willi Schmid, Catholic music critic in Munich, both of whom were executed on the Night of the Long Knives, 30 June 1934, and Friedrich Ritter von Lama, author of her story and also a supporter of Marpingen, who died in Stadelheim concentration camp in 1944 (Blackbourn 1993: 378). She became popular with American Catholic servicemen as the war ended; they flocked to see her and to seek her advice.

Neumann's fame made her a powerful ally in establishing the popular status of visions such as those of Léonie van den Dijck of Onkerzele in Belgium (see Chapter 8 within this volume). Therese sent letters of support to Léonie (Schellink 1994: 212–13); Onkerzele's devotees made much of the link to Neumann, whose reputation made her popular across Catholic Europe. Therese provides a strong example of the Catholic archetype of female spiritual giftedness often at odds with the hierarchy; she was renowned as a popular prophet and spiritually sensitive adult woman who received many visitors at her home (rather than an established shrine or religious house). Michael O'Sullivan notes that Therese is not necessarily an example of radical Catholicism, as she and her supporters did not seek confrontation with the Church, and that, as an apparently influential female, she was not critical of Catholic gender hierarchy and remained dependent on men (her priest, father, and brother) for the means of maintaining her work (O'Sullivan 2009: 12–14). Léonie van den Dijck follows the pattern of female prophet and stigmatic that Therese represents. She sought cooperation with the local priest who was initially supportive; only the Church at a higher level refused her claims. A mother of nine children who had been abandoned by her husband (unlike the celibate Therese), she needed the help of male supporters, notably Gustaaf Schellinck, whose memoirs are important in preserving her life story.

Ursula Hibbeln of Bochum (1869–1940), a tertiary Franciscan, was another visionary known and admired by Therese (Ernst 1988; Bouflet 2003: 133–44). She too was bedridden and highly regarded as a reader of souls. She had suffered the death of eight of her nine children and was said to have a special relationship with the souls in purgatory, for whom she prayed. Bouflet describes this kind of seer in helpful detail and is worth quoting in full. He situates her in a German Catholic tradition:

> ... of pious women of humble background who, amongst other things, perpetuate the medieval tradition of the Beguines, even of recluses. Taking up a life of seclusion, devoted to prayer and thankless tasks, they keep to themselves the care of maintaining the parish church, the cemetery, country chapels in the neighbourhood. Often affiliated to the Franciscan Third Order, which lends them a vague institutional legitimacy, people consult them on occasions of bereavement or testing times, because they have the key to a spiritual interpretation, which consoles, comforts, helps understanding. People credit them with extraordinary clairvoyance, even mystical graces, and especially familiarity with the souls in purgatory, with the world of angels, with celestial visions. (Bouflet 2003: 135, my translation)

He gives other examples of this type of female wise woman who like Ursula Hibbeln were said to despise the Third Reich: Barbara Weigand (1845–1943) who predicted the defeat of Germany and referred to Hitler as 'the monster vomited from hell'; and Mariella Klimaschka (1895–1969), associated with the Dresden priest Alois Andritzky who died in Dachau (Bouflet 2003: 135–6).

William Christian records the presence of *divinas*, seers or diviners, mainly older women living alone, in Cantabria, Spain (Christian 1989: 195–6); as his work was on rural areas, the role that they performed often involved the spiritual discernment of the whereabouts of missing animals. He writes:

> Attitudes towards women are implicit in the ascription of both benign and malign occult powers to them. Women are sources of uncertainty in the society. They have a tap on the unknown. Perhaps this is another reason for the use of Mary as the most important divine figure. (Christian 1989: 196)

The close proximity between this figure and the stereotype of the witch is all too apparent, that is, the concept of a witch as a benign rather than malicious magician, probably closer in meaning to the modern use of the word 'shaman'. The shaman (see e.g. Harvey 2002) is understood as a person with spiritual powers and the ability to communicate with souls, but with the endorsement of their community (although respect may be tinged with fear). The *bruja* of Mexican witchcraft is of this type. This is different from the early modern European understanding of witchcraft that led to the deaths of many women; the witch in that context was seen as a weak, licentious person, vulnerable to the temptations of the Devil and often causing harm unwittingly (beliefs in the witch as unwitting protagonist can also be found in Africa). Clearly, this image is solely a justification for victimization and scapegoating. The Marian female visionary is not like a witch in that sense, but a type of shaman, although there is a substantial difference: the wise women (or men) of Catholic Europe would probably not have used formulas, rituals, or spells to bring about ends. Their power is based in knowledge of circumstances rather than the ability to change them; as visionaries, they claim the gift of seeing and knowing what Mary or Christ sees and knows, and communicating with saints or the souls in purgatory.

WOMEN AS POPULAR THEOLOGIANS

In the nineteenth and twentieth centuries, therefore, women's vision-ary experiences have influenced generations of Catholics but, until the Second World War, the most famous were nuns or became nuns. These included: Catherine Labouré of the Rue du Bac; Mélanie Calvat of La Salette (although she left the convent); Bernadette Soubirous of Lourdes; Lúcia (dos) Santos of Fátima; and Faustina Kowalska. Such women are among the best-known Catholic personalities of the modern period: Catherine, Bernadette, and Faustina have been canonized, their lives and writings recorded in detail (Laurentin 1983; Taylor 2003; Kowalska 2012). Lúcia's memoirs have been translated into many languages, as has the more recent *Calls from the Message of Fatima* (2005), based on her letters and reflections. The Catholic popular theology of modern apparitions has been developed primarily by women and their followers have often been women too. Badone (2007: 465) records how the shrine at Kerizinen in Brittany was supported mainly by women; however, she adds that: 'This predominance of women at Kerizinen may have been a factor hindering its investigation and recognition by the official Church' (Badone 2007: 466). The shrines at both Kerizinen and Amsterdam have been maintained by the foundation of new female religious orders, although the order at Kerizinen has not been recognized by the Church (see Chapter 10 within this volume).

Feminist critiques of Mariology, while identifying and analysing the patri-archal culture of Catholicism, have perhaps underplayed the fact that Mario-logical ideas are often developed, promulgated, and taken seriously by women. Marina Warner, in *Alone of All Her Sex*, claimed that 'the moral code she [Mary] affirms has been exhausted' (Warner 1990: 338), meaning a code in which women were subjugated, given secondary status, and their sexuality heavily circumscribed. However, she also stated in a subsequent edition that, if she were to undertake analysis again, 'I would have tried to pay more attention to the voices raised in Mary's praise, and to distinguish more scrupulously between women's and men's conception of the Mother of God...' (Warner 1990: 344). Elisabeth Schüssler Fiorenza regards the image of Mary to be open to 'feminist reconstructions of mariology' which 'assume that a discourse on mariological dogmas from the perspective of women is not only possible but also necessary since otherwise women would have to relinquish the mariological heritage of women's devotion to Mary that has been accumulated over centuries' (Schüssler Fiorenza 1994: 173).

Yet how far does the image of the exalted woman Mary contribute to the maintenance of patriarchy in Catholicism, even when expressed by women? Gebara and Bingemer conclude that the devotion of the subjugated manages, despite the hegemony of the powerful, 'to maintain a degree of independence, a tenuous expression of freedom and of the yearning for recognition and self-determination' (Gebara and Bingemer 1989: 157). On the other hand, 'even the image and cult of a woman who is worshipped by women can cement structures of oppression' (Schüssler Fiorenza 1994: 173–4). Apparitions that reveal a powerful Marian image may support both the patriarchy of the Catholic culture, and sometimes also an implicit subversion of that culture, promoting popular theological ideas conceived by women and establishing a source of authority outside the clergy. Female visionaries often demand something of the priesthood (as in Lúcia's request for the consecration of Russia to the Immaculate Heart), and sometimes criticize it (Lúcia did not explicitly, but others did, such as Mélanie Calvat and Ida Peerdeman of Amsterdam). Yet it must be conceded that the women visionaries have not enjoyed the educational or cultural resources with which to contradict or critique the patriarchal Catholic theology of the magisterium. Their role is rigidly delimited in the Catholic Church.

From the rise of the ultramontane movement in the mid-nineteenth century, the Marian movement has generally promoted a particular stereotype of woman based on identification with the Virgin Mary, i.e. chaste, modest, and pious, engaged primarily with the domestic sphere and committed to educating and raising Catholic children (illustrated in Francoist Spain by Morcillo 2008; in nineteenth- and twentieth-century France by Burton 2004: xx–xxv; in interwar Germany by O'Sullivan 2012). This did not abate until Paul VI, in *Marialis Cultus* (1974), declared that Mary could be the role model for a 'new woman' with a professional career. There is nothing surprising about the association of Mary with conservative views of gender; feminism has challenged patriarchal attitudes across all cultures and religions, and this is not limited to Catholicism. However, the rise of women's emancipation gained momentum in Protestant countries and under republicanism in Catholic ones, and so the entrenched Catholic Church regarded the liberated woman as the fruit of anti-Catholic forces. There is a danger of generalizing this: O'Sullivan (2012: 206–9) gives the example of the Catholic women's association in interwar Germany, the *Heliand-Bund*, which attracted younger women and achieved a carefully managed transition between traditional Catholic roles and preparing women for professional careers (O'Sullivan 2012: 211). Neverthe- less, the general case is that apparition cults arise in contexts where Catholics are concerned about what they see as modern licentiousness promoted by anti-Catholic forces in society. It is interesting that Lúcia Santos, the stereo- typical visionary-turned-nun, should have been disappointed as a child that her parish priest banned dancing as an immoral activity (Bennett 2012: 83), a vignette that captures succinctly the dilemma of the loyal Catholic woman for whom devotion to Mary implies a particular lifestyle, but who has passions and interests that contradict these norms.

Perhaps, to some extent, women visionaries contribute to an overturning of the normal gender hierarchy in Catholicism. Writing about nineteenth- century visionaries, Blackbourn suggests that the Church did offer women partial escape from male domination: in religious orders, for example, away from 'the trials of nineteenth-century reproduction' (Blackbourn 1993: 46). Female visionaries also gained some measure of autonomy in an otherwise harsh and demanding environment, and their followers, disproportionately women, likewise: 'For village women it was their world that now eclipsed the normal world of affairs, however briefly' (Blackbourn 1993: 46). With twentieth-century apparitions, this situation continued, although it should not be overstated. Where female visionaries accepted clerical supervision, it was possible that their message could be heard; if they did not, they risked the charge of disobedience to the Church, in ecclesiastical criteria a clear mark of inauthenticity. The power of visions provokes a hierarchical strategy of tight control over popular devotions, subjecting them to assessments that insist on orthodoxy, humility, and obedience, while selecting only a privileged few to promote and support. The classic apparitions of recent centuries, Lourdes and Fátima, have been ones in which women were the visionaries, but they were then sequestered in the convent while the clergy controlled the interpretations and developments. The 'secrets' that they claimed to have received provided their sole remaining means of power; Bernadette declined to reveal hers and any self-seeking on her part was clearly suppressed in the convent (as estab- lished by the historical data in Taylor 2003). While women have been very important in the growth and maintenance of official shrines, Lourdes in particular, they do not normally aspire to be leaders (Harris 1999: 306, 359–61). Michael O'Sullivan (2009), focusing on Heroldsbach, Fehrbach, and Rodalben, shows how the German apparition cults in the post-Second World War period resonated with Germans experiencing the aftermath of wartime trauma and so the shrines received many victims of the war, includ- ing prisoners of war and concentration camp inmates. The events therefore involved many male pilgrims and supporters, which resulted in the fact that, despite the majority of female followers, the movements that followed the visionaries were generally led by men.

The most influential woman visionary in the twentieth-century Catholic Church was Lúcia Santos of Fátima. She corresponded with popes and met three: Paul VI, John Paul I a year before his election, and John Paul II. Her life is eulogized by Cardinal Bertone (Bertone and de Carli 2008), the Vatican secretary of state and former secretary for the Congregation for the Doctrine of the Faith. She died in 2005, aged ninety-seven, and may yet follow her fellow visionaries Francisco and Jacinta Marto into canonical sanctity; they were beatified in 2000. It is true that the Vatican held back from publishing her 'third secret' for forty years, which may suggest some reservation on behalf of the papacy. Ultimately, John Paul II regarded her secret as being integral to his life and vocation, as he thought that her prophecy of a pope being shot corresponded with the assassination attempt on his life on the sixty-fourth anniversary of the first apparition at Fátima. So Lúcia's story is perhaps one of the most prominent examples supporting the argument that visionary experiences have been the one medium through which Catholic women have been able to make a contribution in spirituality that has influenced the whole Church, including its hierarchy. This appears to have been the only such means in traditional Catholicism. The Fátima cult, with its shrine, pilgrimages, and devotions, would not exist without her revelations. Of course, Lúcia claimed that the origin of these messages was a divine one; she would not agree that she had played any active part. Bernadette of Lourdes had stated that she was like an ox ploughing a field or a broom sweeping a room; these were used and then put away (Taylor 2003: 263). Lúcia used the metaphor of a paintbrush being thrown away after the work is done (Bertone and de Carli 2008: 9). This is the general Catholic understanding of a visionary.

Yet there is another way of looking at it. The Church itself understands the subjective element even in what is regarded as an authentic vision. Although a visionary's revelations are understood as having objectivity from without, nevertheless it is only through her pronouncements that the ideas have taken shape. A religious person who is not a visionary may contribute ideas that they consider divinely inspired, but because of a lack of an 'other' perceived through a vision, they would be regarded as the author of such inspirations. From the phenomenological point of view, all that is in view is the visionary and her messages, along with those who help her express them. Of course, the visionary draws, consciously or unconsciously, on the context, social or ecclesial. Bernadette had declared that her vision was the 'Immaculate Conception' only four years after this title was defined dogmatically by Pius IX. Lúcia said that the lady of her vision had asked people to pray the rosary for peace just eight days after a letter from Benedict XV asking for the same thing was read out in parishes; Our Lady of the Rosary was important to the pope's peace crusade of prayer in 1917 (Bennett 2012: 127). As children, it is no surprise that their messages drew on ideas current in ecclesiastical thought. Yet Bernadette and Lúcia gave tangible shape to current Mariological thinking in the Church in the form of specific devotions centred on a shrine: Lourdes and Fátima became the predominant places of pilgrimage in Western Europe. In Lúcia's case, this was expanded when she became an adult nun. She continued to have visions and locutions throughout her life until her death in 2005 (Bertone and de Carli 2008: 83). Yet, after the Second World War, she was already a global personality, a Catholic visionary who expressed the hopes, fears, and Mariological ideas of a substantial number of Catholics in her own and succeeding generations. She was at the centre of a movement that articulated a popular theology.

Jeff Astley refers to 'ordinary theology', 'the theology and theologizing of Christians who have received little or no theological education of a scholarly, academic or systematic kind' (Astley 2002: 56). Popular theology is ordinary theology, except that it articulates ordinary theological ideas in ways that appeal to a large number of fellow believers. Of course, popular or ordinary theology often diverges from the theology defined by the ecclesiastical authorities, and a conflict arises between 'official' and 'popular' religion (as defined by Vrijhof and Waardenburg 1979; see also Badone 1990). Popular theology is often uncomfortable for people of theological learning as it might not be very profound, original, or reflective; indeed, as the most famous visionaries were relatively uneducated, it is likely to be simple and derived from what the visionary has heard. Note Ratzinger's comments: 'private revelations often spring from popular piety' and 'the concluding part of the "secret" uses images which Lúcia may have seen in devotional books' (Bertone and Ratzinger 2000: 35, 42); Fernandes and d'Armada (2007) present several parallels between published devotional works and Lúcia's messages. What defines popular theology is not its intellectual depth or novelty but that it is *popular*. The rosary, Immaculate Conception, and Immaculate Heart were already very prominent and deeply rooted in early twentieth-century Portuguese Catholicism (Martindale 1950: 11–14; Bennett 2012: 211). However, Lúcia inspired millions by her claim that Mary said to her: 'My Immaculate Heart will triumph'. Even when derived from currents of thought in the visionary's context, the ideas will be framed in such a way as to suggest a new revelation of some kind. Even though Fernandes and d'Aramada consider Lúcia's later messages to have been framed within the tutelage of her Jesuit confessors (2007: 167–206), they accept that 'Lúcia was sufficiently creative not to copy. She gathered ideas and became inspired by certain models' (2007: 176).

It is clear, therefore, that the notion of 'popular theology' is quite different from the traditional concept of 'theology', that is, 'official theology' or the theology sanctioned and supported by the Church. The 1990 Vatican instruction *Donum Veritatis* refers to the theologian as one who is 'attentive to the epistemological requirements of his discipline, to the demands of rigorous critical standards, and thus to a rational verification of each stage of his research' (Ratzinger and Bovone 1990: para 9). Other denominations would follow equivalent definitions (while perhaps preferring gender-inclusive language in some cases; the male pronoun is quite instructive in the argument being developed here). Of course, in the Catholic context, *Donum Veritatis* goes on to insist that theology must be undertaken in obedience to and in consultation with the Magisterium, the teaching hierarchy of the Church. In contrast, it cannot be said that visionaries work critically and rationally within the constraints of a professional discipline. The visionary mode of theologizing is mystical and appears to be dictated by a supernatural other.

Visionaries do not articulate their ideas in a vacuum any more than 'official' theologians. It is very difficult for them to escape the public pressure and priestly oversight arising in the local context. This will entail an editing of the messages to remove heterodox, folk-based, parochial, or political material, a process that is more likely to lead to a wider acceptance in the Church. Those denouncing Medjugorje (e.g. Sivrić 1988: 61) raise questions about the origins, as the messages seem to shift from unorthodox ideas to established doctrine under Franciscan influence, but they fail to recognize that most apparitions have their origins in rural belief and folklore. Harris (1999: 33, 53–4, 58–9, 77–8) demonstrates this for Lourdes: the lady appeared in a grotto associated with spirits and was thought by some to have been a fairy or departed soul. Fernandes and d'Armada (2007: 151–5) bring to public attention the fact that the apparition lady of Fátima was originally described as wearing a knee-length skirt that contradicts the familiar long dress of orthodox Fátima images and traditional Catholic modesty. Apparently, this can be found in documents made public in 1992 that include additional records of the original interrogations in Portuguese. Admittedly, if proved conclusively to be the case, this would be an unwelcome surprise for Fátima devotees, but a model of apparitions that excludes any folkloric and unusual elements—which may seem to contradict orthodox Catholicism or rational belief—is not an accurate or truthful one. Popular and official beliefs often do conflict with each other; canonically approved apparition cults move the popular belief system nearer the expectations of doctrine, but it is never an easy marriage and may involve the suppression or marginalization of some aspects.

To conclude, the classic 'popular theologian' of Marian apparitions in the twentieth century is female. Apart from Lúcia, whose case has been explored further in Chapters 2 and 3 within this volume, other cases may be investigated to show the dynamics of the process by which popular theologians develop their ideas in the light of experience and response. In the middle years of the twentieth century, the apparitions at Kerizinen in Brittany (Jeanne-Louise Ramonet) and Amsterdam (Ida Peerdeman) provide fascinating examples of the role of women as popular theologians. These cases will be explored at more length in Chapter 10, while Angela Volpini provides another interesting example, and she will be included in Chapter 11.

6

Children as Visionaries

CHILDREN AND IMAGINATIVE PLAY

The prominence of children, particularly girls, is even more marked than that of women in twentieth-century apparitions of Mary. At Fátima in Portugal in 1917, the children were aged only ten, eight, and seven. A person unfamiliar with the Fátima story (see Chapter 2 within this volume) could be forgiven for being surprised that interchanges between such young children and a supposed vision could lead to a worldwide Catholic cult of such importance. The children were watching sheep, thought they saw lightning, and then a teenage girl in white appeared standing on a tree. Lúcia, the eldest and the only one who spoke to the apparition, asked questions. The girl in the vision pointed at the sky: she had come from heaven. They were to return to see her on the thirteenth of each month. Lúcia then asked about her own destiny: yes, she would go to heaven, so would Jacinta, but Francisco only after saying many rosaries. Lúcia also enquired whether Maria, a recently deceased child, was in heaven and this was affirmed by the vision; a girl called Amelia, however, would be in purgatory until the end of the world.

The scenario, including its questions and answers, is typical of children's play. It would be natural for the outsider to conclude that Lúcia, leading the dialogue, was making a child's judgements on other children as she had experienced them: she, Jacinta, and Maria were worthy of heaven; Francisco, a boy, needed to be more pious. Amelia, whoever she was, seems to have fared worst in this series of assessments. The argument that the first apparition involved children's fantasy is strengthened by the fact that Lúcia did not want the adults to learn about it. Jacinta's revelation of an apparition of 'Our Lady' to her family when the identity of the vision was not yet definite (Martindale 1950: 33) was one that she and Lúcia regretted, as it led to a period of considerable harassment. Bennett, in his book on Fátima, discusses the ability of children to create fantasy and then to mould it according to adult responses: 'They [the child seers] made personal contributions to the apparition drama . . . as the children increasingly experienced the adult desire that they personify holiness and act as seers, they converted this desire into a demand and acted on it accordingly . . . ' (Bennett 2012: 139).

Why, then, do Catholics believe in the visionary reports of children? Cardinal Ratzinger, the future Benedict XVI, writing on Fátima, suggested that: 'Perhaps this explains why children tend to be the ones to receive these apparitions: their souls are as yet little disturbed, their interior powers of perception are still not impaired' (Bertone and Ratzinger 2000: 37). Bennett (2012: 86) records the 'faith and purity' associated with female children in Portugal at the time of Fátima. It is likely that the Catholic positive assessment of the purity of children's apparition experiences is enhanced by the fact that visionary children repeat simple devotional ideas and demonstrate relative ignorance about social and political matters. The belief that children are better channels for inspiration than adults was also held by the psychoanalyst Carl Jung, who saw the proliferation of visions of Mary at the beginning of the nuclear age, coinciding with the declaration of the doctrine of the Assumption in 1950, as indicating 'a deep longing in the masses for an intercessor and mediatrix' (Jung 1954: 166). 'The fact, especially, that it was largely children who had the visions might have given pause for thought, for in such cases the collective unconscious is always at work' (Jung 1954: 165).

Despite the emphasis on innocence and purity, Catholics themselves do not overlook children's ability to fabricate experiences. The reactions of many visionaries' own families show that those closest to them were under no illusions about the possibility that the stories were the product of a fertile imagination. At Fátima, Lúcia's mother, in particular, did not believe the story and subjected her daughter to some pressure to admit its falsehood (as is clear from Lúcia's memoirs, Santos 1973: 129–31). She took Lúcia to the local priest, the first of many Catholic clerics to doubt in the early days, although he suggested that the fault may not have lain with the children but could have been a deceit of the Devil (Santos 1973: 133–5). Other members of her family and many neighbours were also sceptical throughout the five-month period of apparitions, and this caused Lúcia a great deal of stress (Bennett 2012: 91–111, drawing in part on Lúcia's memoirs). The children's refusal to back down despite all this adult pressure led to people believing in them, and the fact that they said little about the experiences—as local hostility turned them in on themselves—made the apparitions all the more compelling, the children appearing extraordinary to the point that people began to accept the truth of their story (Bennett 2012: 128–9, 138, 156). They were also helped by the fact that Francisco and Jacinta's father was one of the earliest believers. However, the negativity of Lúcia's family was increased because of the financial repercussions of the visions: Lúcia, a working child, was distracted by visitors and the family property trampled on and its productivity reduced (Zimdars-Swartz 1991: 86, also using Lúcia's memoirs). The family only came to accept the apparitions in the face of mass popular support for the cult.

The possibility of children as visionaries, initiating and shaping a cult that involves thousands of pilgrims, has been accepted in Roman Catholicism in the past, but one could argue that it has become less likely in recent years because of changes in social attitudes towards childhood. In Europe and also in Roman Catholicism, the age of majority or adulthood is generally eighteen, while the age of consent is usually sixteen. Concern about the vulnerability of children under the age of sixteen has increased during the latter period of the twentieth century and they are seen to need protection against the abuse and manipulation of adults in an unequal power relationship. There has also been a gradual transition over the century from the use of children as resources in the economy of the family, able to work and take responsibility at a young age, to an emphasis on protecting the rights of children to enjoy play and concentrate on education away from pressures to work. In the nineteenth century, Bernadette Soubirous, France's most famous visionary at fourteen, would have been regarded as close to adulthood, but now there would be concern for her youthfulness in the face of such intense public scrutiny. Fátima's children were even younger, but the question has been seldom asked as to whether, in general, small children's prominence in the community as visionaries may have been harmful for them or even abusive. It is true that there was concern for the health of Fátima's visionaries because of the persistent questioning. Canon Formigão, who interviewed the children, thought that Francisco and Jacinta looked weak and depleted (Bennett 2012: 110). These two died in childhood from the influenza that spread as an epidemic after the First World War. Martindale talks about the fatigue of the three children (1950: 89, 96) and Bennett, drawing on Lúcia's own memoirs, notes that they were 'tortured, doubt-ridden, frightened, frustrated and socially isolated' (Bennett 2012: 138) during the apparition drama. One hundred years later, children such as these may well have attracted attention from social services.

If Jacinta di Marto, aged seven, was vulnerable, what is one to make of the very young infant visionary Gilles Bouhours of Espis in France, the subject of a recent hagiographical book that revives his memory as a visionary (Guiot 2010)? His first recorded vision occurred when aged two in his family home in 1947 and then, at this same age, he joined a number of visionaries at the open-air site in Espis that included other children as young as four years old, becoming the most celebrated of them. Guiot (2010: 101) includes a photograph of him kneeling in vision, the crowd behind him, at the age of five. This continued until he was six, when Gilles's family decided not to return to Espis because of the disapproval of the bishop; the apparitions at Espis were rejected by the bishops of Montauban in 1947 and 1950 as not being of supernatural origin and orchestrated by misguided nuns (Guiot 2010: 79; Laurentin and Sbalchiero 2007: 300–1). However, there is little in the Catholic memory of Espis to suggest concern about the extremely young age of the seers. Laurentin and Sbalchiero state that Gilles's 'young age and his clear self-confidence attracted the attention of the group' at Espis (2007: 142, my translation). However, he was also vulnerable, a sickly child who had suffered from meningitis as a baby, and he would not survive past the age of fifteen.

Despite the Church's negative decision on Espis, Gilles seems to have been made a special case and regarded more favourably by the Church than the other seers; he met Pope Pius XII in 1949 and 1950, and is credited by devotees with encouraging the pope to proclaim the Assumption of Mary, which occurred on 1 November 1950 (Laurentin's preface in Guiot 2010: 10; Laurentin and Sbalchiero 2007: 142). The chapel that was built at Espis some years later has a prominent plaque remembering this encounter. Gilles continued to experience visions throughout his short life. Extraordinarily, he was also known to have celebrated Mass at a young age in his home; Guiot (2010: 113) refers to him as a 'child priest' and refers to 'the purity of infancy . . . placed in the service of the most beautiful causes' (Guiot 2010: 11, my translation).

CHILDREN'S SPIRITUALITY

A critique of the Catholic tendency to overvalue the play-making of young children and of the possible naivety involved in regarding them as pure vessels of the divine (a view not necessarily shared by their families) need not necessarily lead to its opposite, i.e. the undervaluing of children's spirituality. Researchers of religious development in Britain and the United States see this as the danger of a strongly secular environment where religious and spiritual experiences are often suppressed as being embarrassing or indicators of poor mental health. Hart (2003), with many examples, argues that listening to children can yield insight and wisdom. Coles (1992: 10–21), a psychiatrist, recounts an early career encounter with an American Catholic girl aged eight who had been sent to him because of behavioural problems. Originally a Freudian, he was keen to find the relational issues that lay beneath her wishing to talk about religious themes, but the child was reluctant to discuss anything other than faith. Eventually, she got the better of the stand-off and taught him about the importance of hearing children on their own terms, which eventually led him to write *The Spiritual Life of Children*. It is interesting that the girl wanted to talk to Coles about Bernadette of Lourdes, whose life she had seen in the film *Song of Bernadette*. She identified with Bernadette and Joan of Arc as role models of virtuous resistance to authority (Coles 1992: 14).

In the general literature on children's spirituality, experiences that are recorded include seeing and hearing spiritual entities; sometimes these are clearly 'in the mind's eye' of the imagination, sometimes they are more realistic. Hart gives the example of a three-year-old who saw auras and

interpreted their meaning for the people concerned (Hart 2003: 126); nevertheless, he points out that the mystic tradition warns against becoming 'overly
fascinated by these powers' (Hart 2003: 143) as such abilities should be
accompanied by intellectual and emotional development. Hyde adds instances
of children perceiving energy, hearing voices, or seeing visions: 'Some children
are able to tune into these intuitive capacities, and these types of experiences
are more common than many believe' (Hyde 2008: 15). To dismiss these may
be a missed opportunity to gain an insight into the rich world of a child's
spirituality. Nye gives the case of a six-year-old who saw a 'bishop kind of
alien' and thought it was the Holy Spirit, but his parents did not want to
have anything to do with this (Nye 2009: 30). Coles (1992) likewise recorded spiritual experiences amongst children from various backgrounds:
Muslim, Jewish, Native American, Catholic, and Protestant. These children
described their encounters with Allah, God, or the world of ancestors and
spirits with expressions such as 'seeing', 'hearing', 'meeting'. In most cases,
they knew that these experiences occurred within their imaginative world
and were not the same as encounters with flesh-and-blood people, but
they regarded them as real nevertheless. In a context where believers hung
on the words of these children, could they not have become 'visionaries' in
the same way as Gilles Bouhours and others? Carroll (1985: 59) notes the
special dispensation of children and adolescents for eidetic vision, i.e. the
ability to project vividly their imaginative ideas into three dimensions. Hay
and Nye discuss the importance of the imagination in children's development and its realism:

> Indeed, their natural ability to become absorbed in a guided imaginative exercise
> is so evident that teachers are urged to use such methods with care and only after
> appropriate training... The mystery-sensing created in imaginative acts is per-
> haps as much or even more significant than children's responses to what 'adult'
> religion has defined as sacred. (Hay and Nye 1998: 70)

Lack of interest by adults can contribute to a rejection of former experiences
by the growing child. Nye writes that: 'Children can report feeling embarrassed by the "silliness" of the spirituality of their younger selves, even
questioning their sanity' (Nye 2009: 94). In the apparition tradition, on the
other hand, acceptance of the phenomena by adults can lend objectivity to
them. Despite this, there have been instances of child visionaries coming in
early adulthood to doubt their experiences, in the cases of Pontmain and
Garabandal, for example. At Garabandal, this only lasted for a short time
(although long enough to convince the local diocese of the lack of value of the
visions); the visionaries returned to their former belief. The strength of the
Garabandal movement and the fact that the visionaries' own belief was crucial
to it may have contributed to this turnabout, coupled with the idea that the
period of disbelief had been prophesied in the visions themselves. Nevertheless,

these retractions show how apparition experiences in children may eventually seem to them to belong to an earlier and distant stage of their lives. Taylor writes of Bernadette of Lourdes, who as a nun was pressured to remember the detail of the apparitions by historians: 'All of this had become completely distant in the intervening years, Sr Marie-Bernarde had little in common with the fourteen-year-old girl who had run through the streets of Lourdes and pulled her stockings off to wade through a millstream' (Taylor 2003: 245–6).

Children use the only language available to describe spiritual experiences, that which is learnt from adults (Hay and Nye 1998: 102–3). Hence there is the danger of circularity in regarding children's experience as revelatory. The way in which children articulate it to adults may be entrancing, as it is common for adults to be amazed by the ability of young children to express themselves. Adults often remember their childhood experiences of spirituality as vivid and meaningful for the whole of their lives and, like the poet Wordsworth, lament the passing of mystery into the rationalism of growing older (Hay and Nye 1998: 44–5; Nye 2009: 11). Children's experiences may then represent a mysterious relationship with the world of spirit that adults recognize as belonging to the depth of their being, from a time of childhood innocence and openness. The contents of Gilles Bouhours's visions, unsurprisingly for his age, contained no novelties. His description of the Virgin matched those already reported at Espis: he saw Mary crying tears of blood, a cross in the sky, and Thérèse of Lisieux with flowers. The Virgin told him to pray the rosary at the bottom of the wood where a spring would run, an as-yet-unknown source of water echoing the story of Lourdes. He held up rosaries for the Virgin to bless (Guiot 2010: 27–8, 49–50). None of this was revelatory, yet the charismatic demeanour of the little boy and reported healings held the attention of the pilgrims.

In several Marian apparitions, adult religious tradition in the form of symbols, stories, and doctrines intersects with children's imaginative spirituality in ways that have contributed to the unfolding of new visionary narratives. Roman Catholicism, while maintaining the primacy of public theology over private experience, has allowed a space—albeit one that is subject to hierarchical control—for the publicization and sharing of private experiences and devotion. This leads to the danger of sensationalizing visions, which are actually commonplace, in contexts of heightened social anxiety and the seeking of the miraculous. The concern of recent decades for the protection of children will tend to suggest that children should not be subject to the public scrutiny that fame as visionaries would bring them, and the issues over child safety in the Roman Catholic Church, in particular, will exacerbate this anxiety. However, this does not mean that a secular hegemony, in which children's visions and experiences are suppressed, disregarded, or discouraged, is the only alternative. In the general move towards what Laurentin (1991: 119,

211) calls a 'democratisation' of visions, by which he means that apparitions may be healthier if each one is not seen as the latest global sensation but a modest local renewal, children's insights and experiences may play their part in community prayer and spiritual discernment.

VISIONS AND ADOLESCENCE

Adolescents (those aged at least eleven or older at the beginning of the visions) feature as much as small children in the well-known Marian apparitions in the modern period. Adolescent visions are among the most famous and include La Salette and Lourdes in the nineteenth century, and Beauraing, Banneux, Heede, Gimigliano, Garabandal, and Medjugorje in the twentieth. Of the adolescent visionaries at those sites, girls make up the great majority, nineteen to two. While some of the points made about children may also apply to adolescents, clearly this is an age group for which other factors come into play. First, they are more articulate and aware of social issues than small children. Phillips's research notes that girls of this age growing up in faith communities are able to handle relatively complex theological ideas, constrained only by their life experience and breadth of language; they are also known to experience the presence of the transcendent, 'some with physical manifestations' (Phillips 2013: 83–4).

Secondly, this is an age which presents particular challenges, with physical changes and sexual awareness provoking psychological stress. Feminist psychologists point out that early female puberty is often experienced as bereavement caused by the loss of child relationships with peers and parents, which results in a drop in self-worth (Gilligan 1991; Phillips 2013). As a response to this, an apparition of Mary could be regarded both as providing comfort and expressing anxiety (as many visions include these aspects). However, it is important to remember that psychological analysis of individual visionaries themselves is not sufficient as an explanation for Marian apparition cults, as visions to individuals are very common but large-scale responses to them by people of all ages less so. Any psychological explanation would need to be social (as in Carroll 1986, in his Freudian assessment of the Marian cult, but he also analyses individual visionaries: Carroll 1985). What can be said in that respect is that adolescent girls have often been chosen as suitable channels of divine communication by the Catholic community. One of the obvious reasons for this is that they are icons of the Virgin Mary as she is presented in images of the Immaculate Conception: a pure and innocent young girl, not yet at the time of the Annunciation.

Just as it does for children, fantasy plays an important role for girls coming to adolescence in the development of a relationship with the divine; play space is important in this liminal moment in the life cycle (Phillips 2013: 85). Once again, there could be dangers in taking very seriously the pronouncements and experiences of adolescent girls, as in Marian apparitions. However, on the other side of the coin, Gilligan's sample of adolescent girls shows how commonly they dismiss their experiences and voices as part of the process of patriarchal socialization (Brown and Gilligan 1992: 217). Certainly, Catholic girls in the contexts where apparitions occur are under this pressure. While they are not encouraged to be silent because apparition experiences can be valued, the voice of the Marian visionary is not considered to be their own, but that of the Virgin Mary. Furthermore, even when accepted by some people in the community, the visionaries usually go through harassing tests to prove themselves worthy of the visions. If they succeed and stay firm in the face of opposition, they will gain a public voice, which is unusual for an adolescent, not to mention a woman, in a Catholic community.

Could the adolescent female visionary be an example of what Gilligan refers to as 'resistance' to the initiation of the adolescent girl into the socialization of patriarchy?

> This resistance is manifest in an honest voice, reflecting our ability to pick up and register the feeling of what happens and the desire for relationship or mutual understanding. Because it is resisting, it is not necessarily a nice voice, a voice that other people want to hear. It is a voice that can make trouble in families, schools, and communities. Consequently, it is a voice that girls begin to cover. (Gilligan 2011: 63)

Girls' voices in apparitions, expressed as the voice of the Virgin Mary, are often raised in protest against the 'sins' of society and one could read that as resistance to injustice. It certainly unsettles many Church leaders and others in authority. Yet the Catholic visionaries are often interpreted as expressing the resistance of Catholic culture to another (republicanism, communism, secularism), one patriarchy against another, rather than crying out against patriarchy and its divisiveness as a whole. Boss (2000: 169–74) notes how Mary's goodness can be used to serve dualistic ways of thinking because it is often contrasted to the supposed evil of those who oppose Christian orthodoxy. This was a tendency present in the medieval world, where the perceived 'others' were often the Jewish minority communities, but it has been magnified in recent centuries during the travails of the Catholic Church in dealing with more powerful opposition.

Journalist E. Michael Jones, in his denunciation of Medjugorje, *The Medjugorje Deception*, claims that Mirjana Dragicević, sixteen years old when the visions began in 1981, was their instigator. He suggests a possible explanation for the drives behind this, based on Mirjana's sensitivity to the violent history of the region in which she was born: 'Judging from the psychological evidence, Mirjana may very well be a "medium", i.e. a person who has an unusually sensitive relationship to the fears and hopes and sins and guilts which drive her community' (Jones 1998: 86). Whatever the merits of Jones's other arguments about Medjugorje, this is a helpful insight into the psychology of a young visionary. Those seers who become famous are normally born into times and places that are undergoing profound social and political change, with many unresolved matters from the past, including violence and deeply divided societies. In Catholicism, the Virgin Mary provides a transcendent moral voice with which to express this angst and the fears and hopes for the future. Yet it is extremely hard for young visionaries with sensitivity to the fault lines of society to present a critique of their immediate community. At Medjugorje, the early calls by the *Kraljice Mira* ('Queen of Peace') for inter-community harmony were swamped in the nationalist cause and the young Croat visionaries always referred their analysis of a sinful world outwards towards a global horizon rather than interpret it in terms of the terrible civil war that was about to engulf their nation and in which Croat nationalism played its part (see Chapter 13 within this volume).

Along with the other challenges of her calling, an adolescent girl visionary also faces the difficulty of projection by attracting interest based on her appearance. In addition to perceived innocence and simplicity, a physically striking visionary is more likely—although this is by no means essential—to become a suitable physical mediator for the Virgin Mary, who is always conceived in terms of great beauty as well as kindness and maternal concern. In Italy, Caterina Richero of Balestrino and Angela Volpini of Casanova Staffora (aged nine and seven respectively when their visions began, but these continued into the teenage years) delighted the crowds with their broad, pretty smiles and demonstrative gestures that heightened the drama and convinced people that the Virgin Mary was behind the phenomenon. They became local celebrities. Twelve-year-old Conchita González of Garabandal was photogenic, like Bernadette of Lourdes a hundred years before during the early days of photography. At Ezkioga, Christian reported (including adults and males in his observation): 'Those present at the visions have pointed out to me that beauty enhanced credibility . . . Photographs of seers in vision show that some quite ordinary faces took on a special attractiveness when rapt, and spectators likened the young seers to young saints' (Christian 1996: 246).

In summary, the Catholic world has believed that children's innocence makes them particularly suitable for perceiving the presence of the divine, a viewpoint that has a parallel in the Romantic understanding (as one finds in Wordsworth, for example) of childhood as a time of magic, reinforced by the fact that many adults remember and treasure their own childhood encounters with the sacred throughout life. Older children face the particular challenge of adolescence and they may have become sensitive to the social issues and histories into which they are born. In the case of girls, adolescence may be an especially stressful time in a patriarchal culture such as the traditional Catholic in which there is ambivalence about women's voices in public; they are also subject to projection, being at a similar age to Mary at the time of the Annunciation, an image that has been captured in artistic depictions of the Immaculate Conception.

7

Basque Raggle-Taggle

Ezkioga

THE ACCOUNT OF WALTER STARKIE

In the Introduction to this volume, four types of literature about apparitions were identified: the social scientific, the theological, the devotional, and the sensationalist. It is therefore quite refreshing and informative to find a description of an apparition that does not fall into any of these categories, but which describes the events just as they are, human experiences, individual and collective. This is the case with the first-hand account of Walter Starkie (1894–1976), an Irishman travelling across Spain with a violin in the summer of 1931 and, by chance, coming across Ezkioga (this is the Basque spelling; in 1931 it was known in Spanish as Ezquioga) in the rural agricultural area of Gipuzkoa. Starkie was a professor of Spanish at Trinity College, Dublin, as well as a theatre director and British cultural representative in Spain. However, on his travels he wished to emulate the gypsy *juglar*, a travelling minstrel and jester well known in medieval Europe. Therefore, while he encountered people and places just by wandering and playing for his keep in taverns, he also wrote an articulate account of his journeys; his work belongs to the genre of travel writing. Although a Catholic, he is clearly not particularly inclined to believe visionary phenomena, but he gives a warm portrait of all those he meets. Whether everything he wrote was a true first-hand account or sometimes based on second-hand reports, it is not possible to know, but certainly the most comprehensive work on Ezkioga, the anthropological survey by William Christian (1996), accepts it as genuine testimony.

Starkie's book is called *Spanish Raggle-Taggle: Adventures with a Fiddle in Northern Spain* (1934). 'Raggle-taggle' refers to things or people that present an eclectic mixture of different parts from various sources: one such is the gypsy *juglar* and his music, the inspiration for Starkie's book. However, the term also provides a very apt description for the apparitions at Ezkioga, which brought together a great crowd of contrasting personalities as visionaries.

Starkie spends just three short chapters on his visit to Ezkioga, which lasted a few days (Starkie 1934: 112–50), but his account brings the events to life and illuminates the social world of the apparitions. He encountered visionaries who also feature in Christian's account: the original visionary children, a cheeky boy aged seven and a serious girl aged eleven; an older teenage visionary, Dolores (Lolita) Nuñez, who moved Starkie during her apparition and on whom he became briefly fixated (Starkie 1934: 141–7); Francisco (Patxi) Goicoechea, a twenty-four-year-old man who mocked the visions at first but became one of the most prominent seers. These were all working people of modest means. Another important feature of Starkie's writing is his witness to the tension in 1931 between supporters of the newly formed Spanish Second Republic and those Catholics who saw the republic as a threat to their traditional way of life and to the Church itself. He recalled Doña Carmen Medina, a wealthy aristocrat and ex-nun who supported and promoted the visionaries:

> Dona Carmen touched me by her piety: though she was a daily communicant and spent a great deal of the day in prayer, she was a very active and practical woman, and directed many organizations connected with the Church and the exiled monarchy... In my mind I felt quite convinced that she was doing her best to use Ezquioga apparitions as a political lever. (Starkie 1934: 124)

There were many more visionaries that Starkie did not come across, notably the mid-teenage servant girls Ramona Olazábal, a stigmatic, and Evarista Galdós, as well as nine-year-old Benita Aguirre (Christian 1996: 49–65, 81–4). Most of the seers were from farming communities and many visited Ezkioga from elsewhere in the Gipuzkoa region (Christian 1996: 20).

Starkie describes the scrambling of the crowds up the hill towards the trees that were the site of the visions. The immediate area became quite desolate as the trees were stripped bare by souvenir hunters (Starkie 1934: 126). Prayer was exacting and intense: 'After the Rosary there was silence for a few minutes... and then came the Litany to the Blessed Virgin which had to be recited kneeling with arms outstretched in the form of a cross' (Starkie 1934: 132), which embarrassed Starkie as he had to give up his kneeling position despite the old and infirm maintaining theirs. This was one of Ezkioga's peculiar features, along with the fact that the visionaries fainted after their experiences and needed to be supported or carried down the hill. Starkie captures the emotion of the experience:

> I felt as if the devotional excitement of those thousands and thousands of people had enveloped me and lifted my soul out of my body. Suddenly I heard a cry piercing through the buzzing rhythm of the Litany. All those who were kneeling near me started up and looked around. Many rushed towards the place whence the sound came, and stood in a cluster above the kneeling masses... It was a young woman who had seen Our Lady. The crowd pressed round and suddenly

I saw her lifted up on the shoulders of five men and carried down the hill as though she were a corpse. (Starkie 1934: 133)

After the apparitions, seers and pilgrims gathered in the village tavern, providing opportunities for the local innkeeper and his family because of the visitors who came from all over the region. The family illustrates the divided nature of both Basques and Spaniards during this period, since the father was a republican while his wife and daughters were Catholic believers. A son, Florencio, a trendy French speaker and self-confessed *libre penseur*, had returned to the village to help his father make money: 'He thought there were possibilities to be exploited in Ezquioga, for it might turn out to be a Spanish Lourdes . . . Florencio's one obsession was the miracle that must take place' (Starkie 1934: 118). The anticipated miracle would have established Ezkioga as a major shrine.

EZKIOGA AND THE SPANISH SECOND REPUBLIC

The Spanish Second Republic emerged from the election of 12 April 1931 and abdication of Alfonso XIII two days later, after eight years of dictatorship (Preston 1994: 38). Republicans and socialists made great gains in the cities at the expense of the conservative parties. The history of republicanism in France and Portugal, and the momentum of socialism after the Bolshevik Revolution in Russia, led many Catholics to fear that the fall of monarchy and the existence of the republic represented a perilous situation for the Church and its moral monopoly. The conservative reaction to the republic was particularly strong in the countryside, just as it had been in France and Portugal. The city and tourist sites, especially along the coast, were regarded as hotbeds of immorality by people living in rural areas (Christian 1996: 33–6). The anti-republican right generally agreed that political activity within the republic was, initially at least, a better tactic than outright resistance, and so the politics of Spain in the first half of the 1930s was fraught with tension within the government. Political propaganda fuelled inaccurate interpretations of political persons and actions, and there was a constant threat of a military uprising (Preston 1994: 38–73). This all came to a tragic conclusion at the outbreak of the civil war in 1936, which was won in 1939 by the conservative forces of Francisco Franco. He remained in power as dictator until his death in 1975.

The Church considered itself under siege during the period 1931–6. Crucifixes and religious artefacts were removed from schools (Christian 1996: 18). Reports of the burning of churches and religious houses spread across the country; later, Franco saw these as the events that defined the republic and his opposition to it exemplified the way in which conservative elements in the army allied with the Church at this time. Although Preston points out that 'the origins of the incendiarism remain obscure' (1994: 43) and may have been the work of right-wing *agents provocateurs*, the general understanding in Spain was that republicanism and socialism stood for the overthrow of Catholicism, monarchy, and traditional privileges (Preston 1994: 38–73). This polarization found its expression in the republic's constitution of 1931, which instituted equal rights including religious freedom, votes for women, civil marriage, divorce, secular education, and at the same time removed state funding for the Church and religious orders, limited the wealth of the Church, and attempted to dissolve the Jesuits because they swore allegiance to Rome (Paz 2001; Schneider 2013).

In the initial period of the republic, Marian visions associated with resistance to anticlericalism were reported in Torralba (Aragón) and Mendigorría (Navarra, a Spanish-speaking area in the Basque country). Ezkioga continued that sequence but became the most famous, being promoted by the press (Christian 1996: 13–20). The apparitions articulated a Marian response to the advent of the republic, proclaiming her assurance and protection. As Christian puts it: 'Mary's sorrowful opposition to the Second Republic was the central interest of believers and seers at the Ezkioga visions in the summer of 1931' (Christian 1996: 41).

A complicating issue was the regional struggle for independence of the Basque country and Catalonia from Spain. The urban areas of these regions gave a great deal of support to the republic, which was seen as a better option for regional autonomy (a view that proved reasonable after the republic's defeat by Franco led to the suppression of Basque and Catalan aspirations for independence). However, many Basques and Catalans from rural areas opposed the republic (Starkie 1934: 119–20). It is from this pool that much support from the visions came and so the messages do not display any support for Basque separatism; they are far more concerned with the republican threat to the Church across Spain. Despite interest from Basque nationalists at the outset of the visions, 'in contrast, not one of the major promoters had any interest in the visions as a Basque phenomenon' (Christian 1996: 161). Pilgrims to Ezkioga came from several nearby regions: there were many Catalans in addition to pilgrims from the Basque districts of Gizupkoa, Navarra, Bizkaia, and Alava. The Catalans adopted Benita Aguirre as their representative visionary, although she was from a village close to Ezkioga (Christian 1996: 81–92).

Starkie's account of conversations that he had in Ezkioga show how concerned the devotees were over the recent establishment of the republic, while republicans saw the visions as a fabrication by the Church, in particular the Jesuits (Starkie 1934: 112–13, 125, 136–7; note that Ezkioga is close to Loyola, the home village of Ignatius, founder of the Jesuits). The political dimension of the visionary messages is demonstrated by one of the most famous prophecies at Ezkioga, that of Patxi on 28 July 1931, foreseeing a civil war in the Basque country between Catholics and non-Catholics; the latter would win at first, but ultimately the Catholics 'would triumph with the help of twenty-five angels of Our Lady' (Starkie 1934: 135). Patxi, along with others, saw Mary holding a bloody sword, a detail which turned the leftist press from mockery to concern, asking for government intervention (Starkie 1934: 135; Christian 1996: 31). Mary was often seen as the *Dolorosa*, sorrowing Mary, reflecting Catholic concern for the state of the nation; other titles were the Immaculate Conception and Our Lady of the Rosary (echoing Lourdes and Fátima), along with Our Lady of Aranzazu (Christian 1996: 28), a Basque devotion which had been exported elsewhere in Spain and overseas. However, while the visions generally expressed hostility to the republic, the situation is far from simple: Christian notes that Ezkioga seers fought on both sides in the civil war (1996: 375). The visionary focus changed from political issues in Spain to general and global sinfulness. Furthermore, even though they had regarded the republic as their adversary, the visionaries did not receive support from either the Church or, later, Franco's nationalists. After Franco's victory in 1939, they were condemned by his government because of the fear of Basque separatism (Christian 1996: 377).

EZKIOGA AND THE CATHOLIC CHURCH

The Spanish Church is not traditionally as friendly to apparitions as the Church in other countries such as Italy or France. Christian describes periods of suppression of visionaries in Spain, particularly in the thirteenth, sixteenth, and late eighteenth and early nineteenth centuries (Christian 1996: 2–6). Therefore, Christian suggests that 'the visions at Ezkioga were the first large-scale apparitions of the old talking but invisible type in Spain since the sixteenth century' (Christian 1996: 6). Nevertheless, the popularity of the nineteenth-century French apparition shrines did extend into Spain, and Basques considered Bernadette Soubirous, a Bigourdan from the Pyrenees, to be a Basque. In the twentieth century, there were famous cases of moving crucifixes in northern Spain: Limpias (Cantabria) in 1919 and Piedramillera (Navarra) in 1920. Pilgrimage to these sites was modelled on Lourdes. Thurston (1934: 45–65) reports that many pilgrims to Limpias saw the statue move, including priests and doctors, although the majority did not. While the Church was very interested in the affair and set up a commission of enquiry, no episcopal pronouncements were forthcoming.

Ezkioga is situated in the diocese of Vitoria. Initially, the apparitions enjoyed the support of the parish priest, Antonio Amundarain, and the clandestine attendance of the bishop of Barcelona. In 1931, the bishop of

Vitoria, Mateo Múgica Urrestarazu, had suffered exile from Spain due to restrictive measures imposed by the republic against what it regarded as Church agitation; the primate of Spain, Cardinal Pedro Segura of Toledo, was likewise expelled (Christian 1996: 14). It was therefore left to the vicar general of the Vitoria diocese, Justo de Echeguren, to make a pastoral decision on Ezkioga (Christian 1996: 128). At the beginning of the visions, he allowed priestly involvement in organizing devotions and leading the rosary. The Catholic press was in support, which was encouraging. However, his visit to Ezkioga changed the atmosphere dramatically (Christian 1996: 49–52). The chief protagonist in the case was the teenage seer Ramona Olazábal who, like others in July 1931, began to anticipate a miracle. She predicted that she would be wounded and that the Virgin would give her a rosary; on 15 October, stigmata appeared on her and a rosary was found attached to her belt. This caused great excitement and many new pilgrims arrived. The parish priest, Father Amundarain, called the vicar general to the site. For some reason, Ramona denied predicting these 'miracles' in advance, but the vicar general learned that she had and was therefore lying. There was also evidence that the wounding was caused by a razor blade. These incidents caused the diocese to prohibit priestly involvement and to issue edicts prohibiting devotion at Ezkioga. Father Amundarain resigned just over a year later. Patxi was ordered to dismantle the stage on the hill at Ezkioga that had been erected for the apparitions, although it stayed intact for many months afterwards. All this effectively turned the visionaries of Ezkioga into a sect, supported by Catholic mavericks (Christian 1996: 67–127).

A visit by Carmen Medina and the seers to the exiled bishop in France did not help their cause, as this simply served to bring him into the argument on the side of the vicar general. Added to this, Patxi continued to prophesy miracles that did not occur (Christian 1996: 128–9). The hopes for canonical approval of the apparitions ended with the arrival of the Jesuit José Antonio Laburu in October 1931 (Christian 1996: 129–35). Laburu was a psychologist and his interest in extraordinary experiences led him to film the visionaries in their trances. While they were willing to cooperate, unknown to the seers Laburu was constructing a theory that compared them to mental patients. This became the main argument in a series of lectures that Laburu gave in 1932; the apparitions could be explained as natural phenomena, a kind of mental contagion. The disqualifying factors against a supernatural provenance that he listed included the ability of visionaries to have apparitions at will; the childishness of the messages; the false theology of prophecies of punishment against those who did not believe the apparitions; the behaviour of seers (drinking, dancing, boasting, kissing); frauds, especially Ramona's 'miracles'; exhibitionism rather than signs of the supernatural; pressure on the seers to have visions including bribes and public adulation sometimes resulting in the seers not having to work; their refusal to remove the stage despite the diocesan instruction; and the night hour of the visions. Therefore, for Laburu, the pilgrims' piety, while a good thing, was based on a phenomenon that was not supernatural (Christian 1996: 130–2).

Laburu's objections are informative about the difficult relationship that exists between the clergy, keen to protect the respectability and dignity of the Church, and the exuberant proponents of popular and visionary Catholicism. The latter do not always behave according to the expectations of the Church as it seeks signs of divine inspiration and pious holiness. The possibility of isolating the original visionaries of Ezkioga as the genuine articles amongst less credible mimics was lost because they did not have the strong, charismatic personalities that Bernadette Soubirous or Lúcia Santos presented. By the time Walter Starkie arrived, only three weeks or so after the first apparitions, the eldest girl had become morose:

> I have rarely seen such a tragic expression on a child's face ... Doña Carmen told me that she was very sad, because the Blessed Virgin had not appeared to her lately, although she had appeared to many other pilgrims. And so the poor little thing shut herself up in her room and refused to play with the other children. (Starkie 1934: 127)

The brother, a 'mischievous little urchin' (Starkie 1934: 126), aged nine or ten according to Starkie's observation but only seven according to Christian (1996: 48, also in Laurentin and Sbalchiero 2007: 310), was unlikely to have been able to carry the burden of chief seer. These original seers were abandoned because they did not enter the intense trance states of new seers (Christian 1996: 274). So the multiplication of visionaries from far and wide complicated the phenomenon and made it unmanageable from a Church perspective, resulting in official prohibition which began in Vitoria and extended to other dioceses (Christian 1996: 163–84). Furthermore, other marks of popular Spanish Catholicism were present: the seers saw the dead (Christian 1996: 326–7) and there were visions of the Devil (Starkie 1934: 129); witches were also seen and this was linked to the fact that the Basque country had had an outbreak of witchcraft accusations in the seventeenth century (Christian 1996: 26–7, 211–12).

In 1932, the seers were under pressure from both Church and state (their isolation is highlighted in a fictionalized Spanish account in the 2001 film *Visionarios*). Bishop Múgica returned to his diocese in May 1932 and in August 1933 sent a negative report on Ezkioga to the Holy Office of the Vatican, which formally supported him in December of that year and prohibited books on Ezkioga in 1934. In September 1933, the bishop published a denial of the supernatural nature of the phenomena, pointed out that prophecies had not been fulfilled, prohibited the cult, and declared the site off limits (part of the text can be found in Laurentin and Sbalchiero 2007: 311). He also denounced Padre Burguera, a one-time Franciscan who had become a champion of the seers and wrote about the apparitions in *Los Hechos de Ezquioga ante la Razón y la Fe* (1934) (Christian 1996: 151–9). Burguera seems to have acted as a mentor to the seers and weeded out the less impressive ones from among them, while the seers themselves vied for authenticity (Christian 1996: 143–50). Another interested party and would-be promoter, among several, was the fascist Léon Degrelle from Belgium; he visited Ezkioga after the apparitions at Beauraing in 1933, but was prevented from writing on Ezkioga by the bishop's pastoral letter. Meanwhile, the state governor had visited Ezkioga and the chapel was dismantled; a judicial enquiry in October 1932 resulted in some of the seers spending a short time in a mental hospital (Christian 1996: 138–41). Burguera spent a week in prison and was then exiled from Gipuzkoa.

Church prohibition led to the seers organizing secret meetings or moving to places where the priests were more lenient and allowed them communion. Clandestine support groups included priests and religious (Christian 1996: 200–3, 217–42). The suppression of Ezkioga continued over the years; in 1936, Bishop Múgica threatened excommunication of the woman who tended the statue, as well as all those who disobeyed the Church by continuing the cult (Christian 1996: 373–4). In the 1940s, a new bishop repeated the negative evaluation and the Ezkioga visions were omitted in local histories (Christian 1996: 378–82). Thus, by the time of Christian's research in the 1980s and 1990s, some child seers 'lived with fear until their death', the Basque witnesses of the phenomena were 'ashamed of their own enthusiasm', and the families of the seers bore 'the stigma of Ezkioga in total silence for sixty years' (Christian 1996: 400–1).

THE MIRACLE AND THE CHASTISEMENT OF EZKIOGA

In the 1960s at San Sebastián de Garabandal in Cantabria, Spain, Marian apparitions took place where the focus of prophecy was on three great signs: a warning, a miracle, and chastisement (see Chapter 12 within this volume). Similar announcements have been made at Medjugorje, Bosnia-Herzegovina, from the 1980s on (discussed in Chapter 13 within this volume). These prophecies have become famous in the Catholic world and the relationship between Garabandal and Medjugorje is obvious. For believers, this consistency is proof of the reliability of these messages (despite variations between them); for non-believers, it suggests that visionaries know of previous cases. Ezkioga is not so famous but it is clearly a predecessor of Garabandal, not many miles away in northern Spain; Ezkioga supporters who befriended Garabandal seers and devotees are mentioned by Christian (1996: 398). La Salette and Fátima, with their secret prophecies, precede both. At Ezkioga, a miracle, chastisement, and the imminence of the end-times were foretold; the sequence shifted from the miracle coming second to its coming first, but both were thought to precede the coming of the reign of Christ (Christian 1996: 352–5, 362–5). Another phenomenon parallel to other visions was the children being taken to heaven; they thus gained power: 'by obeying the minors, people were obeying and humbling themselves before the divinities for whom the minors spoke' (Christian 1996: 195). There was also a case of 'miraculous' or invisible communion at Ordizia, not far from Ezkioga, where seers gathered because the priest was lenient (Christian 1996: 200–1). This echoed Fátima and anticipated Garabandal, both places where the communion was said to have been given by angels; the concept of communion being given without a priest being required can be interpreted as representing a lay challenge to priestly authority. This was certainly the case at Ordizia, where 'no longer confessing with the parish priest, these believers felt themselves to be under direct scrutiny, judgment, and penance' without priestly mediation (Christian 1996: 201).

At Ezkioga, people became excited about small-scale individual miracles, such as the healings that began to be reported a few months after the apparitions began, and anticipated great miracles as announced by seers from the first month, the non-occurrence of which led to disillusionment (Christian 1996: 27–9, 268). Despite this, just as at Fátima, Garabandal, and Medjugorje, many believers at Ezkioga believed in a future punishment that transcended their own national context: it would be global (Christian 1996: 161). The visionary messages—increasingly as the seers came from further and further afield—evolved from concern over civil war, healings, local people disbelieving, and the fate of the dead to a greater sense of universal malaise that could only lead to divine chastisement (Christian 1996: 347). Patxi was instrumental in this shift (Christian 1996: 354). Apocalyptic prophecies took on various traditional elements mixed with more recent prophecies, such as the secrets of La Salette (Christian 1996: 352, 356–8). Another idea promulgated at Ezkioga, and later at Garabandal, was the belief that communism would enjoy global domination for a time (Christian 1996: 372). On the other hand, belief in the imminence of the reign of the Sacred Heart of Christ, as promoted by the Jesuits and present at Limpias, was rearticulated in a vague sense in the Ezkioga visions (Christian 351, 362–9). This was encouraged by the establishment of the republic as this was regarded as the antithesis of Christ's kingdom (Christian 1996: 350–2). The seer Luis Irurzun reiterated a centuries-old Catholic prophecy that the chastisement would include three days of darkness (Christian 1996: 359); this idea has become popular in contemporary Catholicism.

Both Garabandal and Medjugorje visionaries speak of a permanent sign that will be seen by everyone (in contrast to the visions, which are only available to a few). Believers at Ezkioga had foreseen 'a vision of the Virgin that everyone could see, some act of God that was counter to nature, or a miracle through a given person' (Christian 1996: 353). Patxi explained that this visible-to-all vision of the Virgin would be one in which she would stand on a half-moon accompanied by three angels and St Michael on a white horse (clear references to the Book of Revelation), lasting for six and a quarter hours. This is a natural and logical progression if a visionary wants to convince people that what they alone are experiencing has universal relevance: everyone will be affected by it and eventually will be able to see it for themselves.

Suffering is often interpreted by visionaries as their sacrifice for the sinfulness of the world (Zimdars-Swartz 1991). Expressions of disapproval and anxiety about social developments may also be made in the form of stigmata, bleeding from the head, hands, and feet re-enacting the Passion, or in the poses adopted during trances. At Ezkioga, a tradition emerged in which seers lay down and spread out their arms in crucifixion poses and observers followed their example (Christian 1996: 101–2, 264). There is thus a symbolic relationship made between Christ's suffering for the sins of the world and the suffering of seers for sin in the contemporary context. They are co-sufferers with Christ. The martyrdom of seers was sometimes prophesied (Christian 1996: 365), a logical conclusion from the connections being made.

However, the message of Ezkioga was not spontaneously generated from the seers' experiences. Just as at other apparition sites, there was a weeding-out process, in which questionable visions that would not have impressed the Church, messages that were disturbing to devotees or appeared to be fabricated, and bizarre poses were all rejected in favour of those that addressed collective concerns (Christian 1996: 401). Despite this, the Church, through its official channels, remained unimpressed and Ezkioga never achieved the honour of canonical approval. Nevertheless it was influential on the Catholic Marian apparition tradition of the twentieth century.

8

Between the Wars

The Belgian Visionary 'Epidemic'

TEXT AND CONTEXT

In Belgium in the 1930s, Marian apparitions were as intense as in any other period in modern Catholic history. They bring into sharp relief the nature of the relationship that exists between the historical context and a religious phenomenon such as a series of apparitions. The concept of 'alternative history' describes how Catholics experience visionary phenomena as confirmation of the belief that God is ultimately in control of events and that human history relates to a divine purpose. This is particularly important when devotees feel powerless in the face of economic, social, and political change. When there is a collective perception of suffering or threat, then it is more likely that an apparition will gain a large following (Zimdars-Swartz 1991: 7–8, 263–70). The very large number of apparitions in Belgium (the word 'epidemic' has been used to describe them) originating in the year between November 1932 and November 1933 reflects a communal angst; in this period, it is clear that the interest in apparitions related to political and economic uncertainty (van Osselaer 2012: 2).

The first Belgian apparition in this period, on 29 November 1932, occurred in the small Walloon (French-speaking) market town of Beauraing, a very short distance from the French border, close to Dinant and the River Meuse (see Laurentin and Sbalchiero 2007: 120–3 for a summary; Toussaint and Joset 1981 for a more detailed Catholic account). After the First World War, the Catholic Church in Wallonia had experienced anticlericalism whilst universal suffrage gave impetus to socialism in that region: the socialists were more popular than the Catholic party, and there was growing support for communists (Genicot 1973: 424; van Osselaer 2009: 381). The Church responded with a missionary effort against 'dechristianization' (Delfosse 1969: 245; van Osselaer 2009: 392 discusses the role of the 'Catholic Action' movement); this shows that Belgium was an appropriate setting for the perennial apparition concern for the 'conversion of sinners'. To add to the general atmosphere of pessimism, all Europe was suffering the effects of the Great Depression that followed the Wall Street Crash of 1929. Yet there is nothing in the account of the original Beauraing apparitions to children that refers to suffering or threat, at least not in the received tradition of visionary messages established at the shrine. The messages followed traditional patterns for children's visions: requests for the building of a chapel and pilgrimage; exhortations to 'be good', to make sacrifices, and pray a great deal; promises to convert sinners; identifications of the vision using Mariological formulae: 'I am the Immaculate Virgin' and 'I am the Mother of God, Queen of Heaven'. Thus the uncertainties and anxieties of the context cannot be related explicitly to the content of the visions but rather, implicitly, to an underlying need for consolation on the part of the children and certainly to the mass public *response* to their experiences.

It is clear that a dialogic model is the most accurate one for visionary phenomena, as opposed to seeing the seers as a one-way medium for divine initiatives. The community plays its part in the construction of the story. The Virgin Mary at Beauraing said that she was 'the Immaculate Virgin' only after a question using this epithet had been put to her via the visionaries. Derselle, a Catholic opponent, pointed out that the messages were solicited by questions and that clarity was lacking in the earliest accounts of the visions (Derselle 1933: 25–6). Probably most visions are subject to these objections. The Namur commission in 1942, when the diocese pressed for authentication, had to draw on the concept of the 'homogeneity' of the messages as a whole to counter them (Charue 1946). It would have been reasonable for Derselle to respond that homogeneity emerges from the work of visionaries, devotees, editors, and supportive theologians as the believing community move towards harmonizing the different aspects of what was originally an outburst of enthusiasm, not without its chaos and confusion. Yet then Derselle would have had to condemn all apparitions and thus contradict the Catholic Church, which accepts a small number as genuine encounters with the divine.

The received narrative of the Beauraing visions focuses on the simple presence of the Virgin and the hope that her presence would continue to be marked by a shrine in the years that followed. At the centre of all Marian apparition cases—while they may vary with respect to the messages reported and the themes that become important—is the presence of Mary, a presence marked by her power and authority. She has theological titles; she heals; she converts sinners. She is described in terms of supernatural beauty and all-encompassing light. At Beauraing, her presence did have implications for religious belief and practice, but not anything unusual or specific to a time of crisis, although one can speculate that prayer and sacrifice might have greater urgency and intensity in such a period of history. The Roman Catholic template that seems to be most comfortable for the hierarchy is one in which social turmoil elicits only quiet and resolute piety; therefore, Beauraing is another example of the general observation that the straightforward messages of children, which lack socio-political reference, are more likely than adult visions to be acceptable to bishops. For Beauraing, the diocesan bishop's support would be needed in the face of Roman Catholic opposition to the excitement over visions: the apolitical nature of the messages was helpful to his cause, but not the politically charged nature of some elements in the ensuing cult.

If there were contextual triggers for the popularity of visions in Belgium in this period, then it could be asked, why did the Belgian apparition phenomena start in Beauraing in particular? An answer to this is inevitably speculative and can derive only from describing associated events and circumstances. In August 1914, German armies invaded and rapidly conquered most of Belgium before confronting the Allied forces. While Belgian resistance in general was not very effective, isolated harrying of German troops in some towns led to their populations—men, women, and children—suffering atrocities by the invading forces, most notably in Leuven/Louvain and Dinant (Lipkes 2007). Dinant is Beauraing's larger neighbour from where many pilgrims came in 1932–3. Lipkes argues that anti-Catholicism constituted a major factor in the treatment of Belgians by the German army, and the majority of Belgian territory remained under German occupation throughout the war until November 1918. Understandably, Belgians were anxious when Hitler rose to power in Germany just fourteen years later; the apparitions in Beauraing began in the same month as one of the series of elections that established the National Socialists as the largest party in Germany (6 November 1932). Although this election was not as successful for the Nazis as that held on the preceding 31 July, it was not long before Hindenburg appointed Hitler as chancellor on 30 January 1933. The Nazis gained strength in a further election on 5 March 1933 after which opposition was progressively silenced. In these circumstances, it is reasonable to suggest that the Roman Catholic community in Wallonia in areas most affected by the First World War would have been sensitive to the possibility of divine intervention and consolation. Devotional accounts agree that this period was a traumatic time when one *would* expect the Virgin Mary to comfort the faithful; in relating crisis to visitation, devotees and social historians concur despite their different perspectives.

THE APPARITIONS AT BEAURAING AND BANNEUX

At Beauraing, five children (aged between nine and fifteen) from two families, the Degeimbres and Voisins, formed the visionary group. According to their testimonies, a shining young woman, her feet hidden by a small cloud and golden rays around her head, hovered above a railway bridge. She appeared as they passed a Lourdes grotto in the grounds of a convent. After more visions over the next few days, the figure moved closer, among the branches of a hawthorn bush. The eldest girl saw a golden heart on her chest, causing supporters to locate Beauraing within the tradition of devotion to Mary's Immaculate Heart. There was also a phenomenon of a ball of light, apparently visible to several onlookers. The apparitions (thirty-three in number) ceased on 3 January 1933, the crowd having grown to somewhere approaching 30,000 (Laurentin and Sbalchiero 2007: 120–3). Thurston (1934: 1) records how pilgrimage to Beauraing attained an estimated 1.7 million between November 1932 and September 1933, nearly twice the annual pilgrimage to Lourdes at that time.

Apparitions occur in an unfolding metanarrative of Catholic devotion in which certain themes evolve and in which prominent cases form templates. Beauraing's visions owe something to the precedent of Lourdes, having taken place next to a Lourdes grotto; like Lourdes, they share the reference to the Immaculate Conception and the request for a chapel. The vision of the heart is often said to be a confirmation of the Fátima messages, but this is unlikely to have been consciously realized by the visionaries at the time. The parallels are not particularly strong. The Immaculate Heart was an established devotion (Boss 2007), while the Fátima revelations of the 1920s were not well known across Europe in the 1930s. Nevertheless, the first Namur diocesan commission investigating Beauraing in 1935–6 felt the need to deny that the visionaries had been given a leaflet on Fátima (Joset 1981–4: V. 39–75).

There is a long-held Catholic belief that Mary appears to people who have no particular predisposition to visions nor merit them. Furthermore, the age-old principle of the prophet not being believed in their own home (Mark 6.4) applies to apparitions; they often bring conflict with parents. The child seer Gilberte Degeimbre (who died in February 2015, the last survivor of the Beauraing and Banneux visionaries) demonstrates these two principles. In 2009, she was interviewed for the DVD *Beauraing, 76 ans après: Gilberte raconte*, in which she recalls the apparitions when aged nine and clearly still has a strong belief that they were a genuine encounter with the Virgin Mary. She describes how the children were involved in a game of what in Britain is known as 'knock-down ginger' (ringing doorbells and running away), just before the first apparition. She also recounts how the visions, experienced by herself and her older sister Andrée, attracted the jealousy of the eldest sister Jeanne, who was a very pious young adult but could not see anything. The apparitions also brought on the anger of her mother—the father having died the year before—who did not believe either of her girls and severely castigated them for lying. Although their general comportment during the apparitions is an important criterion for authenticity, visionaries are not necessarily expected to be saintly or especially remarkable. Despite the tradition of visionaries becoming priests and nuns, the Beauraing visionaries all married, which has become the norm for child visionaries since the 1930s.

Even more Lourdes-like were the apparitions at Banneux in the hills near Liège, where eleven-year-old Mariette Beco experienced visions between 15 January and 2 March 1933 with far fewer witnesses than those at Beauraing (see Laurentin and Sbalchiero 2007: 111–15 for a summary; Rutten 1985 for a more detailed Catholic account). Banneux was a remote hamlet (although the famous racing circuit at Spa, built in 1921, is only twenty kilometres away). Mariette reported a lady in a white robe and blue sash who prompted her to pray and helped her find a healing spring, all details that echo Lourdes. Just as 8 December, the feast of the Immaculate Conception, became a key date at Beauraing during the visions, 11 February, the feast of Our Lady of Lourdes, was similarly central at Banneux. Like the Beauraing case, Banneux's visions centred on the presence of the Virgin and her relationship with the visionary who stood as an intermediary for other faithful people. Above all, the Virgin Mary wanted a great deal of prayer. Lourdes was famous for the local priest's somewhat sceptical request for a miraculously sudden blooming of roses to prove the apparitions and this was not granted to him. In response, the Virgin only smiled; thus Bernadette gained the upper hand (Harris 1999: 68). At Banneux, the dynamics of this exchange were repeated. In response to the local priest's request for a sign that proved the authenticity of the visions, Mariette replied that Mary had said: 'Believe in me, I will believe in you'. The figure referred to herself as the 'Virgin of the Poor', and later, 'the Mother of the Saviour, Mother of God', a final message not dissimilar to that at Beauraing two months earlier: indeed, Mariette was accused of mimicking Beauraing (Laurentin and Sbalchiero 2007: 112).

Thurston (1934: 4–5, 33) points out that the Beauraing and Banneux visionaries' families were not regular churchgoers, a factor that generates conviction that the visions are genuine. Their faith practice was renewed after the visions, so that the families became examples of 'conversion'. However, Mariette Beco's traumatic adult life is popularly regarded as another good example of the way in which quite ordinary people appear to be chosen by the Virgin Mary. The adult Mariette divorced, then cohabited, and she suffered the death of two daughters. Mariette owned a pilgrim hotel at the site and therefore did not move far from her childhood home (which was incorporated into the shrine proper as a memorial of the location of the apparitions). She died in 2011.

There was an emphasis on healing and the relief of suffering at Banneux; therefore the messages align more closely than Beauraing's with Zimdars-Swartz's paradigm (1991: 8) in which suffering or threat is included in the content of visions, although the suffering seems to have been understood by Mariette in terms of poor health rather than the effects of social, political, and economic circumstances. Nevertheless, she perceived an international dimension: the spring was 'reserved for all nations . . . to heal the sick'. This is a good example of 'alternative history'. The German border lies only a short distance away from Banneux and across it in 1933 a newly installed Nazi government was beginning to make plans that would engulf many nations in total war. While it cannot be claimed that eleven-year-old Mariette was aware of the ramifications of the political situation, she grew up in a culture where there would have been intense concern about the international situation, particularly acute since the onset of the depression. In this context, the Virgin Mary was believed by devotees to have created a shrine 'for all nations' that would outlast the war and mark her healing presence through the coming decades. This was emphasized by the first healing made famous there, that of a man who walked from Barcelona in the summer of 1933, supposedly an anarchist (Thurston 1934: 38–40). Thus, in the eyes of the supporters, the twin fruits expected of a Marian apparition—healing and conversion—were realized.

There were positive signs from the dioceses in their responses to Beauraing and Banneux from an early stage. Parish priests took an interest by interviewing the visionaries and were gradually won over. As early as December 1932, the bishop of Namur, Monseigneur van Heylen, forbade clergy to attend among the growing crowds at Beauraing, but soon afterwards he admitted that he was happy to see Marian piety developing in the diocese, visited the shrine in June 1933, and sanctioned the building of a chapel (Joset 1981–4: I. 17–42; Servais 1933: 57–61). At Banneux, Monseigneur Kerkhofs, bishop of Liège, authorized the building of a chapel in May 1933 and was arguing for the likelihood of the authenticity of the apparitions by the end of 1934 (Beyer 1959: 203–14).

However, the extracanonical history of Belgian apparitions had not yet begun in March 1933. It is not unusual for the intensity of interest in apparition phenomena to inspire new visions among the pilgrims and very often children are displaced by adults whose social knowledge seems to provide them with a greater motivation to unveil the secrets of the future. Thus an apparition site evolves. Beauraing saw a renewal of apparitions in June 1933, this time to fifty-eight-year-old security guard Tilman Côme, a pilgrim from Pontaury near Mettet, about thirty kilometres away, who claimed to have been healed of spondylitis and osteitis at Beauraing (van den Steen 1996; 22–36; Toussaint and Joset 1981: 115–19). Thurston (1934: 11, 25) comments how healing miracles, despite being prayed for, were not common during the children's visions at Beauraing, but, along with conversions, they became much more prevalent during the middle months of 1933. The few words of simple devotion that characterized the children's apparitions contrast with Côme's conversations with the Virgin. 'I [Mary] have come for the glory of Belgium and to preserve this land from the invader. Hurry up!' People understood this to refer to Nazi Germany (although Côme is reported to have interpreted it as meaning the influx of enterprise as Beauraing became a centre of pilgrimage: van den Steen 1996: 29).

Côme maintained that Mary had come to bring grace to the afflicted and to the visionaries, which included himself. Several elements were familiar in the apparition tradition: the importance of prayer which would soon be answered; the request for a chapel; the conversion of sinners; a 'secret'. He seems to have misspelt Beauraing, referring to 'Notre-Dame de Bôring', and some other messages were seen to be incoherent. Côme's own lack of sophistication came through in his account and this soon led to ecclesiastical disfavour. He was unorthodox in naming 5 August as 'my [i.e. Mary's] feast day' and asking for a great pilgrimage on that date. It was assumed that he had confused this date with the Feast of the Assumption on 15 August, as the 5th was a little-known feast of Our Lady of the Snows, but Côme held firm. Therefore, an estimated 150,000 attended on 5 August. Côme had a vision of his desired chapel and its interior, but some thought it looked like the church at Mettet. Disillusionment with his testimony grew and negative contrasts with the children were made, especially by clergy. However, Côme—despite never being regarded as one of the authentic visionaries of Beauraing by the main body of pilgrims—had his supporters, including Pierre Burnon, who published a booklet entitled *Le Vrai Visage de Tilman Côme* (Burnon 1933). A few followers continued to go to Beauraing on pilgrimage on 5 August for many years afterwards (according to van den Steen 1996, who recalls that they were referred to as 'Cômistes').

The simplicity and devotional orthodoxy of the children's visions at Beauraing and Banneux finally allowed them to take their place in the canon; they displayed aspects of non-controversial originality despite the obvious but inevitable references to Lourdes. They eventually became the subject of theological interpretations by priests who drew out the symbolic meanings and relationships with the Gospel which are essential for a genuine apparition in the Catholic tradition (e.g. for Beauraing, Joset 1981–4 III; Bossard and Chenot 1981; for Banneux, the contributors to Kerkhofs 1953–9 II). Scheuer articulated an idea popular at Banneux when he wrote that the Virgin Mary beckoning Mariette to the healing spring symbolizes the way in which she draws the believer to Christ, the Water of Life and source of salvation (*source* = spring in French) (Scheuer cit. Wuillaume 1982: 275). Nevertheless, the eventual canonical separation of the initial apparitions at Beauraing and Banneux from the rest that followed in Belgium was hard won, much more difficult than at Lourdes where Bernadette's visions in 1858 were also followed by many others.

CONTROVERSIES

Arguments within the Catholic community began to rage in early 1933 over the credibility of the Beauraing apparitions. As a criterion for diocesan commissions, strong Catholic disagreement is decidedly a negative one. At the outset, a certain Dr Maistriaux supported the apparitions of the children and attempted to give them medical backing; he was the first to put in writing the accounts of the phenomena (Maistriaux 1932). As Gilberte Degeimbre recalls, the children at Beauraing were plagued by doctors. At most apparition sites, the medical profession has taken a great interest in the phenomena, testing the trance states by inflicting pain and taking lack of response as a positive sign. Psychologists were present at Beauraing too. The Leuven/Louvain University investigator, Dr van Gehuchten, thought that the agreement between the children was caused by 'unconscious simulation' complicated by 'auto-suggestion'; like his colleague Dr de Greeff (who remarked on the 'inanity' of the phenomenon), he did not think they were guilty of fraud but deceived by psychological factors (van Gehuchten 1933: 24–30; de Greeff 1933: 173–4).

These psychologists teamed up with a Carmelite, Bruno de Jésus-Marie, in publishing doubts about Beauraing in a volume of the *Études Carmelitaines* (de Jésus-Marie et al. 1933), the publication through which Belgian Carmelites expressed opposition to Beauraing. De Jésus-Marie was correct in arguing that the Carmelite mystical tradition, in particular the writings of the sixteenth-century saints Teresa of Avila and John of the Cross, recommended scepticism with respect to popular visions that claimed objectivity on the basis of an apparently realistic image. This heritage is often used to urge caution about new visionary claims. The Carmelite mystics also expressed concern about the possibility of demonic influence in religious phenomena. Drawing on this, Derselle's publication *Et si c'était le diable?* (Derselle 1933) represented strong Catholic opposition to the apparitions on the basis that the problematic aspects, as he identified them, could suggest that a diabolical origin was more likely than a divine one. Derselle developed his thesis by claiming that a local spiritualist in Beauraing had inspired the visions (Derselle 1933: 58–61), something countered by the first Namur commission in 1935–6 (Joset 1981–4: V. 39–75). De Greeff, on the other hand, concluded with much stronger justification that the crowd had influenced the visionaries (de Greeff 1933: 87–8). The English Jesuit Thurston lent support to the conclusions made by van Gehuchten and de Greeff. He regarded them as sincere Catholics and competent analysts of the phenomena at Beauraing (Thurston 1934: 14). He expressed his disappointment with the extreme denunciations of doubters made in Catholic pro-apparition publications and their unquestioning acceptance of the visions (Thurston 1934: 17–18). He also pointed out some facts that could tell against the divine origin of the Beauraing apparitions: the period of ten days before Maistriaux's account, which was the first attempt to create a proper record; that the concurrence of the children's accounts was illusory; that the so-called 'ball of fire' coincided with a journalist's flashlight. At the same time, like van Gehuchten and de Greeff, he did not believe that the children were lying, but that the phenomenon complied with the general category of 'collective hallucination' (Thurston 1934: 10–22).

Nevertheless, while Catholic scholars debated the theological and psychological factors, popular support continued unabated. Publications were set up that supported the new shrines and disseminated information about them. For Beauraing, there was the *L'Officiel de Beauraing*, produced by the 'Pro Maria' movement in French and Flemish; at Banneux, *Tancrémont-Banneux* (Tancrémont is an older shrine with a miraculous cross about two kilometres from Banneux). Then *Les Annales de Beauraing et Banneux* published material on both shrines from 1933 to 1940 (Toussaint and Joset 1981: 121, 216). By the summer of 1933, pilgrims were arriving at both sites from across Europe (Thurston 1934: 38–40). Banneux's emphasis on 'all nations' led to the founding of the 'International Union of Prayers' by the German Catholic welfare society, Caritas. Banneux consequently developed with a more international focus than Beauraing (Kerkhofs 1953: I. 168–79), an emphasis that has continued to this day.

Another source of support for the cause of the apparitions, particularly at Beauraing, was the fact that they were promoted by the Belgian 'Rex' movement (Rex = Christ the King), which had arisen from the 'Action Catholique de la Jeunesse Belge', part of the European-wide Catholic Action movement (see van Osselaer 2009). Starting with Dr Maistriaux, a local president of the movement, their *Éditions Rex* supported the Beauraing apparitions, including those of Tilman Côme. While important for the promulgation of the Beauraing shrine in its early period, this association eventually became less helpful for the shrine's reputation among Catholics. Despite the apolitical principles of Catholic Action, the leader of the Rex movement, Léon Degrelle, took it in a fascist direction and they stood against the Catholic Party (van Osselaer 2009: 383). They were denounced by the Catholic Church in 1937 for electoral misconduct (Genicot 1973: 427–8; Delfosse 1969: 244), the same year as the pope spoke out against German Nazis for their anti-Catholic policies in *Mit Brennender Sorge*. While he was anti-Nazi at first, in keeping with Belgian anti-German nationalism, Degrelle became a collaborator during the Second World War and was consequently disgraced. Nevertheless, Beauraing survived and outgrew its connections to the Rex movement.

MANY APPARITIONS IN FLANDERS AND WALLONIA

While Beauraing and Banneux are situated in the French-speaking Walloon southern half of Belgium, the proliferation of apparitions later in 1933 belongs mainly to the Flemish-speaking north. They began on 4 August in the small town of Onkerzele on a hillside near Geraardsbergen. Once again, as is common in this period, Lourdes played its part in the origin of the apparitions, as they took place at a Lourdes grotto below a small chapel next to the parish church wall. The visionary was Léonie van den Dijck, who had been on pilgrimage to Beauraing in June; one of her first messages referred to the 'Virgin of the Poor', a clear borrowing from Banneux, something which would not have helped her cause. Léonie's visions also referred to the tradition of Mary being unable to hold back the arm of her Son in judgement (a medieval theme repeated at La Salette in 1846); this was caused by the sins and blasphemies of humanity for which prayer, conversion, and penitence were necessary. The messages of Onkerele have much in common with the controversial and threatening elements of La Salette and Ezkioga, another disqualifying factor. Nevertheless, Léonie was not at all out of step with popular Catholicism; the tradition of warning of future catastrophe is more common in the modern apparition tradition than the gentle healing spirituality of Lourdes and Banneux. Chastisements were threatened, Léonie's 'country' was in great danger, but Mary would protect it. The vision asked for an enlargement of the chapel and a new small shrine at the place of the apparitions dedicated to Our Lady of Sorrows, where people could come on pilgrimage, especially on the feast day (15 September). The image of the sorrowful Mary was therefore paramount. There were also references to the Immaculate Heart of Mary (Schellink 1994: 73–7; Laurentin and Sbalchiero 2007: 683).

While the main period of apparitions lasted only until October, there was an occurrence that echoed Fátima with a 'miracle of the sun' on 18 December, a duplicate solar disc which spun and vibrated while resplendent with a variety of colours (Jacobs n.d. 13–16). While the Fátima story was not widely known outside Portugal and Spain until the 1940s, there was nevertheless some knowledge of it (e.g. in Germany, Scheer 2006: 79–91), and the miracle of the sun was probably the most famous feature, having been covered in Portuguese newspapers in 1917. Prophetic visions continued over the years, although not apparitions of Mary, confined to 1933; later, Léonie had visions of the Sacred Head of Christ (Schellink 1994: 135–8). Her prophecies apparently included foretelling of the deaths of the Belgian king and queen in 1934 and 1935. According to the testimony of a supporter, Gustaaf Schellink, Léonie predicted the coming of the Second World War and denounced Hitler, which alienated some of her devotees and upset some German pilgrims (Jacobs n.d. 18–22). In this account, she also foresaw details of destructive battles in Belgium and deportations to concentration camps. The coming war, as in the revelations of Lúcia of Fátima, would be a punishment for sin; however, at the end of the war, Léonie foresaw even greater chastisements for humanity to come. From 1940 until her death in 1949, Léonie was also a stigmatic (Jacobs n.d. 23–7), following Therese Neumann at Konnersreuth in Bavaria, whose stigmata and redemptive sufferings had become famous in the

1920s. Léonie's home became her shrine and today is a museum in Onkerzele in the same way as that of Therese Neumann.

After Onkerzele, other apparition cases were then reported in Flemish towns such as Herzele, Etikhove, Wielsbeke, Naastveld (a suburb of Lokeren), Olsene, Uitkerke, and Berchem and Wilrijk (suburbs of Antwerp). Onkerzele seems to have functioned as an inspiration and centre for these, as visionaries appeared at Onkerzele from other neighbourhoods: Jules de Vuyst (Herzele), Berthonia Holtkamp (Lokeren and Berchem), and Henri Kempanaers (Lokeren and Wilrijk) (van Osselaer 2012: 144). Walloon visions continued at Tubize, Melen, Houlteau, the older pilgrimage site at Foy Notre-Dame, and Verviers. All these cases began in 1933. In 1934, the continuation of apparition enthusiasm threatened public order at times, especially at Lokeren-Naastveld where new visionaries emerged, pilgrims came into conflict with local people, and predictions of miraculous cures were not realized (van Osselaer 2010: 1177–9). The ensuing disorder caused the senior churchman in Belgium, Cardinal van Roey, archbishop of Mechelen/Malines and Brussels, to make a statement on 25 August 1934 in partnership with the bishop of Ghent. He dismissed the claims at Lokeren-Naastveld and advised Catholics to stay away (Bouflet and Boutry 1997: 249–50; van Osselaer 2010: 1177). Nevertheless, some Catholic journalists were keen to show that apparitions were not out of keeping with modern times; they continued to support the visions in defiance of the Church and in opposition to some fellow Catholic writers and the liberal and socialist press. The interest in the media from all sides helped to keep the apparitions in the public eye (van Osselaer 2010).

Dictionaries and lists of apparitions give fifteen cases in Belgium in 1933 (combining Bouflet and Boutry 1997; Hierzenberger and Nedomansky 1996; Laurentin and Sbalchiero 2007; the University of Dayton and Miracle Hunter websites), and none for the rest of the 1930s except at Ham-sur-Sambre (beginning in 1936). However, van Osselaer (2012: 131) reproduces a map of the time identifying thirty-two Marian apparition sites for the period 1932–5, evidence for the prevalence of apparitions in Belgium during that period. In this environment, the Church hierarchy felt called on to act. Clergy were forbidden to organize pilgrimages or publicly support the apparitions, although some sent letters of private support for the apparitions to bishops (van Osselaer 2012: 156). An interdiocesan commission was set up in 1933 and continued its work into 1934 (Joset 1981–4: I. 33–4; Laurentin and Sbalchiero 2007: 121). It is clear by this time that the bishops of Namur and Liège were supportive of the claims at Beauraing and Banneux, but progress towards approval was halted, both by national ecclesiastical control over the first diocesan commissions and also by the Holy Office of the Vatican, which was suspicious of the number of apparitions occurring (Beyer 1959: 219; Joset 1981–4: I. 35–6).

Although 1933 is known as the year of apparitions in Belgium, this did not see the end of new cults. In 1936 in Ham-sur-Sambre, a small town in the Walloon region between Charleroi and Namur, an adult woman claimed to see the Virgin Mary in a tunnel that carried a spring under a road next to a row of Stations of the Cross, and an eleven-year-old girl also reported visions there. The Church rejected these as it had all those apart from Beauraing and Banneux, but the following at Ham was persistent and processions to the shrine continued through the war and into the 1950s. The bishops of Namur announced prohibitions on the cult in 1938, 1942, 1943, 1946—the same period during which they promoted Beauraing—and again in 1958 (Bouflet and Boutry 1997: 294–6). The Ham apparitions were so famous that Alfredo Ottaviani, the future Secretary of the Holy Office in Rome, included them in a list of deviant visionary movements in a statement published in *L'Osservatore Romano*, 4 February 1951. Ottaviani pointed out that religious sentiment is liable to deviation and must be subject to the guidance of both reason and Church governance. Where this is not the case, Ottaviani argued, disobedience against Church authority results.

THE AUTHENTICATION OF BEAURAING AND BANNEUX

As for Beauraing and Banneux, the supportive bishops of Namur and Liège refused to be dissuaded by controversy and the uncertainty of the national hierarchy and the Vatican. They were encouraged by the fact that there was plenty of Catholic and Catholic press support for these apparitions, although doubts were expressed about other influential visionaries such as Léonie van den Dijck and Tilman Côme (Thurston 1934: xii–xiv, 30–1). However, the bishops' cause was not helped by diocesan commissions in Namur (1935–6) and Liège (1935–7), whose members felt unable to come to a definite decision (Joset 1981–4: V. 39–75). The character of Mariette Beco and the subjectivity of the priest at Banneux were called into question at Liège (Beyer 1959: 215–25). The national commission of 1935–8 expressed its doubts about the concordance and sincerity of the witnesses and referred to the discord that Beauraing had provoked (Joset 1981–4: V. 76–84), while not discussing Banneux extensively (Beyer 1959: 224). However, there seems to have been a sea change for Beauraing and Banneux with the coming of war; both shrines functioned as places of pilgrimage during the German occupation. In 1940, the bishop of Namur, van Heylen, announced to pilgrims that he 'daily invoked Our Lady of Beauraing' and, in 1941, agreed that 4,000 people could gather there to pray for peace (Joset 1981–4: I. 37–41). Van

Heylen died shortly afterwards after forty-two years as bishop of Namur; he was succeeded by Monseigneur Charue who, after initial hesitation, continued the cause of Beauraing (Laurentin and Sbalchiero 2007: 122). The bishop of Liège, Kerkhofs, authorized the cult of the Virgin of the Poor of Banneux on 2 January 1942. Then Cardinal van Roey made a new statement on 25 March 1942 (Bouflet and Boutry 1997: 251–3). In this, he allowed the local dioceses to reopen commissions on Beauraing and Banneux. However, he declared that the Onkerzele and Lokeren-Naastveld visions lacked the characteristics of the supernatural; Etikhove, Olsene, and Tubize presented no element which would support a case; and all others were not worthy of attention.

Given this clear support for the original two shrines, new diocesan commissions were set up (Namur 1942; Liège 1942–4) and Charue now felt enabled to authorize the cult of Beauraing on 19 February 1943. However, Kerkhofs was stymied by his own commission, some of whom thought that Mariette Beco was prone to hysteria, others that she had deliberately copied Lourdes (Laurentin and Sbalchiero 2007: 114). So he employed a sympathetic priest, René Rutten, to undertake an exhaustive study (which was finally published in Rutten 1985) and simply overruled the doubters. Charue in Namur also felt he had to answer doubts—in this case about the one male visionary of Beauring, Albert Voisin—by setting up an enquiry into his character. These final investigations gave the bishops justification for formally approving the apparitions in 1949 (on Marian feast days as they stood in the liturgical calendar then: Beauraing on 2 July, the Visitation, and Banneux on 22 August, the Immaculate Heart).

Beauraing and Banneux are today well-established shrines with steady groups of pilgrims from Belgium, other parts of Europe, and further afield. Beauraing has developed local pilgrimage routes for walkers through the Ardennes countryside. Banneux, with greater space in the rural woodlands, is the larger of the two and has developed its international network more extensively, with small shrines in the precinct linked to various countries as far away as Vietnam. There is a memorial to 1950s German chancellor and Catholic, Konrad Adenauer, as a testimony to his work for peace in post-war Europe. A chapel dedicated to St Michael is a copy of one in Rhöndorf, Adenauer's natal village near Cologne, where, during the war, people gathered to pray for the prisoners of war from all nations; the chapel at Banneux was opened by Adenauer's son, a priest, in 1960. In this way, Banneux has stayed true to Mariette Beco's testimony that the Virgin wanted the spring 'reserved for all nations'. Banneux's location, so close to the borders of Germany and the Netherlands, lends itself to this symbolic vocation.

NON-AUTHENTICATED APPARITIONS

Only one of the shrines that emerged after Beauraing and Banneux has survived as a place of pilgrimage, that at Onkerzele. Léonie van den Dijck's main legacy there was to restore a seventeenth-century procession to Our Lady of Sorrows that followed stations through the town. Of the seven stations, only one remained at the time, but Léonie raised money for their reconstruction; by the time of her death, four stations stood and by 1970 all seven had been reconstructed (Schellink 1994: 127–8). Her best-known prophecy was that her body would be exhumed and found incorrupt with the stigmata still visible. According to supporters, who provided photographs and doctors' reports in support, this was found to be true in exhumations in 1972 and 1982.

Onkerzele is an example of how the persistence of 'popular religion' (the term used in Vrijhof and Waardenburg 1979, for example) or 'popular faith' (the terminology used by Badone 1990) causes the 'official' Church, the Roman Catholic hierarchy, to moderate its original position. This is explored in relation to the apparitions in Amsterdam (discussed in Chapter 10) by Margry (2009a, 2009b). With respect to Onkerzele, the 1942 statement by Cardinal van Roey was not the end of the matter: 'The events lack any supernatural characteristic . . . consequently, all activities of the cult that proceed from these events or having any relation to them will be regarded as prohibited' (Laurentin and Sbalchiero 2007: 683, my translation). Contemporary devotees do not regard this as a final statement and, while acknowledging the Church's reluctance to approve the apparitions, argue that the inauthenticity of Onkerzele was never finally established in the Church. Therefore the memory of Léonie and her visions continues. The stations of the Seven Sorrows of Mary continue to be the focus of a monthly procession on the first Saturday of the month that proceeds from the grotto chapel around the seven stations and back to Léonie's grave in the churchyard. The curators of the museum that has been opened in Léonie's old house describe how the Church has relaxed its position in stages from the 1990s: the Onkerzele parish priest began to allow Mass to be said by priests visiting with pilgrims and, subsequently, he provided Mass himself to coincide with the first Saturday procession. The fact that the pilgrims sing a hymn to 'Our Lady of Flanders' gives a clue as to the persistence of Onkerzele in the face of the decline of all Belgian 1930s shrines except for Beauraing and Banneux. The two approved shrines are in French-speaking Wallonia, and so Flemish-speaking Flanders has no twentieth-century apparition shrine. The most famous medieval Marian shrines in Belgium are in Flanders (Scherpenheuvel/Montaigu), Wallonia (Walcourt), and close to the border (Hal/Halle). This symmetry is not continued for approved modern apparitions.

Other 1930s shrines were either suppressed or neglected. They are only recalled by the faintest vestiges and memories; it takes an effort to locate them (research visits in 2012). Local people seem embarrassed or unaware of the mass gatherings of the 1930s. Ham's Stations of the Cross and 'apparition tunnel' are overgrown by brambles and not easy to see from the road. Staff at Etikhove's community centre can just about tell the visitor where the apparitions occurred but add that it is on someone's land and there is nothing to see there now. Olsene has a small memorial but its most popular shrine is a Lourdes grotto built in 1876 where there is no record of any visions other than Lourdes. Melen's 1933 chapel, built because of the apparitions, serves as a garden shed today, while Naastveld's apparition site is marked by a neglected statue in a small, broken, glass-fronted box.

Belgium of the 1930s illustrates the varied fates of Marian apparitions in the devotional life of popular Roman Catholicism. First, like Beauraing and Bannuex, they may gain approval and then the nascent shrine will be supported, visited, and expanded to become an international place of pilgrimage. Secondly, they may fail to be recognized by the Church but because of the persistence of devotees, local and visiting, pilgrimage may be maintained, as at Onkerzele. Websites and pamphlets will keep the story alive and there may be tacit acceptance on a wide scale. Only if the Church bestows a good measure of support will the shrine grow to a reasonable size; as will be seen in Chapter 11 within this volume, this has happened at some pilgrimage sites in Germany but it has not yet been the case at Onkerzele. The devotion there centres on Léonie's grave, the grotto and pre-existing chapel, which has been enlarged, and the stations of the Seven Sorrows of Mary, which were rebuilt at various sites through the town. Thirdly, once the Church rejects the case, popular support may die out quickly or after a decade or two. Only a faint vestige remains or nothing at all; the case is noted in lists but there is no live support. This has been the case in all the Belgian apparitions of the 1930s with the exception of Beauraing, Banneux, and Onkerzele.

9

'When the Gestapo Hounded the Apparitions'

Mary in Nazi Germany

THE QUESTION OF CATHOLICISM
AND THE THIRD REICH

Marian apparition shrines originating in 1930s Europe inevitably bear memories of those times and the coming world war. At shrines that emerged in Germany during Nazi rule, German Catholics remember that the Church was persecuted by the Third Reich; memorials of Nazi opposition to the apparitions can be found at many of these sites. Yet the debate over the role of the Catholic Church under Nazism is a complex and often bitter one. At the heart of it stands the question of responsibility for the Jewish Holocaust. Guenter Lewy's well-known book from a Jewish perspective and based on exhaustive research into diocesan papers, *The Catholic Church and Nazi Germany* (1964), charges the German Catholic Church with complicity during Hitler's regime. In a more recent edition, Lewy argues that his original judgement still stands: that the Church in the 1930s and 1940s had reneged on its prophetic mission and remained silent on the Jewish persecution (Lewy 2000). A Catholic biography of Pope Pius XII, by Gerard Noel (2008), agrees that the pope could have done more in speaking out against Nazism, but he prioritized the safeguarding of the Catholic Church and regarded communism as the greater enemy.

On the opposite side of the debate, it is true that members of the Catholic Church suffered considerably at the hands of the Third Reich, despite Hitler being raised a Catholic and the Catholic contribution to the early Nazi movement in Bavaria. After the failed 1923 Munich *putsch,* Nazi support lay chiefly in Protestant parts of the country, while Nazism was predominantly anti-Christian (Hastings 2010: 182–3). John Frain's defence of the Church in Nazi Germany, *The Cross and the Third Reich,* reports that the German Catholic bishops argued against the possibility that a Catholic could also be a Nazi (2009: 111). Included in his book are maps indicating voting patterns in the 1932 elections, which show clearly that the *Nationalsozialistische Deutsche Arbeiterpartei* (NSDAP: colloquially, the Nazi Party) gained the least electoral support in the major Catholic regions: the Rhineland, Baden-Württemberg, and Bavaria (Frain 2009: 45). This was due to the support in those places for the Catholic Centre Party which, along with other opponents of the Nazis, was prohibited from running for office after March 1933, so that Hitler gained an overwhelming majority in the November 1933 election.

The Vatican–German Concordat of July 1933 safeguarding Catholic institutions proved to be as lacking in value as many of Hitler's other agreements. The Nazi objective of an integrated society obedient to the Führer in a common nationalist cause meant that Catholic loyalties to the Church, pope, and bishops were regarded as secondary. The foundations of Catholic culture were undermined just as they had been under French or Portuguese republicanism or, in Germany, during the *Kulturkampf* of the 1870s. Catholic youth organizations and newspapers were banned or closed down and Catholic religious education subject to strict limitations (Bouflet 2003: 145–7; McDonough 2001: 33–5). Priests and nuns were implicated in manufactured scandals and monastery buildings were confiscated. Many Catholic priests, German as well as those from conquered countries, were sent to concentration camps. Several prominent Catholics were assassinated during the 'Night of the Long Knives' on 30 June 1934 (Bouflet 2003: 51). Only on the orders of Hitler, fearing a backlash, did Nazi officials stop short of removing crucifixes from schools. In 1937, Pope Pius XI responded by publishing the encyclical *Mit Brennender Sorge* ('With Burning Anxiety'), criticizing the regime in Germany because of its repressive measures against the Catholic Church.

The religious orders were targeted; one of those to suffer the greatest persecution was the Pallottine Fathers, a missionary movement founded in 1835. In 1914, the German Pallottine Joseph Kentenich established an international movement of prayer of Marian devotion with orders of priests and sisters based at Schönstatt in the Rhineland. The movement's objective was to promote Catholic Christian mission in the context of twentieth-century society based on a 'covenant of love with Mary'. Schönstatt is the site of a medieval Augustinian abbey in Vallendar near Koblenz, and the twentieth-century Marian shrine there is probably Germany's largest. The Schönstatt movement is global; Schönstatt chapels are built to the same model all over the world and contain an image of Mary 'Thrice Admirable' and Child, surrounded by the Latin words *servus Mariae numquam peribit* ('the servant of Mary will never perish'). Joseph Kentenich was one of many priests imprisoned in Dachau, which he survived, living until 1968. However, other Pallottines in Dachau, such as Richard Henkes and Albert Eise, died there and their memorials can be found at Schönstatt. Another Pallottine Father, Franz Reinisch, was executed in Berlin (Schönstatt International 2010: 16; Frain 2009: 259–67).

Schönstatt is a shrine that remembers Catholic suffering in the Nazi period; it is not an apparition shrine but it has influenced Marian devotion in modern Germany (for example, providing inspiration for the apparition shrines at Wigratzbad and Marienfried).

However, despite all this, the commitment of German Catholics in resisting Nazism is questioned; as Lewy points out, there was very little Catholic opposition to the Nazi persecution of the Jews. Frank McDonough says that 'active resistance against Nazism was undertaken by less than 1 per cent of the German population' (McDonough 2001: 1). The most prominent of the Catholic anti-Nazi heroes, the beatified Bishop von Galen, known as the 'Lion of Münster', was the subject of a hagiographical account by his chaplain, Heinrich Portmann, in 1953 (Frain 2009: 186–95). Yet Beth Griech-Polelle's study of Bishop von Galen questions his credentials as an anti-Nazi. In her view, he defended Catholics but did not intervene on behalf of other persecuted groups; while some sermons (especially those in 1941) famously resisted the state, he also 'sought to prove his obedience and loyalty' to it (Griech-Polelle 2002: 166). She concludes that von Galen, raised to cardinal shortly before his death in 1946, was an important symbolic figure in the process by which the German Catholic Church reconstructed its image, even before the war was over, as the robust opponent of Nazism (Griech-Polelle 2002: 2). Catholics wanted to distance themselves from the horrors of the Third Reich. Michael O'Sullivan remarks that 'the Church confronted its ambiguous Nazi past by inaccurately depicting religion exclusively as a bulwark against National Socialism' (O'Sullivan 2009: 1).

Any study of the Marian apparitions in Germany in the 1930s has to contend with this debate and ask critical questions about the hagiographies of Catholics in the Third Reich. Catholic historian and Vatican consultant Joachim Bouflet's work, *Quand la Gestapo Traquait les Apparitions* ('When the Gestapo Hounded the Apparitions', 2003) is quite remarkable for tackling the subject of Marian visions persecuted by the Nazis, otherwise ignored by Catholics writing about apparitions. As welcome as this study is, it is subject to the same reservations concerning the accuracy of the data that show visionaries and their supporters to be strongly anti-Nazi. For example, while Bouflet links many of the Marian visionaries of the 1930s with the emergence of the White Rose resistance movement from 1942, it is on this issue that he cites the least sources in evidence.

MARIAN VISIONS DURING THE THIRD REICH

Notwithstanding the debate about the extent of Catholic–Nazi collusion, the memorials of the Nazi period at the Marian shrines in Germany illustrate how the Virgin Mary has been understood to intervene, console, and assure her devotees in perilous circumstances (Table 9.1 lists apparitions in the Third Reich period and provides basic details). Heede and Wigratzbad recall Catholic visionaries who suffered harassment by the Gestapo; Marpingen saw new apparitions at the nineteenth-century shrine. Other 1930s cases cited by Bouflet have not resulted in fully fledged shrines, although there are some remnants. Like those in the nineteenth century, the German apparitions of the 1930s follow Lourdes in one or more of the following elements: requests to pray the rosary; calls for penance; requests to build a chapel; visions occurring at a Lourdes grotto; Mary dressed in white and blue as in the Lourdes case; and reference to the Immaculate Conception.

As Bouflet's book is not translated into English, it is worth giving a summary overview of the apparitions in 1930s Germany that he describes. At Marpingen, a chapel was built at the edge of the Härtelwald in 1932. The shrine saw further apparitions in 1934 and 1999, although the 1876 visions remained at the centre of devotion. In 1934, an anonymous woman ('E. B.'), praying at the chapel, experienced visions of Mary who called for prayer, penance, and conversion, classic themes in apparitions (Bouflet 2003: 50–3). From this uncontroversial beginning, more diverse themes emerged: Mary appeared as Our Lady of Sorrows; there were apparitions of Jesus; there were warnings of the coming danger; and criticism of the inaction of the Catholic hierarchy. Bouflet regards some of the messages as plagiarized from Léonie van den Dijck of Onkerzele, by then well known across the border. German Catholics had visited the new Belgian visionary shrines in large numbers until being prevented by the Nazis from crossing the border in the mid-1930s; this led to greater interest in Germany's own new apparition sites (Blackbourn 1993: 371).

Bouflet suggests that Belgian visionaries were also influential for Odilia Knoll, the seer of Marmagen in the Eifel (Bouflet 2003: 29–45). In 1933, visionaries at Beauraing (Tilman Côme), Onkerzele, Houlteau, and Lokeren visualized chapels that were to be built; Odilia did so too. In the summer of 1934, she was inspired to build a chapel at the bottom of her own garden and it still exists, the family continuing to own the house. There are still signs of the chapel being used, although there is no official parish involvement. Odilia's visions were known to the public in 1934, but she claimed that earlier apparitions of Our Lady of Lourdes and the Trinity in 1932 had led to her being healed of a potentially fatal puerperal fever. In 1966, Odilia revealed further messages that she claimed were from 1934, but Bouflet (2003: 36–7) points out that these (referring to sexual immorality and the television) belong more clearly to the 1960s context and are therefore likely to be fabrications.

Salvatoris Kloke, a nun at the convent hospital of the Daughters of Charity in Bad Lippspringe, claimed visions in 1933 along very similar lines to those of her French forerunner in the order, St Catherine Labouré. Sister Salvatoris's

Table 9.1. Marian Apparitions in Germany from 1933 (all sites were the subject of research visits in 2011)

Location/Diocese/ Region	Duration of visions	Visionaries (all females; adults except at Heede)	Political involvement claimed by Bouflet and other Catholic writers
Bad Lippspringe/ Paderborn/North Rhine Westphalia	15 Aug. 1933–59	Salvatoris Kloke (nun)	Secret warnings about the Third Reich (Bouflet 2003: 50)
Berg/ Rottenburg/Baden-Württemberg	7 Dec. 1933–14 Aug. 1934	Frau Brauchle	Prayers for Germany (Bouflet 2003: 22–3); resulting groups of prayer expressed resistance (Bouflet 2003: 26)
Marmagen/ Cologne/North Rhine Westphalia	(Healing/vision 26 Dec. 1932) then 29 Jul. 1934, 19 Aug. 1934	Odilia Knoll	None
Marpingen/Trier/ Saarland	1 Oct. 1934–36	'E. B.'	In resistance; criticized Church passivity (Bouflet 2003: 52)
Mannheim, concerning chapel at Guttenberg/ Rottenburg/Baden-Württemberg	Three times: 1936	Katharina Schladt	In resistance: White Rose (Bouflet 2003: 61)
Wigratzbad/ Augsburg/Bavaria	1st visionary (Healing/vision 1919) Nov. 1936; Dec. 1936; 8 Dec. 1938	Antonie Rädler	First visionary imprisoned on several occasions (Bouflet 2003: 153–65; Gebetstätte Wigratzbad 2010: 36–9), and was linked to White Rose (Bouflet 2003: 161)
	2nd visionary 22 or 23 Feb. 1938	Cäcilia Geyer	Second visionary died in 1939 while the Gestapo planned to arrest her (Bouflet 2003: 157)
Heede/Osnabrück/ Lower Saxony	1 Nov. 1937–3 Nov. 1940	4 girls (aged 11–13 at outset)	Girls committed to mental hospital by Gestapo which also harassed believers (Bouflet 2003: 72–86; Brinkmann 1999; Sarrach 1997: 41–99)
Bochum/ Paderborn/North Rhine Westphalia	15 Aug. 1938–Easter 1940	Ursula Hibbeln	In 1931, visionary prophesied tyranny of Hitler and in 1940 his downfall (Bouflet 2003: 138, 143; Ernst 1988: 92); she was regarded as an enemy of the state and died just before arrest by the Gestapo (Bouflet 2003: 134, 143)
Oberpleis/Cologne/ North Rhine Westphalia	1 Oct. 1938–1955	Anna Gaggenmeyer	Asked for new chapel despite state prohibition; founded a secret religious community to help the poor (Bouflet 2003: 148–9)

description of the apparition resulted in an altarpiece in the convent chapel, just as Catherine's had been immortalized on the Miraculous Medal. Salvatoris also distributed a prayer to 'Mary, Refuge of Sinners', which formed part of a 'Little Rosary', a new rosary in a shorter form than the traditional version. The case was kept relatively quiet; the visionary also passed on prophecies concerning the Third Reich that were not revealed by the diocesan authorities (Bouflet 2003: 48–50). The Little Rosary is still distributed on prayer cards by the order in Bad Lippspringe and the altarpiece remains on display.

The apparitions at Berg, near Friedrichshafen on the Bodensee, followed a conventional pattern: they took place at a Lourdes grotto, which was and still is in the grounds of a home for the elderly. Priests had gathered people there for prayer retreats; Bouflet (2003: 19–28) adds that this was partly due to anxiety about the rise of Nazism and the need to reflect on and pray about it. The visionary, Frau Brauchle from Ravensburg, had been on such a retreat. This explains the content of the visionary messages that are full of concern about Germany: 'Germany does not wish to receive Mary'; 'I will protect Germany'. The devotees were urged to pray for the *Vaterland* (here Bouflet distinguishes between the Nazi state and the *Vaterland*, i.e. the country with its traditional heritage). The apparitions lasted nine months from December 1933 to August 1934; crowds gathered, but in June 1934, the diocese acted to keep the phenomenon within limits and prohibited access to the grounds of the home. The bishop's interest in the case was terminated with his removal from the diocese by the government. The grotto is still used for gatherings annually in May, although it is not clear whether these recall the apparitions in 1933–4.

Bouflet (2003: 55–61) also reports a story in which Katharina Schladt, a war widow from Mannheim, experienced dreams in 1936 in which Mary urged her to recover an abandoned altarpiece depicting Mary as Mother of Mercy in an unknown chapel; the altarpiece was locked away and neglected. The dream included a scene in which Mary led her to the chapel. These experiences persisted and became more urgent. Katharina met someone who identified the chapel as she had described it; it turned out to be in the grounds of Guttenberg Castle owned by Protestants. Her visit to the site resulted in the chapel being opened up for pilgrims; the altarpiece was referred to as 'the Abandoned Mother' and it is on display today in the castle museum.

Wigratzbad's shrine dates from 1936 and has been an Augsburg diocesan shrine since the 1960s, along with the post-war shrine Marienfried. As it is a well-known centre, the sources describing its origins are more diverse than other 1930s Marian apparitions in Germany (the story is given in Gebetstätte Wigratzbad 2010: 36–9; Laurentin and Sbalchiero 2007: 1007–9; Bouflet 2003: 157–62). Wigratzbad is busy today with two churches, a grotto, a pilgrim hostel, a seminary, and three bookshops. The grand *Sühnekirche Herz Jesu und Mariä* ('Heart of Jesus and Mary Reparation Church'), built in 1976, recalls the emphasis on reparation in the Fátima visions (and this is attested to in the shrine literature). However, it is also a strong symbol of Catholic resistance to Nazism. The visionary Antonie Rädler, as a young woman in 1919, had experienced healing from Spanish influenza at the same time as a vision of Mary. In 1936, Rädler was supposed to have refused to replace a Schönstatt image with a picture of the Führer in her father's butcher's shop and would not greet people with *Heil Hitler* rather than the traditional South-German Catholic greeting *Grüss Gott*. In consequence, she was pursued by the Gestapo and claimed to have been protected by a mysterious cyclist whom she referred to as 'a guardian angel on a bike'. Her parents, who owned land, constructed a Lourdes grotto in gratitude and this was consecrated by the parish priest. Rädler saw the statue in the grotto smile at her in November of that year and she heard a prayer: 'Mother of Victory [*Mutter vom Sieg*], conceived without sin, pray for us'. A month later, while praying the rosary at the grotto, she heard an angelic choir singing: 'O Mary! Immaculate, conceived without sin, Mother of Victory, pray for us'; the German word *Sieg* can be interpreted as countering Nazi propaganda with Marian imagery. Antonie's final apparition of Mary was dated on the feast of the Immaculate Conception, 8 December 1938 while she was incarcerated in a Gestapo cell because of her disrespect for the regime. She reported that the vision promised her release before Christmas and that this was fulfilled. In the 1940s, she was to be imprisoned again and eventually had to go into hiding.

It is surprising that government approval for the building of the chapel was obtained in 1938, given the state's suspicion of Antonie. The gathering of a women's prayer group at the grotto was one of the reasons for Gestapo displeasure (Gebetstätte Wigratzbad 2010: 37–8) and it would be expected that the chapel may have made the situation worse. However, other sources describe a second visionary at Wigratzbad, Cäcilia Geyer, who had a vision on 22 (or 23?) February 1938. While Antonie Rädler's apparitions have not been approved formally by the Church, they are accepted *de facto*. In contrast, Cäcilia's memory is still suppressed at the shrine and in its literature, although it is preserved elsewhere (in, for example: Laurentin and Sbalchiero 2007: 1007–9; Hierzenberger and Nedomansky 1996: 310–11; Bouflet 2003: 154–7). In her apparition, she found herself at the grotto and was told by the Virgin Mary that a chapel should be built. She replied that it would not be permitted. The apparition responded: 'I will guide the hand of the person who has to sign the authorization. The chapel will be built. I will trample underfoot the head of the infernal serpent. I will crush all opposition' (Bouflet 2003: 155, my translation). Bouflet goes on to describe the visit of the state architect three days later, a Protestant, who designed the site as Cäcilia had foreseen it. This story, whatever its veracity, is interesting as it fills in an obvious gap in the official history and represents an alternative tradition.

Heede, a village in Emsland near the border with the Netherlands, is the site of an official Marian shrine in the diocese of Osnabrück. As the shrine receives a reasonably large number of pilgrims, its story, like Wigratzbad's, is well attested to in devotional literature (Bouflet 2003: 63–131; the shrine booklet by Brinkmann 1999; Laurentin and Sbalchiero 2007: 427–30; Sarrach 1997: 41–99). On All Saints' Day, 1 November 1937, in the Heede cemetery, four girls reported visions of Mary crowned with the child Jesus: Maria Ganseforth, aged thirteen, her sister Grete, eleven, Susanne Bruns, thirteen, and Anna Schulte, eleven. Pilgrimage grew rapidly; within a week, the crowds were dispersed by the SS and the parish priest was forced to retire. Echoing the treatment of the Mettenbuch seers in the 1870s by the Church, the state then sent the four Heede visionaries to receive psychological tests in a mental hospital many miles from their homes in Göttingen and then Osnabrück. A potential breakdown of public order was seen as a threat to the state although the messages were not political and focused mainly on the need to pray: Mary was referred to as 'Queen of the Universe and Queen of the Souls in Purgatory'. The period of incarceration, over two months, and a subsequent report from the authorities discounting the testimonies did not discourage the girls and apparitions continued until 1940, although they were forced to avoid gathering in the cemetery. A secret was revealed by the vision under the orders that only the pope could read it, and this purportedly reached Pius XII in 1940 (so Laurentin and Sbalchiero 2007: 430, but Bouflet 2003: 119 admits that this is not certain).

After a diocesan enquiry, the bishop of Osnabrück approved the Marian devotion at Heede and sent a positive report on Heede to the Vatican in 1943 (the text is given in Brinkmann 1999: 5–16). Nevertheless, there was no formal approval of the apparitions themselves, although permission was given to erect a statue of 'Mary, Queen of the Universe'. The shrine enjoyed some Church support and a larger church for pilgrims was built to complement the existing parish church in 1977, but the continued lack of official status led to frustration. The shrine booklet of 1999 states: 'It is a fact that faithful pilgrims go to Heede. The public explicit approval of the bishop is still outstanding in 1999, in spite of devout wishes and pleas of many people' (Brinkmann 1999: 23). This plea was heard and in a new and more positive atmosphere (see Chapter 11 within this volume), Heede became a diocesan shrine in 2000, although the apparitions have still not been given the canonical status of cases such as Beauraing and Banneux from the same period. In Heede, memories of wartime Nazi oppression are perhaps emphasized more than at any other German 1930s shrine. Because of its location in Emsland where several concentration camps were situated, 'some people look upon Heede as a religious memorial to the victims of national socialism' (Brinkmann 1999: 22). Susanne Bruns and Grete Ganseforth have died and now lie in the cemetery, the site of the first vision; Grete Ganseforth became a 'victim soul' (see Chapter 5 within this volume).

A fascinating character also discussed earlier in Chapter 5, Ursula Hibblen of Bochum had a lifetime of spiritual experiences, including apocalyptic prophecies. According to her biographers, in 1931 she had the first of several premonitions of the coming war and also foretold that a government under Hitler would be a tyrannical one (Ernst 1988: 92; Bouflet 2003: 138). However, she remained prudent and avoided publishing messages with political content; therefore, despite coming to the attention of the Gestapo, she was not arrested, an aged and invalid woman being an unlikely source of insurrection. A specific period of Marian visions came during 1938–40, the last two years of her life. These comforted her despite visions of the future war. Finally, in May 1940, just before her death, Ursula is quoted as having predicted that Hitler would be victorious at first, but would never conquer Europe; after a short while, God would intervene to bring a better time (Ernst 1988: 92; Bouflet 2003: 143). Bouflet adds that, when this became public, the Gestapo set out to arrest her but arrived too late; she had already died.

The visions and prophecies of Bochum followed those in Belgium, and then at Berg and Marpingen in Germany, in predicting war and having a gloomy outlook on the future. The Nazi state did not want to have this kind of message circulated. From 1934, Catholic bishops made regular public pronouncements about the Nazi threat to the Church (Mariaux 1942 quoted in Frain 2009: 81–5). In June 1934, an SS report complained about the activity of Catholic priests in creating pessimism and regarding National Socialism as a passing phase compared with the longevity of the Church (Matheson 1981 quoted in McDonough 2001: 37–8). This negativity about the near future was reflected in the 1930s Marian visions in Germany: they gave consolation in a time of trouble rather than proclaiming the glorious future of the Reich. For this reason, it would have been natural for the Nazi regime to suppress and discourage Marian visionary cults.

Finally, Anna Gaggenmeyer of Oberpleis had visions of Mary for several years between 1938 and 1955 (Bouflet 2003: 145–51). She and several companions had a vocation to help the poor of the area and were angry that the laws of the Reich prohibited Mass in nearby Thomasberg because it did not have a parish church. They decided on two objectives: to build a chapel in Thomasberg and to found a new community there. The priest in Oberpleis pleaded with them to wait for easier times. However, Anna took a secret name as Sister Maria and then in 1938 had a vision of Mary as the *Christusbringerin*, the 'Bringer of Christ', a traditional German title used by the Schönstatt community. Anna claimed that subsequent visions gave support to her projects: the founding of the community, the building of a chapel, and organizing reparatory prayer vigils and processions. The priest found the visions to be so numerous as to be unrealistic and preferred caution. The messages remained unknown to the public although people heard that there had been apparitions in Oberpleis and Anna's community was never recognized even after the fall of the Third Reich. She continued to have visions until 1955 and died in 1966. In the meantime, she did see one dream come to fruition: a church was built at Thomasberg between 1949 and 1951. This church became the centre of a new parish in 1955, the year that Anna's visions ceased. However, the foundation of the new church and parish was and still is attributed to Hans Bernard Wichart, parish priest of Oberpleis from 1944. He continued to advise silence about the apparitions and Anna's apparitions are all but forgotten today.

None of these apparitions were authenticated in the full sense; as Laurentin points out, Beauraing and Banneux were exceptions during a time when the Church preferred not to endorse apparition cults (Laurentin 1991: 18, 22–3, 26). Nevertheless, Antonie Rädler of Wigratzbad and the girls in Heede received Church support (Gebetstätte Wigratzbad 2010; Brinkmann 1999). These places developed into diocesan shrines, one in each Catholic region of the country, where Catholic suffering under Nazism is remembered in a narrative that distances the history of the German Catholic Church from the Third Reich. There were also other instances of Church support: the Bishop of Rottenburg's investigation into visions at Berg and his interest in the chapel at Guttenberg Castle were interrupted in 1938 by his being one of only three bishops deposed by the Nazi government (Laurentin and Sbalchiero 2007: 126–7, 416). The diocese of Paderborn gave some encouragement to the visionaries of Bad Lippspringe and Bochum (Bouflet 2003: 48–50; Ernst 1988). On the other hand, Marmagen, Marpingen, Oberpleis, and the second visionary of Wigratzbad (Cäcilia Geyer) were all ignored by ecclesiastical authorities and parish priests alike; Bouflet is unusual in resurrecting their memory.

The war years also saw apparitions in Fascist Italy: those at Voltago from 1937 apparently included a denunciation of Mussolini and a prophecy of a war into which Italy would be dragged (Laurentin and Sbalchiero 2007: 999–1000). They were denounced by the bishop of Belluno and one of the visionaries was excommunicated in 1943. Successive episcopal prohibitions could not check the cult. In 1943, the 'victim soul' Maria Valtorta, a Servite tertiary living in Viareggio, received personal messages of love from the Virgin Mary amongst a life of revelations, which were written down as *Poem of the Man God* between 1943 and 1951 (Laurentin and Sbalchiero 2007: 989–90). This publication was placed on the index of forbidden books by the Vatican because of its claim to supernatural guidance; nevertheless, the work remains popular and was praised in the 1980s by one of the visionaries in Medjugorje.

Plate 1. Fátima, Portugal: 13 October 1917. Pilgrims look at the 'miracle of the sun' (with permission: Santuário de Nossa Senhora do Rosário de Fátima).

Plate 2. Beauraing, Wallonia, Belgium: December 1932. The child visionaries lead prayer during the apparitions (with permission: Sanctuaires de Beauraing).

Plate 3. L'Île-Bouchard, Centre, France: December 1947. The child visionaries (with permission: ilebouchard.com).

Plate 4. Heroldsbach, Bavaria, Germany: early 1950s. The seven visionaries in front of the small original chapel erected at the site (with permission: Pilgerverein Heroldsbach e.V.).

Plate 5. Casanova Staffora, Lombardia, Italy: early 1950s. Angela Volpini experienced apparitions as a child between 1947 and 1956 (with permission: Angela Volpini/Nova Cana).

Plate 6. Casanova Staffora, Lombardia, Italy: early 1950s. Angela Volpini presents an infant to the Madonna (with permission: Angela Volpini/Nova Cana).

Plate 7. Heroldsbach, Bavaria, Germany: early 1950s. Visionaries enact the carrying of the Christ Child in their arms (with permission: Pilgerverein Heroldsbach e.V.).

Plate 8. Beauraing, Wallonia, Belgium: the shrine at the hawthorn tree (author photo: June 2012).

Plate 9. Onkerzele, Flanders, Belgium: the Lourdes grotto at the site of the 1933 apparitions (author photo: June 2012).

Plate 10. Banneux, Wallonia, Belgium: the visionary's house preserved as it was in 1933 and the original chapel, both part of the modern shrine (author photo: June 2012).

Plate 11. Heede, Lower Saxony, Germany: a recently sculpted statue of an angel shows the expansion and modern-day use of the shrine area (author photo: April 2011).

Plate 12. Montichiari-Fontanelle, Lombardia, Italy: the statue depicting the *Rosa Mystica*, based on the apparitions of the nun Pierina Gilli from 1946 (author photo: September 2014).

Plate 13. Kerizinen, Brittany, France: ex-votos and objects left at the site under the image of the two joined hearts of Jesus and Mary (author photo: April 2011).

Plate 14. Espis, Midi-Pyrénées, France: apparitions from 1946 are marked by individual altars (author photo: August 2014).

Plate 15. L'Île-Bouchard, Centre, France: pilgrimage on the Feast of the Assumption, 15 August 2013 (with permission: ilebouchard.com).

Plate 16. Amsterdam, Netherlands: the image of The Lady of All Nations revealed by Ida Peerdeman in 1951 (with permission: Stichting Vrouwe van Alle Volkeren).

Plate 17. Casanova Staffora, Lombardia, Italy: the site of apparitions, a hundred metres or so below the pilgrimage church (author photo: September 2014).

Plate 18. Schio, Veneto, Italy. A photograph of the visionary Renate Baron next to a statue of the Madonna at the summit of the Stations of the Cross (author photo: September 2014). Renate's apparitions continued from 1985 until his death in 2004.

Plate 19. Gargallo di Carpi, Emilia-Romagna, Italy. The small shrine at the edge of vineyards bears witness to the apparitions of Gianni Varini and others between 1984 and 1993 (author photo: September 2014).

10

Hearts and Nations

Visionary Women as Popular Theologians

Women and girls are in the great majority among well-known modern Marian visionaries and in some cases they could be regarded as 'popular theologians' (as discussed in Chapter 5 within this volume). Certain women seers made their own original contribution to the Marian tradition, albeit acknowledging Mary rather than their own creativity as the source of these ideas, and they can be assessed in terms of the impact that their pronouncements and personalities have had on their many devotees. This chapter discusses two women who had a profound influence in the immediate post-war period and continue to do so after their deaths, up to the present. They are Jeanne-Louise Ramonet (Kerizinen, Britanny) and Ida Peerdeman (Amsterdam). The stories of Jeanne-Louise and Ida have several elements in common:

- Both women faced the death of their mother during childhood (Ida at five years old and Jeanne-Louise at sixteen).

- Both remained single and descriptions of 'simplicity' and 'suffering' feature prominently in their biographies.

- Their apparitions began in adulthood: for Jeanne-Louise at twenty-seven and Ida at thirty-nine (although Ida reported that she had had an initial vision at twelve).

- The period of the visions was approximately contemporary: popular support for both began in the late 1940s and the apparitions spanned the post-war years up until the Second Vatican Council.

- Their early messages were dictated to a spiritual director, the first recipient (however, Ida's advisor appears to have been more supportive).

- Diocesan authorities initially rejected both cases; this has not been revoked for Jeanne-Louise in Brittany but Ida's devotional ideas finally achieved diocesan recognition just before her death in 1996.

- The concept of Mary as coredemptrix was important in both cases (which, while traditional and not heterodox, has not been raised to the status of dogma).

- A chapel was erected on the land around their homes and they each founded a female religious order to maintain it and promote the messages.

The several years of visions in each case allow for an analysis that divides the visionary messages into phases, thus charting a development in the framing of the apparition narrative. In Ida's case, the division into three phases is one that is already structured by her own followers; in Jeanne-Louise's, there is no equivalent, but the description of the messages by her supporters yields a reasonably obvious identification of four periods.

JEANNE-LOUISE RAMONET OF KERIZINEN, BRITTANY

Jeanne-Louise Ramonet (1910–95) experienced visions from 1938 to 1965. The main source for her story is the book written by her supporters, *Kerizinen: Messages of Christ and the Blessed Virgin 1938–1965* (Les Amis de Kerizinen n.d.), and there is also an account in an academic article written by the anthropologist Ellen Badone, who shows how the devotional account was constructed: 'versions of events become codified, fixed, and official as they are recorded in written format' (Badone 2007: 453). Bearing that caveat in mind, the narrative describes Jeanne-Louise as a young woman from a rural farming family suffering physical weakness, which disqualified her from entering the convent. It is appropriate, therefore, that the first apparition occurred on 15 September 1938, the feast day of our Lady of Sorrows. After the second apparition on 7 October 1939, the feast day of Our Lady of the Rosary, Jeanne-Louise confided in a spiritual director/confessor (referred to as 'M. B.' or 'Father B' in Les Amis de Kerizinen n.d.: 26, 30) while otherwise keeping the events to herself, although the spiritual director may have said something about this to other priests. The apparitions only became known publicly from 1947 due to a little girl overhearing the visionary's confession, after which the sanctuary grew. In 1949, a small shrine was erected consisting of statues in a glass box with ex-votos around the base, and a spring was discovered in 1952, which became the 'holy water' of Kerizinen. In 1956 a proper chapel was built and in 1978 the present large church was completed, encompassing the chapel, which remains complete inside it. Finally, a modern reception building for pilgrims was completed in 1992. The size of the church and growth of facilities is a testimony to the popularity of pilgrimage at Kerizinen, despite the lack of Church encouragement and approval. The initial Breton enthusiasm for the new shrine was supplemented and to some extent supplanted by a national and international movement of support that grew in the 1960s and 1970s (Badone 2007: 454).

Jeanne-Louise's dominant Mariological theme concerns the union of the hearts of Jesus and Mary. The Sacred Heart (of Jesus) and the Immaculate Heart (of Mary) were important devotional ideas in their own right; the apparition tradition usually distinguished between them, although the Miraculous Medal includes an image of both hearts side by side. In the Kerizinen chapel, the figures of Jesus and Mary stand with hearts interconnected by visible rays of love, an iconographical innovation.

The four stages of the visions of Kerizinen can be categorized as:

(1) The first phase, 1938–49: the period before the building of the original shrine in December 1949.

Twenty-four visions took place in this first phase, all of the Virgin Mary except one that featured an image of the rosary. The messages were recorded in notebooks by Jeanne-Louise (Les Amis de Kerizinen n.d.). Early on, they relate to the Second World War and the belief that prayer would bring an early end to it; towards the end of the war, the messages began to express concern over the spread of communism. There are allusions to Fátima, including the desire for devotion to Our Lady of the Rosary (unsurprising as Jeanne-Louise's birthday coincided with the feast day) and communion on the first Saturday of the month. The focus on 'the Sorrowful and Immaculate Heart' reflects the revelations of both Berthe Petit and Lúcia of Fátima. In the post-war years, Jeanne-Louise, like many other visionaries, did not dwell on the military victory but foresaw new calamities and divine chastisements. In particular, the messages referred to a possible invasion of France by communist Russia and the subsequent persecution of the Church amidst general destruction. In order to provide some light in this darkness, Kerizinen was to become a 'Breton Lourdes' (message of 17 July 1948, Les Amis de Kerizinen n.d.: 35).

There is a four-year lacuna in recorded visions after the building of the shrine. During this period a spring was discovered and water piped through for pilgrims.

(2) The second phase, 25 March 1954–12 May 1955, involves seven further apparitions of the Virgin Mary.

These refer to the dogma of the Assumption (declared on 1 November 1950 by Pope Pius XII) and to Mary crying: 'I suffer because of the indifference of mankind. My Heart bleeds because of the offences, especially those of impurity, directed at My Divine Son. The hour of Divine Justice will not be long delayed in sounding. But be strong, Christians. The Reign of God is close . . . ' (message of 5 March 1955 in Les Amis de Kerizinen n.d.: 50). These messages stand in the tradition of La Salette, Fátima, and Ezkioga: indifference and offence preceding chastisement and, finally, God's victory. Jeanne-Louise also regarded the building of a chapel at Kerizinen as Mary's desire and part of the divine plan of reparation and redemption (this was accomplished in February 1956).

(3) The third phase, 1 October 1955–3 March 1962: visions of the Hearts of Jesus and Mary.

This phase began at a time when Jeanne-Louise claimed to be receiving mystical communion by a divine hand. Apparently, there were witnesses (Les Amis de Kerizinen n.d.: 55; Badone 2007: 460). The mystical communion of Fátima was not witnessed by anyone but the seer, in contrast to those at Garabandal and more latterly at Naju in South Korea, which occurred in front of witnesses and have been photographed. The existence of these photographic testimonies leaves one with a clear alternative between miracle and sleight of hand, which is not the case with apparitions, for which sincerity does not necessarily prove the miraculous. During the Easter Holy Weeks of 1955 and 1956, the hosts were said to have bled.

However, the key characteristic of this period is the shift in emphasis from the Virgin Mary as the sole subject of the apparition to a roughly equal division between visions of Mary and apparitions of Jesus and Mary with hearts conjoined. The first appearance of this type was on 1 October 1955. The messages bring together the traditional ideas of consecration to the Sacred Heart and to the Immaculate Heart: 'Let your families, your nations and the whole World be consecrated in the very same consecration, to the Sacred and Merciful Heart of Jesus and to My Sorrowful and Immaculate Heart—to Our Two Hearts United in the Holy Spirit' (Les Amis de Kerizinen n.d.: 57). This marks a theologically important step in the apparition tradition; the emphasis on the union of Christ and Mary as opposed to the centuries-old distinction between Christ as Judge and Mary as Mother of Mercy.

The messages in this period continue to emphasize the contrast between the worldwide indifference towards God and the graces received through the Eucharist, praying of the rosary, and devotion at the shrine. They are wordier than in the past (the object of criticism, according to Les Amis de Kerizinen n.d.: 97). The theme of the two hearts predominates while references to communism disappear. It is now global secularization that concerns Jeanne-Louise's Mary; the sins of the world are not often specified but there are references to the abuse of science, greed and injustice, and agitation and conflict. Jeanne-Louise sees herself as bringing the news of a new revelation as apocalyptic in tone and content as the biblical one. France remains the focus of several of the messages and the Virgin spoke in French. On 3 March 1956, a priest asked if the apparition could speak Breton, so Jeanne-Louise asked Mary and then reported the reply (which was apparently in Breton):

> If I do not speak Breton when I come down among you, it is because I wish My words to be spread throughout the World, but especially throughout France, this country which I love so much and which I want to support and rescue from all the chastisements which threaten it (Les Amis de Kerizinen n.d.: 64).

(4) The fourth phase, June 1962–1965.

This phase began with a 'Eucharistic Week' and daily apparitions of Christ dressed in white from 21–30 June 1962, spanning the feasts of Corpus Christi and the Immaculate Heart. These messages concern the love of Christ as revealed and poured out in the Eucharist; there were also calls for saintly priests and reflections on blasphemies and indifference against the Eucharist. The final nine apparitions (2 March 1963 to 1 October 1965) coincided reasonably closely with the period of Vatican II (11 October 1962 to 8 December 1965). These are calls to Christians to persevere in faith and to recognize the love and redemptive suffering of Christ. The messages reflect the council's emphasis on ecumenism: Christ, speaking about Mary, says that she 'is therefore the hope for unity in the Church', but they also espouse a high Mariology: 'Without My Mother, no Saviour, no Redemption, no Church!'. There is a call to the priests to retain a Marian devotion: 'You especially who have charge of souls, remain in the school of My Mother' (Les Amis de Kerizinen n.d.: 128–9).

There were four diocesan pronouncements on Kerinzen in 1956, 1961, 1972, and 1975, all prohibitions on devotion and pilgrimage, especially clerical involvement. The last of these was made with Vatican approval. However, Church support was not wholly lacking according to Laurentin and Sbalchiero (2007: 490–1). They write that a priest claimed to have been cured at Kerizinen in 1968 and the authenticity of this was witnessed by a theologian and a doctor. Ellen Badone shows how, after the period of visions, the pilgrimage movement was not wholly harmonious. While early supporters were Breton, 'Les Amis de Kerizinen' was formed in 1972 mainly with outsiders, usually from Paris. This created tension: 'As local interest declined, neighbours were replaced as primary supporters of Jeanne-Louise by *Les Amis de Kerizinen*. For local people the association was viewed in a very poor light' (Badone 2007: 459). These conflicts did not bring an end to local support, however, and believers explain them in terms of the Devil working to undermine the divine plan (Badone 2007: 468).

In the absence of Church endorsement, Les Amis de Kerizinen 'assumed the role of a parallel, lay authority' (Badone 2007: 465) and took on the writing of the accepted text of the apparitions. As in other cases, this involved editing out aspects that could cause the cult difficulty with the Church. Badone notes Jeanne-Louise's reputation for precognition, which is a faculty known in popular religion and not necessarily linked to Christianity; furthermore, oral memories of the apparitions do not associate this with the gift of the Virgin Mary in the way that the published account does (Badone 2007: 461). Here, as elsewhere, elements of folk belief are excluded in order to tie in with the apparitions with orthodox Catholicism. There are also disturbing local traditions that explain personal misfortunes, such as death or serious illness, as being due to the protagonists' obstruction of the growth of the shrine (Badone 2007: 463–8). Furthermore, some pilgrims travelled to Kerizinen to counter witchcraft.

The religious order, 'The Children of Mary of Kerizinen', was first requested in the message of 4 October 1947 (Les Amis de Kerizinen n.d: 26). It was eventually founded in the 1970s and presently includes four women based at the shrine. The lack of episcopal approval for the shrine means that this community is unofficial. The remaining members continue to hope for some recognition, especially given the recent decline in the numbers of pilgrims (visit, 2014). With diocesan backing, the shrine would be much more likely to survive in the face of a continuing reduction in the numbers of regular church-goers in France. Jeanne-Louise Ramonet died in 1995 and the farmhouse is maintained just as it was in her lifetime. The visitor can see her bed, her cooker, and some ornaments. The preservation of the houses of those regarded as holy people is common across Catholic Europe; in this way, the shrine remains focused on the seer and her life as much as it does on the hearts of Christ and Mary.

IDA PEERDEMAN OF AMSTERDAM

Ida Peerdeman (1905–96) has inspired a global campaign of support asking for the papal dogmatization of the Marian titles 'Coredemptrix, Mediatrix, and Advocate'. Ida may have known of an earlier campaign in the twentieth century led by Cardinal Mercier of Belgium to define Mary as 'Mediatrix of All Graces'; however, the bringing together of the three titles is unique to her. Her story is given in publications by her supporters, The Lady of All Nations Foundation (hereafter TLANF), who manage the Amsterdam shrine, and an academic analysis can be found in Margry (2009a; 2009b). As at Kerizinen, at the heart of the maintenance of the shrine is an order of religious sisters. Another parallel is in the Church reaction: the Amsterdam apparitions (1945–59) were investi-gated formally by the diocese (Haarlem-Amsterdam); however, episcopal dec-larations in 1956 and 1974 did not find evidence for the supernatural and returned negative verdicts with Vatican backing. Yet the Amsterdam apparition cult had a different trajectory and a more successful one than that at Kerizinen. There was growing, influential Catholic support, firstly among the Dominicans and the wealthy Brenninckmeijer family in the late 1940s (Margry 2009a: 248), then later from the Marian author Raoul Auclair, who published the messages of Amsterdam and Kerizinen and organized a conference on the Amsterdam apparitions in Paris in 1966 (Laurentin and Sbalchiero 2007: 79–84). Episcopal approval finally came with the pronouncements of successive bishops of Haarlem-Amsterdam in 1996 and 2002, the first authorizing the cult and the second the apparitions themselves.

Ida's contribution to the Catholic Marian tradition was to bring together three traditional ideas about the Virgin Mary into a request for a new dogma just after the definition of the Assumption of Mary as dogma in 1950. The promotion of traditional ideas to dogma means that obedient Catholics *should* rather than *might* believe in them and regard them as essential to the faith. However, while Ida was announcing Mary's initiative for what many Catholics regarded as a natural next step in the development of Catholic Marian dogma, the advent of Vatican II and the playing down of a 'high' Mariology meant that the hierarchy of the Church was not likely to be receptive to the idea during this period.

The first apparition occurred towards the end of the Second World War, on 25 March 1945, when thirty-nine-year-old Ida was at home with her sisters and the Dominican Father Frehe, her confessor and spiritual director. Ida and her followers were acutely aware that this month marked the six-hundredth anniversary of the 'Eucharistic Miracle' of Amsterdam in 1345, the story of a Host that rose out of the ashes of a fire into which it had been thrown and then continually returned to a linen chest from wherever it was placed. In medieval Amsterdam, this event was remembered in an annual procession. During Protestant times, a secret 'Silent Procession' maintained the devotion and this tradition was revived in 1881 and continues today (<http://www.de-vrouwe.info/en/the-apparitions> accessed 31 May 2015).

The Lady of All Nations Foundation identifies three main phases of the visions (the messages can be found on the TLANF website <http://www.de-vrouwe.info> accessed 31 May 2015 and in print in TLANF 1999; Künzli 1996):

(1) The first phase, 1945–50: 'These messages are more general in topic. Mary, the Lady, presents images, warnings and prophecies which clearly predict the political and spiritual turbulence to come in the second half of the twentieth century' (TLANF 1999: 13).

The messages in the first phase have the quality of dreams, with shifting scenes, symbolic gestures and images, and mysterious sayings. Margry refers to the first phase of messages as 'primarily characterized by their chaotic and strongly symbolic style, which is, as it were, a reflection of the times, dominated by political unrest, moral ambiguity and personal anxieties' (Margry 2009a: 245). There are recurrent themes: the presence of the 'Lady' (*Vrouwe*, the way in which the Virgin Mary is described by Ida); Ida Peerdeman's feelings of pain evoked by the Cross, which included her rejection of it as she placed herself in the role of a representative of sinful humanity; concern about the lack of love, truth, and righteousness in humanity; the danger of communism and Russia; and anticipation of various disasters. Ida's Mary made many exhortations: to the nations to have greater faith in the Christian truth (especially England, Germany, and Italy); to Rome to take responsibility for leading the world in a time of political and spiritual struggle; to other denominations to support Rome in this crisis; to the Catholic Church to modernize its 'laws' and its training of priests in order for it to be equal to the task. Ida was concerned about priests who were not committed enough.

This first group of messages on their own would have been unlikely to achieve either episcopal approval or the large-scale Catholic following that has survived into the twenty-first century. Generally, Ida's early revelations are limited by being too mysterious and personal (even though family members and some clerics were involved in the transcription and circulation). They are context-bound in post-war Western Europe, when many other such phenomena relayed the guidance of the Virgin Mary in the face of the threat of communism and renewed war (Christian 1984); they contain too many instructions about pastoral strategy and occasionally admonish the priesthood, even to high levels in the hierarchy. The prophecies are vague and only occasionally can they be related to actual events. These messages reflect the anxiety of a Catholic woman highly concerned about the future of the world in which she was living.

Towards the end of this initial phase, on 16 November 1950, Ida communicated for the first time the full title of the Lady: 'the Lady of All Nations' (*De Vrouwe van alle Volkeren*). The title relates to the many messages given thus far about the dangerous state of the nations of the world; furthermore, Ida will have known of the shrine at Banneux in neighbouring Belgium where Mary was described as having requested a chapel in 1933, 'for all nations, to heal the sick'.

(2) The second phase, 1951–54: 'Following the proclamation of the dogma of the Assumption of Mary into Heaven on November 1, 1950, the messages take on a new direction. The great plan by which the Lady wishes to save the world gradually unfolds' (TLANF 1999: 13).

A new Trinitarian prayer, which had been hinted at in the first apparition, was fully revealed on 11 February 1951: 'Lord Jesus Christ, Son of the Father, send now your Spirit over the Earth. Let the Holy Spirit live in the hearts of all nations, that they be preserved from degeneration, disaster and war. May the Lady of All Nations, who once was Mary, be our advocate. Amen'. The words 'who once was Mary' were problematic for the Congregation for the Doctrine of the Faith, which directed in July 2005 that they be changed to 'the Blessed Virgin Mary' (TLANF 2009: 16). Ida then asked on 4 March 1951 for the circulation of an image depicting Mary standing in front of the Cross and on the globe of the earth surrounded by followers symbolized by black and white sheep. Here Mary is seen as suffering with Christ and thus participating in the work of redemption; Ida identified Mary's sash as Christ's loincloth. This is a pictorial expression of the concept of Mary as Coredemptrix. Both prayer and image have attracted the devotion of Catholics on a global scale; on 31 May

1951—in some dioceses, this had marked the feast day of Mary Mediatrix of All Graces—this date started to become an annual day of gathering and celebration for the Amsterdam visionary movement.

It is clear that the papal declaration of the Assumption inspired Ida to bring together all the disparate elements of her visions; now they became focused on the demand for further Mariological dogmatic definition. The project was revealed between April and May 1951. The Virgin Mary wished to be defined as 'Coredemptrix, Mediatrix, and Advocate'. None of these titles is unknown in Roman Catholicism and they can be found in Mariological writings and debates of the period (Margry 2009a: 247–8; Miravalle 1995). Such a definition would comprise the fifth and final Marian dogma (the other four being the Motherhood of God or Mary as *Theotokos*; Mary as Ever Virgin; the Immaculate Conception; the Assumption). Ida claimed that the Virgin Mary herself had urged the dogma on the 'theologians', as it would change the world for the better. However, the request for a dogma was demanding too much for two reasons (for reservations about the coredemption of Mary as dogma, see Schillebeeckx and Halkes 1993: 17–21; Endean 2007: 290): firstly, in the modern period, popes had only carried out dogmatic definitions on two occasions after widespread pressure in the Church and wholesale consultation; secondly, Marian dogmatic definition was increasingly seen in the 1950s as an obstacle to ecumenism. These concerns culminated in the guarded claims about Mary at Vatican II (see Chapter 12 within this volume).

This second phase also sees a change in the style of Ida's apparitions. The messages became more didactic in nature, with fewer 'scenes' and more in the way of continuous teaching by the Virgin Mary. It seems as if Ida, through her visions, had been searching for a central theme, meaning, and purpose for nearly six years, and had now discovered it, the nucleus of the cult emerging as the title of the Lady, the prayer, the image, and the dogma.

(3) The third phase, 1954–59: 'In grand visions [the Lady] addresses the nations of the world, showing them the way to go, the way leading to the daily Miracle, the Eucharist' (TLANF 1999: 14).

After 31 May 1954, Ida reported only one apparition on 31 May each year up to and including 1959, plus one other vision in February 1958 (which resulted, apparently, in a sealed and accurate prophecy that Pius XII would die in October). The third phase concentrates on the Eucharist, completing the main period of the apparitions (there were occasional further messages, for which, see Künzli 1996: 101–13). The third phase is the least controversial and involves powerfully emotional experiences while at Mass, which reflect an orthodox Roman Catholic Eucharistic and Trinitarian piety. This movement towards the Eucharist parallels the progress of the visions of Jeanne-Louise Ramonet. The evolution from a prophecy-centred to a sacrament-centred devotion in both cases could be said to anticipate the changes at Vatican II itself.

The movement promoting the dogma of Coredemptrix, Mediatrix, and Advocate grew in strength from the 1950s. Its chief promulgator in the English-speaking world is Deacon Professor Mark Miravalle of the Franciscan University at Steubenville, Ohio, who writes articles, publishes video material on the web, and edits a journal, *Mother of All Peoples*. He is also president of *Vox Populi Mariae Mediatrici*, an organization founded in 1993, which continues to campaign for the definition of the dogma (<http://fifthmariandogma. com> accessed 31 May 2015). According to this movement, a petition for the dogma addressed to the pope included seven million signatures and the endorsement of forty-three cardinals and over 550 bishops. The movement has a global following, notably in the Philippines, the region with the most derivative shrines and a strong public devotion to the Lady of All Nations (Margry 2009b: 192). In Akita, Japan, a wooden statue depicting the Amsterdam picture was from 1973 the focus of a cult of apparitions as a 'weeping statue'; the Akita devotion was approved by the local Catholic bishop in 1984. The Amsterdam movement holds regular 'International Days of Prayer', which gather together a large number of supporters. However, the bishop of Haarlem-Amsterdam and TLANF have distanced themselves from the derivative movement 'Community of the Lady of All Nations' or 'Army of Mary', led by Marie-Paule Giguère in Quebec, who has claimed to be an incarnation of the Virgin Mary (<http://www.de-vrouwe.info/en/notice-regarding-the-qarmy-of-maryq-2007> accessed 31 May 2015). This group has been condemned by the Church, diocesan and international, as schismatic and heterodox.

Amsterdam stands, along with several other twentieth-century apparition cases, in the Fátima tradition with its predictions of global disaster and concern over the threat of communism; Ida established this link herself by claiming that she had experienced an apparition as a young girl at the time of the Fátima vision in October 1917 (Margry 2009a: 247). Nevertheless, Amsterdam has its own unique focus, the Lady of All Nations prayer and image, along with the proposed fifth dogma.

JEANNE-LOUISE RAMONET AND IDA PEERDEMAN AS 'POPULAR THEOLOGIANS'

In her analysis of several Marian apparitions, Sandra Zimdars-Swartz (1991) argues that the Marian apparition tradition articulates a narrative of suffering based in the experiences of the original visionary or visionaries, supplemented by the experiences of the people who become pilgrims to the shrines and devotees of the cults. The central theme is that God is angry with the world, but wishes to intervene through Mary's maternal concern for her children in order to warn humanity about impending disaster, and Zimdars-Swartz sees this as indicating dissatisfaction with life, personal, social, and political. Margry's field research on Amsterdam supports this thesis (2009b: 191). Both Jeanne-Louise Ramonet and Ida Peerdeman lived through the horrors of the First and Second World Wars, the first as young children. In that, they are unremarkable but they were both vulnerable individuals. Jeanne-Louise was clearly drawn to a spiritual life but suffered from physical ill-health that prevented her from joining the convent (Les Amis de Kerinzen n.d.: 6–7). Ida Peerdeman's biography shows a highly sensitive woman prone to a belief that she was under demonic attack (<http://www.de-vrouwe.info/en/the-first-35-years/demonic-torments> biography by Father Paul Maria Sigl, accessed 31 May 2015). During the period of the apparitions, she claimed to experience for herself the agonies of the Cross.

These women articulated the concerns of a generation of traditionalist Western European Catholics who regarded themselves as victims of political history and of evil supernatural forces. For Jeanne-Louise and Ida, the remedy lay in prayer, the sacraments, and devotion to Mary. They had their own individual approaches and drew on tradition, but in creative ways that they ascribed to the initiative of Mary herself. Their more famous contemporary, Sister Lúcia of Fátima, urged the Church to consecrate Russia to the Immaculate Heart of Mary to achieve that country's conversion. Lúcia found a new application of the practice of consecrations (of either the world or particular countries such as Spain and Portugal) to the Sacred Heart. Jeanne-Louise inherited the Immaculate Heart tradition, but wished to integrate the devotions to the Sacred and Immaculate Hearts. Ida, in a post-war age when the world emerged as a 'global village', saw Mary as a global mother and co-participator with Christ in the work of redemption. For both Jeanne-Louise and Ida, Mary remained central to an understanding of Christ and redemption; Mary had to be understood in the 'Christotypical' sense and Christianity was Marian. Like many other visionaries, their revelations ran counter to the trend in Vatican II towards an 'ecclesiotypical' Mariology.

Nevertheless, Ida's first phase of messages can be interpreted (and are interpreted as such by TLANF) as encouraging Church reform in the run-up to Vatican II; Ida argued for modernization in the Church to make it more relevant in the post-war world and advocated 'social rights' (message of 16 December 1949). On 11 February 1951, Ida had a vision of a future council about which the Lady said that 'the doctrine is right, but the laws can and must be changed' (TLANF 1999: 85). Later, Ida seems to have become less comfortable with change in the Church; she recorded that Mary had assured her that priestly celibacy would be maintained (31 May 1957). As Vatican II

ended, she claimed that a divine voice had warned her of a possible schism due
to modernism, which included '*false* theories about the Eucharist, sacraments,
doctrine, priesthood, marriage and family-planning... Divine teaching and
laws are valid for all time and newly applicable to every period' (Künzli 1996:
108). Ida's story is typical of many middle-aged people growing more resistant
to social change. On 29 August 1945, Ida praised socialism, as long as it was
guided by the Church (Künzli 1996: 3), but on 20 March 1953, she stated that:
'It is modern humanism, realism, socialism and communism which have the
world in their grip' (TLANF 1999: 134).

Both Jeanne-Louise and Ida wrote down their messages. Ida was adept at
expressing her feelings, as can be judged from letters to her spiritual director
(TLANF 1999: 177–83, 185–9). She often spoke of 'theologians', but clearly did
not regard herself as one. Nevertheless, she regarded her own contribution as
primary, as she believed it to be dictated by the Virgin Mary: 'I have said:
theology must give way to the concerns of my Son. By this I mean to say:
theologians, the Son always looks for the little and simple for His cause'
(TLANF 1999: 94).

While respecting the Catholic Church as an ideal, Marian visionaries have
scolded and occasionally disobeyed the Catholic priesthood. Some of Ida's
messages were directed at Rome itself and the priesthood; she identified a lack
of action by the Catholic Church in what she perceived to be a time of global
crisis. Visionaries and their messages do not conform to any stereotype of the
Catholic woman as humble or self-effacing; if there are stereotypes of the
figure of Mary and Marian visionaries in Catholicism, it would be the feisty
mother and her protégée. Yet, although Ida talked about gender very seldom
in her messages, brief references reflect her traditional views, unsurprising for
their time. Two messages on 10 December 1950 and 31 May 1951 demonstrate
a complementary and patriarchal understanding of the roles of men and
women: men should be 'soldiers for Christ'; men have 'strength and will'
and women need to 'make sacrifices' and 'abandon all your egoism and vanity'
(TLANF 1999: 80, 104). God is Mary's 'Lord and Master' (31 May 1951,
TLANF 1999: 102). The supreme importance of Mary as the Coredemptrix
with Christ is circumscribed by a traditional and orthodox view of their
relationship.

Jeanne-Louise and Ida's work passed through phases of development. As
with any theologian or writer or social commentator, one finds evolution,
maturation, and sometimes contradiction. However, in the traditionalist
Catholic circles in which their messages have currency, they are not recognized as theologians in any sense. They are seen as conduits for Mary's
messages; nevertheless, in the subjective models employed by the humanities
and also by the Vatican, these can be ascribed to the visionaries' imaginative
faculties. The difference is that the humanities will not theorize on a supernatural inspiration behind the creative process, which the Church will do in

cases that are approved. Yet, in both of these subjective models, these women brought previously known Catholic ideas and popular theologies about Mary into new relationships that have enjoyed considerable influence amongst Catholics, particularly those who campaign against the Vatican's reluctance to develop Marian dogma beyond the Immaculate Conception and Assumption, and who are critical of Vatican II norms in which Mariology is not situated within a Christotypical perspective. This implied critique of Mariological development has not helped the cause of Kerizinen: 'According to a diocesan spokesperson, the primary difficulty for the Church with respect to Kerizinen concerns the elevation of the importance of the Virgin in the Kerizinen messages' (Badone 2007: 455).

Overall, it is the development of Marian devotion that is likely to be the most enduring contribution of Jeanne-Louise and Ida. The images created by them and which they ascribed to the initiative of Mary were 'Christotypical', i.e. Mary conceived of as a partner to Christ in the events of salvation. Jeanne-Louise seems to have been sensitive to a possible disjuncture between the devotions to the Sacred Heart and the Immaculate Heart, with the latter becoming dominant in the period following the revelations of Lúcia of Fátima. Therefore her most prominent visionary image is of a union of the hearts; it could be said that, despite being accused by some of inappropriately exalting Mary, she is actually restoring Christ to an equal place in the twentieth-century plan of divine initiative in the face of global disasters. Ida's famous picture leaves the viewer in no doubt—Mary is an *alter Christus*, standing before the Cross with Christ's loincloth for a girdle. Here there is no Christ in the scene, although he is often referred to in the visionary messages. Ida wanted Mary's partnership to Christ as Coredemptrix, Mediatrix, and Advocate to be dogmatically declared as the next logical step after the Immaculate Conception (1854) and Assumption (1950).

The final general point that can be made is that Jeanne-Louise and Ida should be distinguished from the younger women of the apparition tradition, for whom a short period of visions left a series of messages that could be easily written down on a single sheet of paper. Jeanne-Louise and Ida announced a whole series of visionary messages over several years. This allows one to discern a progression in the messages as they interacted with world and ecclesiastical events. As visionaries, Jeanne-Louise and Ida were 'popular theologians' and like any other person whose ideas are eagerly anticipated by a wider audience, they disseminated images and concepts that adapted to new circumstances.

11

The Cold War and the Marian Cult

THE INTENSIFICATION OF THE MARIAN APPARITION CULT

In December 1947, four girls between the ages of seven and twelve in L'Île-Bouchard, a village in the diocese of Tours, reported that they had seen in the parish church an apparition of a sad-faced Mary who said to them: 'Tell the little children to pray for France because she has great need of it' (Laurentin and Sbalchiero 2007: 530, my translation). It had been a chaotic year in French politics, with the very real possibility of communist takeover (Evans and Godin 2014: 133–7). The parish publication on these events makes the link between the apparitions and this situation (Paroisse de L'Île-Bouchard 1988). The political connection worked against official approval, as the Church disliked the expression of political aspirations in apparitions, although the children can only have sensed the general feeling of unease without understanding the politics in any detail. However, the Church did afford some level of approval to L'Île-Bouchard, building a grotto in the parish church and organizing an annual pilgrimage, often with a bishop present, on the feast of the Immaculate Conception, the anniversary of the first apparition (Laurentin and Sbalchiero 2007: 534–5).

L'Île-Bouchard is an example of the very many apparitions in Western Europe during the years 1947–54, the early years of the Cold War between the West and communist Eastern Europe, a period identified by William Christian Jr (1984) as a time when Catholics were particularly sensitive to reports of a Marian intervention. The reasons for this are, he suggests:

- The fear that the newly emerging superpower stand-off could lead to widespread devastation, turning the apocalyptic images and messages into reality.
- Fear that Catholic countries west of the Iron Curtain could fall to communism through the democratic process, a very real one in Italy and France.

He adds that the global apprehension of possible destruction from the skies also led to more sightings of UFOs than in any other period, particularly in the

United States. The lists of recorded apparitions confirm the increase in recorded cases in the years between 1947 and 1954. These provide evidence that political uncertainty has a bearing on this increase: Italy followed by France and then Germany saw the most incidents. Apparitions occurred in Catholic Eastern Europe too, in countries such as Yugoslavia, Poland, Czechoslovakia, and Hungary; although there were fewer than in the Western European countries mentioned and they did not lead to a major shrine, this was probably due to the decreased likelihood of a case becoming widely known and gaining a following under communist rule (Apolito 2005: 24–5).

The ideological battle in Western Europe between Catholicism and communism or secularism in these years resulted in a strategy of reviving faith through missions (in Spain, Christian 1984: 245; in Italy, Poggi 1972: 142, 151). These missions remained in a given location for a few days and were led by accomplished preachers, often from religious orders such as the Jesuits or Dominicans. Sometimes, they used travelling statues: in France during the 1940s, the most famous statue used in this way was that of Our Lady of Boulogne (Christian 1984: 246). The connection made between these missions and consecration to the Immaculate Heart of Mary made the statue of Fátima a highly suitable standard around which to rally in the cause of conversion (Christian 1984: 247; Morgan 2009). The international journeys of this statue across Europe in 1946 and onwards reinforced Fátima as the archetypal twentieth-century Marian apparition; its call for prayer and consecration to overcome communism and its stress on forthcoming miracles (in the original messages) and divine punishments (in the later 'secrets') created a template for new visions. Fátima was also publicized through children's re-enactments of the story of its visions, such as at Ghiaie di Bonate (near Bergamo, Italy) where, on 13 May 1944, the twenty-seventh anniversary of the first apparition at Fátima, a seven-year-old girl had a vision announcing the end of the Second World War and attracted hundreds of thousands to the site (Christian 1984: 250). The Church made a negative pronouncement on the case, as it would do with most Western European apparitions that it investigated formally after the war. Many of these referred back to the Fátima scenario of secrets, miracles, the spinning sun, and the conversion of Russia, and therefore lacked originality (Christian 1984: 251).

Ghiaie di Bonate's seer, Adelaide Roncalli, experienced thirteen apparitions throughout May 1944, which resulted in a Marian cult emphasizing the sanctity of the family (see e.g. the website <http://www.madonnadelleghiaie.it/> accessed 31 May 2015, which promotes the apparitions but includes the full story of the Church's opposition and some original film footage). Adelaide's messages contain echoes of Fátima, such as the suffering of the pope, prayer for him, for the conversion of sinners, and for the end of the war; therefore her visions are referred to by devotees as 'Fátima's epilogue'. However, the Bonate visions are not mere reproductions. Many of the apparitions were of the Holy Family, putting the focus on the family unit (the Catholic stress on the family,

as with some Protestant views, often presupposes a breakdown of family life in
the post-war era and over-romanticizes family unity in the past). Under some
pressure from a diocesan priest, Adelaide did retract her testimony, a
common occurrence among Marian visionary children, but she returned to
her original belief in the genuine nature of her experiences. Nevertheless,
on 30 April 1948 the bishop of Bergamo declared that the supernatural
character of the visions had not been established and prohibited the cult. He
attributed the healings and conversions reported at Bonate to the faith of the
pilgrims as opposed to any special presence of the Madonna (Laurentin and
Sbalchiero 2007: 387–8).

In 2002, the devotions and shrine at Ghiaie di Bonate, although not the
apparitions, were finally legitimated by a later bishop. The recent period,
beginning in the pontificate of John Paul II, has seen several non-approved
shrines that have stood the test of time finally being accepted (as in Germany,
for example). Laurentin (1991: 18, 26) regards 1950–80 as the peak years of an
anti-apparition mood in the Vatican (1949 had seen the approval of Beauraing
and Banneux). This attitude, hardened by the great number of visionary
phenomena that had erupted after the war, was maintained by the influence
of Cardinal Ottaviani in the Holy Office. Ottaviani became famous as the
leader of the conservatives at Vatican II, yet he was not disposed to accept
Marian apparitions any more than progressive theology. In *L'Osservatore
Romano*, 4 February 1951, Ottaviani wrote that the Church stood between
the extremes of atheism and blind religiosity; it did not abandon reason when
discerning visionary experiences. His examples of problematic apparitions
show which cases were in the public eye at the time: he cited examples at
Voltago, Italy, Espis and Bouxières in France, Ham-sur-Sambre in Belgium,
Heroldsbach in Germany (covered later in this chapter), and Necedah in the
United States. This shows the persistence of some cults, as the phenomena at
Voltago, Bouxières, and Ham-sur-Sambre had begun in the 1930s. Yet the
inclusion of Heroldsbach and Necedah, both starting in 1949, shows that these
words would also have been targeted at the recent explosion of cases in the
post-war years.

POST-WAR ITALY

The Italy that emerged from the overthrow of Mussolini's fascist dictatorship
in 1943 was spearheaded by a resistance movement that aimed to remove the
German military and fight with the Allied forces but which was also dominated by communists (Ginsborg 1990: 49). On the other hand, the capitalist
Christian Democrats gained from the fact that American money became
crucial to the revival of the Italian economy after the war. In 1946, Italy

rejected the monarchy and established a republic. Universal suffrage was also introduced; Italian women voted for the first time in 1946 in an election that resulted in a coalition between left and right, which remained locked in political conflict with uncertain outcomes (Ginsborg 1990: 72). Due to electoral union between the Socialist and Communist parties in a hybrid known as the Popular Democratic Front, the left had good prospects for victory in the 1948 election. However, the Catholic Church and the Catholic Action movement unsurprisingly favoured the Christian Democrats and, with their backing, that party gained mass support (Ginsborg 1990: 50). After the party's clear victory in 1948 (Ginsborg 1990: 115–18), the Christian Democrats ruled Italy for decades, although the Communists remained strong as the second party making it necessary for the Christian Democrats to seek coalitions in order to form governments (Ginsborg 1990: 442). During the Cold War period, the Americans and British backed the Christian Democrats as a centre-right party supporting the capitalist economy in Italy, just as they did in West Germany. However, as Italy modernized and its economy became buoyant, Christian Democracy did not always espouse the Catholic values of its origins, accepting rather consumerism and liberalism; tension between the Vatican and the Christian Democrat politicians continued despite the common enemy in communism (Ginsborg 1990: 153, 168). Furthermore, commitment to the Church declined in the late 1950s and 1960s (Ginsborg 1990: 245), and divorce was legalized after a referendum in 1976.

Apparitions are among many Catholic reactions and responses to rapid developments in society that appear to threaten traditional ways of life. Italy's greater number of visions than any other European country may either reflect a national tendency to experience apparitions as Carroll (1992: 52–3) concludes or make something of phenomena experienced but not heralded in the same way elsewhere. Many apparitions in Italy during the 1947–54 period echoed Fátima and its rallying call against communism. However, the most famous, the visions at Tre Fontane in the grounds of a Trappist monastery just south of the Roman city wall, did not; they involved the conversion of a Protestant. Bruno Cornacchiola, at the time of his first vision, was a zealous Adventist (Laurentin and Sbalchiero 2007: 828–32). He had even considered assassinating the pope. On 12 April 1947, he took his three children (aged between four and seven) to Tre Fontane and, according to his testimony, was preparing a talk denouncing Marian doctrine while the children played together. Bruno's recollections are that, at the entrance to a grotto, the children claimed to see a beautiful lady and fell to their knees in a trance; they became heavy and he could not lift them. Then Bruno saw the lady in his turn. She held a book and said to Bruno alone:

> I am She who is within the divine Trinity. I am the Virgin of the Revelation. You are persecuting me: stop now! Join the flock of the chosen, the heavenly court on

Earth. God's promise remains unchanging: the nine Fridays of the Sacred Heart that you observed to please your faithful wife before following the path of error will save you! (Laurentin and Sbalchiero 2007: 829, my translation).

These words refer to the fact the Bruno, raised a Catholic, had originally undertaken devotions to the Sacred Heart to satisfy his Catholic wife, but he then joined the Adventists and insisted that his wife did so too. The apparition told Bruno to present himself to the pope. Two more apparitions followed and healings were reported. Bruno met Pius XII in 1949 and showed him a dagger on which he had written 'Death to the Pope'. The cult of the Virgin of the Revelation was authorized, although the apparitions were not officially approved. The website 'Theotokos' suggests that the reluctance of the Church to take the second step was in part due to further claims of apparitions by Bruno Cornacchiola, 'increasingly apocalyptic in tone', up to 1986 (<http://www.theotokos.org.uk/pages/approved/appariti/trefonta.html> accessed 31 May 2015).

Like many other Marian apparitions, Tre Fontane's visions refer to the need to convert sinners and unbelievers; while they do not include a reference to the battle against communism, it is recorded that the visionary had been a communist at one point in his life. Tre Fontane also includes elements which make the case unique. In addition to resolving Bruno's own inner struggle between Catholicism and Adventism, the visions of Mary holding a book, which is thought to represent the Bible, reflect a Catholic Church coming to terms with its own need to develop a stronger practice of biblical study in the years leading up to Vatican II. Pius XII initiated this trend in *Divino Afflante Spiritu* (1943). Tre Fontane is also the area of Rome associated with the martyrdom of St Paul, whose own persecution of the Church was challenged in a vision. So Tre Fontane has its own peculiar features, while at the same time expressing two familiar Catholic apparition concerns: (1) Catholic fears about the vulnerability of the pope because of the hostility of modern enemies of the Church; and (2), the role of the Virgin Mary in the potential conversion of those enemies. The conversion of males, the gender in Catholic countries most likely to join the communists, was a central aim of post-war missions in Europe (Christian 1984: 244–6).

In the period 1947–54, in addition to Tre Fontane, other Italian cases that merit brief consideration are given in Table 11.1 (details from Laurentin and Sbalchiero 2007: 643–7, 169, 390–1, 110–11). Of course, these are selected from many and are chosen because they are the best known. They all focus on a single female seer; at the outset of visions, one was an adult, one a teenager, and there were two children under ten. The table shows the tendency for suppression in the post-war years, but also indicates a relaxation of strictures in the 1990s for those deemed most worthy among the more persistent cases. In all of these Italian cases as well as at Ghiaie di Bonate and Tre Fontane, chapels remain today as the focus of lively and regular devotion.

Table 11.1. Prominent post-war apparitions in Italy (all included clear references to the message of Fátima or its sun miracle)

Site	Diocese/ Region	Dates of apparitions	Visionary	Original Church decision/ Recent change
Montichiari	Brescia/Emilia-Romagna	23 Nov. 1946–8 Dec. 1947 Feb. 1966–Oct. 1976	Pierina Gilli (1911–91) nun, ill health	Prohibition/Endorsement of cult of Mystical Rose, 1990
Casanova Staffora	Tortona/ Lombardia	Fourth of each month, June 1947–June 1956	Angela Volpini (1940–)	Non-recognition but chapel allowed/Episcopal visits
Gimigliano	Ascoli Piceno/ Marche	18 Apr.–25 May 1948, then various visions until 1985	Initial visions in 1948: Anita Federici, aged 13; later, many others	Negative judgement
Balestrino	Albenga-Imperia/ Liguria	4 Oct. 1949–5 Nov. 1986	Caterina Richero (1940–)	Non-recognition and prohibition/Chapel blessed by bishop, 1991; cult approved as Our Lady of the Cross, 1992

There were visions in all regions of Italy, including Sicily. In 1953, a plaque of the Virgin with Immaculate Heart hung on the wall in a family house in Syracuse where the pregnant wife suffered seizures causing temporary blindness. She claimed that, having recovered her sight on 29 August, she noticed that the statue was weeping. This was accepted as a miracle by the Sicilian bishops. Their statement included these words: 'The Madonna was seen to weep for four days, 29, 30, 31 August, and 1 September, and she wept with such abundance that the tears soaked a number of swabs of cotton wool and they were able to be studied scientifically' (Bouflet and Boutry 1997: 323–4, my translation). Apparently, the commission investigated the statue itself for ordinary explanations of the phenomenon without success; they confirmed that the liquid was constituted of human tears; they studied the reports of healing. All this led them to their positive conclusion and a sanctuary devoted to the *Madonna della Lacrime*, Our Lady of Tears, was built at the site because of the flow of pilgrims (see e.g. <http://catholictradition.org/Mary/syracuse.htm> accessed 31 May 2015). The Syracuse weeping statue stands alone as an approved Marian miracle during this period in Italy; it reflects the main Marian theme of the age, the Immaculate Heart, associated with the Fátima revelations.

CASANOVA STAFFORA: THE VOCATION
OF ANGELA VOLPINI

The story of Casanova Staffora is something of an enigma. The origins of its apparition movement belong to the period of the Catholic post-war crusade against communism in which Fátima was central, but the visionary's initiative took her in a direction that tended to be more left-wing in sentiment than right. For this reason, Casanova Staffora is an important reminder that apparitions are complex, not monolithic, and that each case should be taken on its own merit even when common visionary templates seem to be in evidence. It is also another useful illustration of the role that female visionaries can take in a Church led by male clerics; the power and authority bestowed by the apparition affords an opportunity for them to become spiritual leaders.

In an Italian Apennine mountain village in Lombardy's Pavian province on 4 June 1947, seven-year-old Angela Volpini experienced an apparition of the Virgin Mary. This occurred on wooded hills just outside Casanova di Sinistra, a hamlet so-called because that part of the village Casanova Staffora is on the left-hand bank of the River Staffora (from the perspective of someone looking downstream as the water flows down towards the Po). Angela's apparitions continued over nine years until she was sixteen, but she remained prominent in Catholic devotion in the area. Now, sixty-eight years after the first apparition, she continues to be a local celebrity: a search on *Youtube* will reveal television appearances and filmed lectures by Angela, and updates about her story and the activities at the shrine are regularly covered in the regional newspaper, *La Provincia Pavese* (e.g. Guerrini 2008). She has the function of a spiritual thinker and teacher, and clearly fulfils the role of 'popular theologian' explored in Chapters 5 and 10 within this volume. The case has not been fully documented in English.

The story of Casanova Staffora is acknowledged by devotees to have its roots in the unstable political situation in Italy (as in Sudati 2004: 204–8). The first words that Angela heard the Virgin Mary speak to her were: 'I have come to teach the way to happiness on this Earth ... Be good, pray and I will be the salvation of your nation' (<http://www.angelavolpini.it> 'L'incontro con Maria', accessed 31 May 2015, translation by Laura Casimo). The daughter of farmers, Angela tells how she took the cows out to pasture with other children in an area known as Bocco, outside the main village. This was one month after her first communion (2 May 1947, Sudati 2004: 223). At about four o'clock in the afternoon:

> I was sitting on the grass making some bunches of flowers, when all of a sudden I felt someone taking me under my arms from behind, and lifting me up to carry me in her arms. I turned around, convinced I was going to be face to face with my

aunty, but instead I found myself in front of a very beautiful, sweet, and unknown face of a woman. (<http://www.angelavolpini.it> 'La Storia', accessed 31 May 2015, translation by Laura Casimo)

This case differs from others, as groups of children often see visions together even if one is the main or initial visionary. From the very beginning, it seems that Angela was marked out as an individual visionary.

Angela thought immediately that she had been visited by the Virgin; at the second apparition on 4 July 1947, the vision identified herself as Mary and on 4 August, as 'Mary, Help of Christians, Refuge of Sinners' (Sudati 2004: 164–5), traditional, time-honoured titles of Mary. On 4 February 1948, the vision instructed Angela to tell the priests that she was 'Mary, the mother of Jesus'. Angela later interpreted her apparition experiences in a more profound and original way, stating that her insights were based on the very first apparition, all the rest derived from that one:

> It was a total experience which took my mind, spirit, and also my entire body and senses. I could touch the Mother of Jesus... It was the aim of the human life, it was all human possibilities, it was what gave meaning to every human living. It was the joy of the Creator. With great approximation I can say that I have contemplated the universal world, through the eyes of the Madonna I have seen all mankind... I saw all the story of human beings. (<http://www.angelavolpini.it> 'L'incontro con Maria', accessed 31 May 2015, translation by Laura Casimo)

Here she may be compared to Lúcia of Fátima, who also recalled childhood visions (see Chapter 3 within this volume). Angela makes it clear that she is interpreting childhood experiences with the hindsight of an adult: 'But at that time I was only little and I didn't know how to express myself; now I can, even if it is difficult to explain everything... I believe that this experience has matured my psyche for the rest of my life' (<http://www.angelavolpini.it> 'L'incontro con Maria', accessed 31 May 2015, translation by Laura Casimo).

Pilgrimage grew rapidly; Billet (1973: 33) says that there were several thousand in attendance by October 1947. The photographs in Volpini (2003) and Sudati (2004: 223–321) show Angela being carried by a journalist from *La Stampa* in November 1947 and there was an article on Angela in the Italian weekly magazine, *Oggi* (14 December 1947). Large crowds visited during 1948, walking or travelling in cars and coaches and there were many visiting priests. A small chapel was built at the site during 1950. Angela's apparitions, like others, settled into a series with a clear programme, each fourth of the month, up until June 1956. The serial nature of apparitions, with expected visions known in advance, helps to create a structure of pilgrimage. The series was not unbroken: Billet (1973: 33) records eighty-five apparitions over nine years and adds that a few apparitions took place away from Bocco, notably some in hospital in 1955. The messages echoed previous cases: the Virgin wanted prayer, penance, a chapel and, from 1950, these requests expanded to include the desire for a larger sanctuary. After a break between July 1948 and February 1950, the messages become longer and more complex, as befits an older child (Sudati 2004: 165–74).

Unsurprisingly, the Casanova Staffora case also reflected the growing fame of the apparitions of Fátima in 1917, with the promise of a great miracle, warnings of chastisements, and sensational reports of movements of the sun. At Casanova Staffora, a prodigy of the sun, in which the sun seemed to spin and descend, occurred for the first time on 4 October 1947. A further dramatic instance of the 'solar phenomena' took place on 4 November 1950, three days after the definition of the doctrine of the Assumption by Pius XII (Sudati 2004: 177). Angela's apparitions came to an end in 1956, and she felt it necessary to interpret the meaning of the great miracle that she had prophesied. At Fátima, the miracle was understood to be the movement of the sun on 13 October 1917 but, although this phenomenon had been repeated at Bocco, Angela foretold something else. At sixteen immediately after the final apparition, she announced that the miracle would be a spiritual renewal, which had already begun (Sudati 2004: 174). These were hopeful messages: the mercy of God was holding the majority of chastisements back, and world peace would follow the tribulations that remained (this also echoed the revelations of Lúcia of Fátima). In this, Angela was more optimistic than visionaries who came after her, for whom miracles and chastisements were apocalyptic in nature.

Many priests supported Angela, despite the fact that two diocesan bishops of Tortona, Egisto Melchiori and Francesco Rossi, came to negative decisions in 1952 and 1965, respectively (episcopal commissions had begun work in 1948). However, despite this episcopal refusal to acknowledge the apparitions, permission was granted for the building of a church at Bocco, subject to the donations already received being transferred from the care of the Volpini family to the parish (Sudati 2004: 180–1). The new shrine was to be for the Marian devotion of the area and the diocesan decree made no mention of the apparitions despite these being the inspiration for its location. The first stone was laid in 1958 and it was formally blessed by an episcopal delegate in 1962.

The visionary tried to encourage the renewal that she had foreseen by founding a new association for prayer, 'Nova Cana', in 1958. Its main target membership was youth; its principles were respect and love for humanity, and the unity of political thought and religious life. Given the provenance in post-war Italy, one might have expected this to be a conservative enterprise. However, Billet, listing it among non-recognized and contradictory apparitions, pointed out that the group included long-haired anarchists, students, and workers (Billet 1973: 34). Angela herself recounts how the popularity of the movement caused problems, with many young visitors to Casanova Staffora sleeping and eating in the parish church and she praises the tolerance of the parish priest. However, the years 1972 to 1982 she describes as 'ten difficult years', when the members of Nova Cana were accused of not attending church and of being communist. In conversation with Sudati (2004: 139–41), Angela accepts that the humanitarian project she started did resonate largely with the political left, although not outright communism. She describes her movement thus:

> 'Nova Cana' gave the impulse to the birth of initiatives whose purpose was to value those economic subjects that operated in the local area under the conditions of long term marginalisation. Thanks to the self-esteem boost that Nova Cana was able to inject to the subjects involved, solitary farmers were transformed into modern social entrepreneurs. For example livestock and farming cooperatives were created. (<http://www.angelavolpini.it> 'Nova Cana', accessed 31 May 2015, translation by Laura Casimo)

Laurentin (1991: 179) points out that, although Nova Cana had as its goal the conversion of the world, this could be interpreted as humanitarian rather than religious, as Jews and atheists made up their number. All of this adds up to a movement whose youthfulness, freedom of expression, and left-leaning politics caused controversy in the Church (even today, she is accused by some of being too tolerant of Marxism: see her talk on 'Marxism and Capitalism' on *Youtube*). During the difficult decade, Angela stopped going to church. Billet (1973: 34–5) claimed that Angela admitted in 1969 that she did not pray the rosary and thus contradicted her childhood messages. However, the movement recovered in 1983 and is still in operation; Angela was reconciled to the parish and established herself as an influential Catholic teacher and speaker. Recently, bishops of Tortona have visited the shrine, which continues to attract pilgrims.

POST-WAR GERMANY

After the partition of Germany in 1945, West Germany contained all of Germany's Catholic regions. West Germany was, like Italy, engaged in a process of rebuilding amid national uncertainty; its fear of communism was not so much internal (despite a five per cent vote for the communists in the 1949 election) but external with the possibility of Soviet invasion (O'Sullivan 2009). In the years 1946–52, West Germany abounded with Marian apparitions. Foremost among these are the visions of Marienfried, a shrine near the town of Pfaffenhofen-an-der-Roth in Bavaria, between April and June 1946. The young adult visionary, Barbara (Bärbl) Reuss, claimed to have already had a vision when she was fifteen in 1940, on the anniversary of the first apparition in Fátima (13 May). The difference in emphasis between her 1940 and 1946 apparitions illustrates the shift from the template of Lourdes to that of Fátima during the 1940s. The message of the 1940 vision includes reference to the

'Rosary of the Immaculate' in which the Immaculate Conception (as Mary was described at Lourdes) was to be invoked in prayer for the Fatherland. The 1946 apparitions, however, emphasize the Immaculate Heart of Mary and consecration to it, sacrifices made for Mary for the conversion of sinners, and coming tribulations (Bouflet 2003: 175–87; Künzli 1974: 18–31), which all echo Fátima. Bärbl said that Mary referred to herself as the 'Mediatrix of Graces', drawing on popular campaigns of the time calling on the pope to define that Marian doctrine.

The original chapel at Marienfried was built by the parish priest, Father Martin Humpf, in thanksgiving for the safety of Pfaffenhofen during Allied bombing, by which he fulfilled a vow to the Virgin Mary that he had made in 1944. Marienfried was inspired in part by the Schönstatt international movement of Marian devotion founded in 1914 by Joseph Kentenich (discussed in Chapter 9). Kentenich visited Pfaffenhofen after his release from Dachau at the end of the war (Bouflet 2003: 175), and the Marienfried chapel was built to the Schönstatt model. Bärbl's visions were the means by which Humpf and his sister Anna decided on the appropriate site for the chapel (Künzli 1974: 13–17), and the messages that Bärbl revealed also gave Marienfried its name: 'Peace of Mary' (Bouflet 2003: 177–8). The link with the Fátima messages encouraged support for Marienfried from devotees of Fátima (the German branch of the 'World Apostolate of Fatima' has had an annual meeting there since 1966). Of Germany's post-war visionary shrines, only Marienfried gained some level of ecclesiastical favour; while a commission held during the years 1947–50 did not approve the apparitions as supernatural revelations, it still concluded that there was nothing contrary to Catholic doctrine in them and so gave its permission for the messages to be promulgated (Künzli 1974: 78; Laurentin and Sbalchiero 2007: 608). Marienfried, along with nearby Bavarian shrine Wigratzbad, never experienced suppression and both were eventually accepted as official places of pilgrimage by the Diocese of Augsburg after the consecration of Monseigneur Dr Joseph Stimpfle in 1963 (Stimpfle was an influential bishop, both in Germany and in the Vatican, known especially for his support for the Catholic Church in communist Eastern Europe).

Other German apparition events were recorded at: Tannhausen, Forsweiler, Munich (1947); Düren, Fehrbach, Heroldsbach, Würzburg (1949); Remagen (1950); Rodalben (1952); Pingsdorf (1954) (there are entries for each in Laurentin and Sbalchiero 2007; Hierzenberger and Nedomansky 1996; see also Blackbourn 1993: 379; Scheer 2006: 175–245; O'Sullivan 2009). None of these received ecclesiastical backing. Among them, Heroldsbach in Bavaria remains a relatively important shrine, which is surprising as this was one of the most contentious of the post-war cases. From 9 October 1949 to 31 October 1952, seven girls aged seven to eleven claimed to have seen Mary and then further visions were claimed by adults, a common development in

Marian apparitions (Laurentin and Sbalchiero 2007: 436; Hierzenberger and Nedomansky 1996: 366–73; Pilgerverein Heroldsbach 2009). At Heroldsbach, Mary was initially identified as the Immaculate Conception, just as at Lourdes where Bernadette Soubirous had famously found a hidden spring of water. Likewise, the seers of Heroldsbach were directed to discover a 'mystical source of grace' located at a dry, well-like feature displayed to pilgrims. However, the apparitions took on more characteristics of the Fátima story, as people assembled on the thirteenth day of the month, there were visions of an angel from whom the girls received 'mystical communion', and pilgrims claimed to see phenomena of the sun and lights. In the same way as Marienfried, Heroldsbach demonstrates the important legacy of both Lourdes and Fátima and, at the same time, the post-war tendency for the apparitions to shift from the former template to the latter. However, the case did not go well with the Church, and some seers at Heroldsbach were excommunicated (a censure lifted in 1998) because they did not concur with the negative judgement of the archbishop of Bamberg in which he was supported by the Vatican.

Generally, the German cases after Marienfried did not fare well with Church authorities. O'Sullivan shows how post-war Marian apparition cults in Germany, as elsewhere, formed sub-milieus independent of Church hierarchy (O'Sullivan 2009: 4–5, 14–15). While some priests and religious supported the visionaries, they did not find favour with diocesan bishops. Supporters in some instances likened the Church's view in the late 1940s and 1950s to the Nazi persecution of Catholics in the 1930s. Thus dioceses recorded negative decisions at Forsweiler, Düren, Fehrbach, Heroldsbach, and Rodalben. A similar situation to that in Heroldsbach, leading to excommunication, developed in Rodalben (Laurentin and Sbalchiero 2007: 436, 812). It was decided that Tannhausen's visions contained no proof of the supernatural, but were copies of Fátima. The other cases did not reach the stage of a Church enquiry. For O'Sullivan, there were two main concerns expressed through the post-war apparition cults: in addition to the fear of atheistic communism, there was anxiety about the growth of materialism and consumerism in the emergent Federal Republic due to the incursion of American popular culture. Fehrbach and Rodalben belong to the Palatinate, a region containing many American military bases in this period (O'Sullivan 2009: 2).

However, from 1952, interest in and support for apparitions in Germany waned, just as it did elsewhere in Europe, with new cases provoking suspicion and scepticism. The support from priests declined while laypeople also resisted the visionary movement (O'Sullivan 2009: 7–11). The comprehensive list compiled by the University of Dayton includes no German case after 1960 other than the re-emergence of visions in 1999 at Marpingen, the 1876 apparition site (see <http://campus.udayton.edu/mary/resources/aprtable.html> accessed 31 May 2015).

The German history of apparitions is the same as in Italy and elsewhere: certain cases, where consistent pilgrimage remained respectful of the Church, did manage to overturn the disapproval experienced in the period before John Paul II. The 1990s, in particular, were a time of thawing of relations between the hierarchy and the popular cults. German shrines provide another example to support Margry's argument (2009a, 2009b) that there is a tendency to eventual convergence between the Church hierarchy and popular Catholic expression. Eventually, Marpingen (1876), Heede (1937–40), and Heroldsbach were accepted, like Wigratzbad and Marienfried before them, as places of pilgrimage and prayer; the Church hierarchy responded to the *sensus fidelium*. In the 1990s, Archbishop Braun of Bamberg decided to bring the stand-off in Heroldsbach to a conclusion. He obtained the agreement of Cardinal Joseph Ratzinger, later Pope Benedict XVI, to establish a diocesan shrine at the site (email correspondence with Dr Heinrich Hohl, Notary of the Archdiocese of Bamberg, 3 February 2012).

However, despite this new mood, recent pronouncements concerning Marpingen, Heede, Marienfried, and Heroldsbach (derived, for Marpingen and Marienfried, from new commissions of enquiry) have restated the original non-authentication of the apparitions themselves. Dioceses are careful to point out the distinction between acceptance of the shrine and approval of the apparitions. Archbishop Braun of Bamberg, while accepting that there were memorials of the apparitions at Heroldsbach, pointed out that these were 'documents of the convictions of private individuals . . . unrelated to ecclesiastical judgement' (Braun 1998, my translation). The Augsburg diocesan commission came to its conclusion in 1998: 'It stands as not established that the happenings in Marienfried from the year 1946 have a supernatural character'. Thus 'publications of any sort, which stand in contradiction to this decree, can be neither sold nor distributed on Church premises' (Dammertz 2000, my translation).

Similar decisions have been made for German shrines from other periods. In Trier, the recent Marpingen enquiry, like that in Augsburg, stated that it could not confirm the supernatural character of the apparitions of 1876, 1934, or 1999. Rather, 'the Marian chapel in the Marpinger Härtelwald retains its character as a place of prayer and veneration of the Mother of God' (email correspondence with the Generalvikariat of the Diocese of Trier, statement of 13 December 2005 received 22 December 2011, my translation). Heede had already enjoyed diocesan backing with the building and consecration of a large new church in the 1970s, but the official word did not come until 2000. Even then Bishop Bode of Osnabrück preferred to emphasize everyday devotion at Heede rather than visions: 'Yesterday does not stand at the centre of spiritual interest, rather today and tomorrow: and it is the intense practice of prayer and reconciliation that many people experience today in Heede' (Bode 2000, my translation). Therefore, in Germany, while these shrines are now official, there remains a potential contradiction between ecclesiastical refusal to authenticate the apparition claims on the one hand, and the memorials of the apparitions at the shrines on the other. The official and popular discourses about apparitions have not been wholly integrated, rather they are held together in a compromise because of the continuation of pilgrimage at sites that owe their existence to visionary claims.

Altogether, the many apparitions of the late 1940s and early 1950s, especially those in Italy and Germany, have left a legacy despite the tendency of the Vatican throughout those years to discourage them. Local people, priests as well as laity, have maintained the sites and in some cases they have developed into important shrines, possibly even recognized diocesan sanctuaries, known regionally or nationally. The Cold War origin is remembered in several cases through links with Fátima and its anti-communist message but, since the end of the Cold War in 1991, the shrines are more likely to emphasize the other half of the post-war message: the anxiety over moral liberalism and religious indifference, resulting in campaigns against (for example) abortion or same-sex marriage, along with calls to conversion and the necessity of prayer in combating social evils.

12

Vatican II

Visionary Reactions to Change
in the Church?

The Second Vatican Council (Vatican II) took place between 11 October 1962 and 8 December 1965 (for the council documents, see Flannery 1996). John XXIII summoned all the bishops of the Church to the Vatican to partake in an ecumenical council, in the long tradition of such councils dating back to the fourth century. Theologians and observers from other churches were also invited. Vatican II was as radical as any before, most notably changing the language of the liturgy from Latin to the vernacular, promoting dialogue with and respect for other denominations and faiths, and committing the Church to social justice. It might be supposed that the visionary phenomena that took place during this period should be explicable in terms of these radical ecclesiastical changes. Of course, the process of change was not instantaneous: the liturgical movement, for example, had been inspiring more radical elements of the Church since the nineteenth century. However, at the macro level Vatican II is regarded by most Catholics as the moment of paradigm shift. Put simply, after Vatican II, the Catholic Church placed less emphasis on the *numinous* (i.e. the sacredness and otherness of God), and more on the communal dimensions of the Church and its role in society. Vatican II, as was noted in Chapter 1, set boundaries on the development of Mariology, moving the emphasis of Marian doctrine from Christotypical to ecclesiotypical (Laurentin 1965), so that she is seen as a role model for the believer rather than a female counterpart to Christ in the work of redemption. These developments present obvious challenges to the apparitions tradition.

In fact, Vatican II was a pastoral council rather than one that decided doctrinal development; it did not change any part of the Mariological doctrine of the Church (such as the Immaculate Conception or Assumption). *Lumen*

Gentium 8, the Vatican II statement on Mary, is a strong affirmation of her as the one who 'far surpasses all creatures' and is the 'highest after Christ and closest to us' (*Lumen Gentium* 53); she cooperated in the work of redemption and is therefore Mother of the Church (*Lumen Gentium* 61). However, at the same time the teaching on Mary was placed in the constitution on the Church and not as a separate treatise, despite the largest minority of the whole council being against this (Laurentin 1965: 80). Catholics were reminded that Christ was the 'one mediator' on whom Mary's influence on humanity and role as mediatrix rests (*Lumen Gentium* 60, 62), she has a 'subordinate role' (*Lumen Gentium* 62), and 'false exaggeration' or 'vain credulity' should be avoided, refraining from anything that might mislead the 'separated brethren', the other Christian churches, as to the true doctrine of Mary (*Lumen Gentium* 67; see also the contemporaneous work of Schillebeeckx 1964: 139–43 on the dangers of 'Marianism'). In this atmosphere, it is not surprising that Marian apparitions could be seen as misleading and devotees over-eager to accept any supposed revelation. The unintended result of Vatican II was the decline in parish devotions with Mary as their focus, because of the emphasis on the sacramental liturgy (Spretnak 2004).

The Catholic controversy over apparitions during the Vatican II period is a reflection of the fact that the Church did not see them as helpful to its evolution over the several decades that bracketed the council; Laurentin identifies this time of reserve as beginning in the 1920s, but at its most intense between 1950 and 1980 in response to the great number of new reports (Laurentin 1991: 18, 22–3, 26). So it is to be expected that the two major apparition events that occurred in the lifetime of Vatican II, those that had the greatest impact in the global Catholic community, were under ecclesiastical censure and restriction both at diocesan and Vatican levels of hierarchy. These were the apparitions at San Sebastián de Garabandal (known popularly as 'Garabandal', in the region of Cantabria, Spain, 1961–5) and San Damiano (the region of Emilia-Romagna, Italy, 1964–81). These two cases are given most space by Sandra Zimdars-Swartz (1991) in her analysis of the way in which personal religious experience becomes public knowledge. Garabandal and San Damiano draw from different traditions of Marian appearances, but both include familiar features. Garabandal is of the type where a group of children report a vision as a shared experience in a series of apparitions witnessed by onlookers; Fátima, Beauraing, and Heede are twentieth-century examples of this type. At San Damiano, the seer was a mature woman with a background of health problems, in the same way as seers at Bochum and Kerizinen. In both cases, it is worth asking whether the apparitions contained critiques, implicit or explicit, of the changes brought in by the Second Vatican Council.

THE EVENTS AT GARABANDAL

There were many visions in Spain during the late 1940s and 1950s, some of which Christian describes (1984, with a list on pp. 261–2). Few apparitions received episcopal approval of any kind, although the local bishop recognized the cult of La Codosera in the diocese of Badajoz in 1945 (Laurentin and Sbalchiero 2007: 501–2). So, while the apparitions at San Sebastián de Garabandal came to be the most prominent, they occurred within an evolving national tradition of post-war cases. They began on 18 June 1961 with a vision of St Michael to four girls, three aged twelve and one aged ten, followed by over two thousand apparitions of the Virgin Mary as our Lady of Mount Carmel from 2 July 1961 to November 1965. Zimdars-Swartz's account of Garabandal (1991: 124–56, 225–33) uses two devotional sources as close as possible to the original events: the published diary of the principal seer, Conchita González (in Pelletier 1971), and the work by Pérez (1981), who interviewed villagers present during the visions (although he did not include testimonies from those who did not believe in the apparitions). What emerges from these accounts are the ways in which the visions at Garabandal conform to certain patterns in modern Marian apparition history, but also aspects in which they are distinctive.

Garabandal clearly stands in the Fátima tradition. There can be little doubt that the Fátima story was well known in Spain by 1961, although visionaries always claim a unique and objective experience that does not depend on their knowledge of other cases. Garabandal echoes Lúcia Santos's memoirs in that apparitions of St Michael the archangel preceded the visions of the Virgin Mary and announced their coming. The Virgin Mary appeared as Our Lady of Mount Carmel, one of the aspects of Mary seen at the final vision of Fátima and a common title in that region of Spain. Garabandal also follows Fátima as a serial and public phenomenon with growing crowds, with its child visionaries albeit a little older than at Fátima, the emergence of one of the children as the prominent visionary (Conchita González, who was also the first to see the angel), the requests of the visionaries for a miracle, the anticipation of which became the centrepiece of the apparitions, a 'mystical communion' given by an angel (although at Garabandal this was not a private experience, being witnessed by observers), and a 'frightening vision' that presaged apocalyptic warnings about the future.

Where the reports of Garabandal differ markedly from others is in the many reports of 'paranormal' phenomena: the girls being able to discern the identity of priests, despite the discretion of the latter in avoiding clerical dress, the girls converging on the apparition site simultaneously having been 'called' three times by interior impulses, the girls walking, sometimes backwards, at great speed while looking up at the vision, the girls returning a jumble of various objects such as rosaries, which had been presented for the Virgin to kiss, individually back to their owners. There were also claims that, during trance, the girls became exceptionally heavy and could not be lifted by strong adults and that they were able to levitate. Experiencing the seers' unusual abilities convinced many of those who had come to the site out of interest. Zimdars-Swartz points out that the paranormal events belong to the second phase of the visions. She identifies this second phase as beginning after the summons to Conchita, regarded as the leader, to visit diocesan authorities at Santander in late July 1961 (1991: 131–2). During the first phase, the group were more integrated, in the second, the experiences were not always shared by all four; in the first phase, the visions were all in the evening and in the *calleja*, a lane leading from the village to the grove of nine pine trees overlooking it. In the second phase, apparitions occurred at various times and in several places around the village.

Yet the presence of paranormal phenomena, even though these may be experienced by a number of onlookers and are not easily explicable, does not necessarily convince the Church of the divine origin of a case (see the discussion in Chapter 4 within this volume; Rahner 1963; Schwebel 2004). In fact, they will raise the level of concern in the Church and therefore probably not prove an aid in eliciting a positive ecclesiastical response. It is surprising, perhaps, given the unusual nature of the Garabandal trances, that the diocese of Santander felt that the apparitions were due to 'natural causes' (Pérez 1981: 63–4) and that there was no evidence of the 'supernatural'. However, this statement shows that the Church does accept the possibility of paranormal phenomena as a part of human existence but not necessarily as a sign of God's special intervention. Such paranormal phenomena can include unsettling aspects. The Benedictine Bernard Billet's summary of negative criteria (1973: 46–7) includes bizarre or strange gestures or signs, and an emphasis more on the means by which messages are communicated than their content. He also warns about the accent being placed more firmly on the negative (sin) as opposed to the positive (love, life with God). Therefore, he regarded Garabandal as problematic because its major messages concerned chastisements rather than salvation and also because its devotees claimed obedience to the Church but ignored episcopal discouragement of pilgrimage to the site and the devotions evoked by it (Billet 1973: 38–43).

Garabandal's apparitions constituted a highly public phenomenon in several ways. First, the parish priest, Don Valentín Marichalar from Cosío, was cautiously supportive and interviewed the girls as well as attending apparitions from 22 June 1961 (Zimdars-Swartz 1961: 128). This resulted in many other priests attending, although in time the diocese prohibited them. Secondly, doctors were in evidence; as they had at previous serial apparitions such as Lourdes and Beauraing, they tested the girls' trances, which included the administering of pain and noting the lack of strong reaction. Thirdly, there were many cameras, and so photographs and recordings of the visions can be found today on websites (including *Youtube*). Children's play is in evidence in the descriptions of the Garabandal apparitions (as discussed in the case of Fátima in Bennett 2012: 132–3; see Chapter 6 within this volume). Just as at Marpingen (Blackbourn 1993: 133–4), the everyday nature of the children's conversations with the Virgin caused some to doubt (Zimdars-Swartz 1991: 129). The visionaries said that the Virgin laughed as they talked to her about their lives; responding to criticisms, supporters claimed that this was a natural feature of children talking to their mother. The Virgin kissed objects such as rosaries and medals; this began by her kissing pebbles that had actually been presented to the Child Jesus for him to play with on the occasions that he appeared with her, but he did not take them (Zimdars-Swartz 1991: 136). All this, of course, was invisible to the crowd.

The 'great miracle' of Garabandal (as opposed to the 'little miracle', the miraculous communion) emerged in similar circumstances to that at Fátima, where the visionaries were concerned that people would not believe what they alone could see; thus they made requests to the Virgin for a miracle so that everyone else would believe. At Fátima, the expected miracle occurred on 13 October 1917 and, later, the Second World War was regarded as a punishment for sin. However, Garabandal's great miracle and chastisement are apocalyptic events in the as-yet-unrealized future, divine intervention through the extraordinary rather than through mundane historical events. In this respect, Garabandal is closer in kind to Ezkioga, not far away in distance (albeit in a different region of Spain). It stands in the tradition of apocalyptic prophecy through apparitions, reflecting the concerns of its time, i.e. a perceived social decline in faith and morality and anxiety over the threat of communism (at Garabandal, messages were reported to the effect that communism would come to dominate the world). Despite their terrifying prophecies, Amsterdam and Kerizinen came to be associated mainly with devotional ideas about the Virgin Mary rather than the apocalyptic. Gara-bandal, whose visionaries ceased their experiences by the age of sixteen, remains fundamentally an apparition expressing high anxiety and some hope about an uncertain future. There were two public messages to the effect that God's punishment was being provoked, the first proclaiming: 'The cup is already filling up and if we do not change, a very great chastise-ment will come upon us' (18 October 1961, as revealed by all four girls, Pelletier 1970: 43). There was a need for people, echoing Lúcia of Fátima's writings, to 'make many sacrifices, perform much penance, and visit the Blessed Sacrament frequently. But first, we must lead good lives'. Later, from 1963, Conchita became the sole visionary and it was through her that the prophecies were clarified and intensified (Zimdars-Swartz 1991: 129–30). The second public message referred to the lack of response to the first message: 'Before, the cup was filling up. Now it is flowing over' (18 June 1965: Pelletier 1970: 44).

From Conchita's prophecies, there emerged a series of three future events: a 'warning', a 'great miracle', and a 'chastisement'. 'The warning will be like a revelation of our sins, and it will be seen and experienced equally by believers and non-believers and people of any religion whatsoever . . . The warning is something supernatural and will not be explained by science. It will be seen and felt' (Pelletier 1970: 124). The second event in the series would be the miracle, visible in Garabandal, where a permanent sign would be left in the pine grove; it would take place at 8:30 on a Thursday evening coinciding with the feast of a martyr of the Eucharist (Zimdars-Swartz 1991: 227). This was the only one of these events for which Conchita claimed to know the date and she would reveal it eight days beforehand (Zimdars-Swartz 1991: 227). She stated this in her mid-teens and she is now over sixty-five, but there is yet no sign of a public statement. Another of the visionaries, Mari Loli Mazón, died in 2009, aged fifty-nine.

Just as the miracle of Fátima in 1917 was supposed to have been experienced by Pope Pius XII many years later, so the Garabandal miracle of the future is thought to have been previewed by various people: Father Luis Andréu, a Jesuit who died suddenly after visiting Garabandal in 1961; Padre Pio, who died in 1968; and Joey Lomangino, a blind American who became a fervent supporter of Garabandal after being sent there by Padre Pio himself (Zimdars-Swartz 1991: 226–8). In the case of the last two, this seems to have occurred because Conchita prophesied that they would see the miracle, but they have since died, Lomangino as recently as 2014. Those believing the prophecy to be true have to assume that the miracle was seen by these individuals before their deaths. The messages state that, after the miracle, chastisement will follow if people do not change their lives in the wake of the warning and miracle. All four girls are supposed to have had a preview of the chastisement, in a 'frightening vision' in June 1962 (Pelletier 1970: 126). Whereas the children at Fátima supposedly saw hell in their equivalent of the terrifying vision, the Garabandal girls shouted with terror as they perceived the coming punishment and prayed that children would die rather than have to face it.

Successive bishops of Santander made several statements in which they insisted that the supernatural validity of the apparitions could not be established. Firstly an enquiry was set up in 1961–2, which was accused of a lack of objectivity by supporters (e.g. Pérez 1981: 69–75). At the same time, the diocese asked for Catholics, especially priests and religious, to refrain from visiting and organizing pilgrimages (Pérez 1981: 63). The commission reported on 7 October 1962 that the events were due to 'natural causes' and a further declaration to this effect was issued on 18 July 1965, although this included the encouraging comment that 'we have found no grounds for an ecclesiastical condemnation, either in the doctrine or in the spiritual commendations that have been divulged in the events and addressed to the Christian faithful'

(Pérez 1981: 64; Zimdars-Swartz 1991: 151). The mood became more negative on 17 March 1967 after the girls went through a temporary period in 1966 of retracting their messages after the apparitions had ended (a difficult period which was foretold, according to Pelletier 1970: 120–2; see also Zimdars-Swartz 1991: 147). Thus the Church felt confident in denying the reality of the apparitions and messages and this was repeated in a letter to all Catholic bishops in 1970 (Pérez 1981: 65–7; Zimdars-Swartz 1991: 151–3). The bishop placed a strict prohibition on priests visiting the village, under the penalty of losing their licence to minister in the diocese. The diocesan responses illustrate the impact and persistence of support for Garabandal during the 1960s, even within the ranks of the clergy.

Conchita, her mother, and a supportive priest, Father Luna, visited Rome in 1966 and met Cardinal Ottaviani, prefect of the Congregation for the Doctrine of the Faith, and apparently also met Pope Paul VI. This led to supporters claiming that the pope and Vatican disagreed with the decisions made by the diocese of Santander, a claim denied by both the bishop of Santander in his 1970 letter and the new prefect, Franjo Šeper, in 1969. The latter insisted that the Vatican had no reason to doubt the decisions taken by the diocese, indeed congratulated it 'on the prudence and pastoral solicitude with which your curia has acted', and preferred to leave decisions of this nature to the local bishop (Pérez 1981: 342). The Vatican position was further clarified in a letter from Šeper to the archbishop of New Orleans on 21 April 1970, which shows the global reach of the cult. He supported the bishop of Santander in his 'aim of dissuading the people from participating in pilgrimages and other forms of devotions attached to or founded on the alleged apparitions and messages of Garabandal' (Pérez 1981: 344–6; also in O'Connor 1975: 1019–22, filed as Canon 2019). New diocesan enquiries in 1976 and 1988 failed to overturn the negative verdicts of the 1960s (Laurentin and Sbalchiero 2007: 377). Nevertheless, they are a further indication as to how much pressure was exerted over the years by the supporters of Garabandal. The 1988 enquiry, coming in a time of greater toleration for apparitions and the seeking of compromises where pilgrimage had persisted despite Church restriction (as discussed in Chapter 11 within this volume), did result in a lifting of the edict banning visiting priests from the village, and they were permitted thereafter to celebrate Mass in the parish church.

GARABANDAL AND VATICAN II

The dates for the Garabandal apparitions coincide closely with those of Vatican II, as noted by William Christian Jr. As a young writer in the late 1960s,

Christian undertook anthropological research in the Nansa Valley area of Cantabria in Spain while the memory of apparitions was still fresh (*Person and God in a Spanish Valley*, 1972, new edition 1989). While he did not concentrate on the apparitions, preferring instead to look at the relationships between people, society, and religion in the region, he nevertheless admitted that the location was chosen because it included Garabandal (Christian 1989: xiii). His thesis centred on the social and ecclesiastical tensions present in the area in the years around Vatican II:

> With the breakdown of community boundaries through mobility and the media, with the industrialization of Europe, the rise in standard of living, the circulation of alternatives to Catholic life... a new model for communication with other worlds has developed in the valley. It has been brought in by radio, television, students, returning emigrants, but above all by the young emissaries of the Council, the younger priests... The impact can be measured by the incredible reaction of the village and its gods—through a series of apparitions of the Virgin Mary in San Sebastian in the early 1960's... Many younger priests maintain a reverence and affection for Mary. But they do not regard either Mary or the saints as essential intermediaries with God. (Christian 1989: 182)

The initiative of these young priests as 'emissaries of the Council' does not fully explain the emergence of the apparitions as early as June 1961, a few months before Vatican II began in October of that year. However, other sources confirm that the social changes mentioned by Christian—mobility, mass media, industrialization—were already having a major impact in Spain (Morcillo 2008: 46–76), and also that the changes of the council were foreshadowed by changes within the Church in the 1950s, although these were sporadic (Callahan 2012: 412–39, 470–99). Writing in the 1960s, Becarud (1969: 183–213) stated that there were shifts in Church politics in Spain during the 1950s, with the lower clergy more willing to criticize the injustices of the Franco regime and disagreeing with the caution of the bishops on political questions. The 1960s brought more wholesale change: a fast pace of economic development and 'a full-blown internal struggle [within the Church] the like of which was unknown in the Spanish Church's modern history' (Callahan 2012: 439). Vatican II and its emphasis on social justice and religious freedom challenged the principles of national Catholicism under Franco in the 1960s (Callahan 2012: 500–26). Therefore, the apparition cult at Garabandal coincided with social and ecclesiastical changes in Spain. Although that nation was under dictatorship, unlike all other Western European nations in the post-war period except Portugal under Salazar, these developments mirrored countries elsewhere in that consumerism and a higher standard of living encouraged by American economic influence challenged traditional Catholic lifestyles and commitments. Despite the efforts under the Franco regime to restore Catholicism after the Second Republic and civil war, the 1960s saw the onset of a period of decline in Church adherence in Spain (Callahan 2012: 638). Finally, the impact of the Cold War cannot be underestimated in any European context during this period. During the early 1960s, concern over potential nuclear war and the strength of the Soviet military reached its height. The perceived growth of global communism concerned nearly all Western European apparitions from Fátima until the 1960s and it was certainly a factor at Garabandal. Therefore, as with most apparition cases, the issues framing the cult at Garabandal have to be regarded as social, political, and economic as well as ecclesiastical.

One message that was revealed at Garabandal encouraged those who thought that the apparitions implicitly criticized the changes being wrought by Vatican II: 'Many cardinals, many bishops and many priests are on the road to perdition and are taking many souls with them' (message of 18 June 1965 near the end of the apparitions: Pelletier 1970: 44). Given the date of this message, in the last year of Vatican II, it is easy to see why it *could* be interpreted as expressing opposition to the council. There were also warnings about the neglect of the Mass in the next sentence of the same message: 'Less and less importance is being given to the Eucharist'. At Vatican II, the liturgy of the Mass went through extensive change in form: from Latin to the vernacular; the position of the priest; and greater emphasis on community involvement. Nevertheless, these changes did not diminish the *importance* of the Eucharist and attendance at Mass; indeed Vatican II emphasized the sacramental liturgy. The message is more likely to be referring to the fact that, from the 1960s onwards, churchgoing in the Catholic Church (as well as in Protestant churches) declined. One could as easily see Vatican II as an attempt to anticipate and arrest these changes in attendance, as opposed to being the causal factor in them.

Peter Margry sees most apparitions in the perspective of a traditionalist view against change in the Church. He argues that:

> The phenomenon, and the cults which arose around them were, in the context of their social construction, employed by the visionaries and their adherents as instruments to combat the changes, such as communism, growing secularism and renewal within the Roman Catholic Church itself, all of which were sometimes interpreted as 'apocalyptic'. (Margry 2009b: 261)

In his view, Marian apparitions are tools in what he refers to as 'ideological wars' in the world and the Church. A Catholic subculture uses visions as support for the promotion of pre-Vatican II-type Catholicism, which of course is idealized by its protagonists (Margry 2009b: 245). This also conforms to the analysis of Marian apparitions made by E. Ann Matter, for whom Marian apparitions are a 'Janus faced expression of Catholic identity' in that visionary messages point forwards to apocalyptic events but also back in time to a traditional Catholic spirituality, particularly that before Vatican II (Matter

2001: 141). However, these analyses overlook the fact that many post-Vatican II developments have been promoted by messages at, for example, Amsterdam (see Chapter 10 and Zimdars-Swartz 1991: 256–9) and Medjugorje, where Bible-study groups, interfaith tolerance, and charismatic renewal have been important as well as the more traditional call for the revival of Mass and Confession (see Chapter 13; for the early period of Medjugorje, see Laurentin and Rupčić 1984). While it is true that San Damiano was associated with anti-conciliar groups for a time, this has not been a strong feature of the Garabandal cult. A search on the web will discover arch-traditionalist material that opposes Garabandal *because it is supportive of Vatican II*, and also material by Garabandal supporters who are keen to dismantle the myth that Garabandal was hostile to the council (which, of course, implies that some people have thought that it was).

Apparition cults do appeal to more conservative members of the Church, but not necessarily those who resist the reforms instigated by Vatican II. Most Marian devotees will probably not agree with the more radical interpretations of Vatican II, such as liberation theology, interfaith relativity, and a tendency to demythologize the Bible or traditional theologies of the Eucharist. This is evidenced by a priest, Richard Gilsdorf writing in the *Garabandal* magazine that the apparitions had 'saved my priestly life' (Gilsdorf 1990); he explained that he had found a strong spirituality that countered post-conciliar liberalism. Yet, liberal interpretations have not been popular with the Magisterium either and certainly not since the accession of Pope John Paul II in 1978, so this does not make Garabandal anti-conciliar per se. There are also many members of the Catholic charismatic movement among the ardent devotees of apparitions and this is most definitely a post-conciliar phenomenon. As Hastings (1991: 636–40) points out, there are at least three tendencies in post-Vatican II Catholicism: the traditionalist right wing; the progressive left; and the charismatic movement, more comfortable than the traditionalists with female (non-ordained) leadership, ecumenism, and liturgical creativity, while agreeing with the right wing on matters of morality and authority. The charismatic movement in Catholicism is certainly not in favour of undoing the reforms of Vatican II.

There is one important sense in which the Garabandal apparition cult gained by changes in the Church. Liberalization in the rules on circulating information about non-canonical apparitions occurred in 1966; Paul VI revised (and, in practice, abolished) the process relating to the index of forbidden books and with it canons relating to censures against publication of non-approved material by Catholics (*Integrae Servandae*, establishing the Sacred Congregation for the Doctrine of the Faith, 7 December 1965, followed by clarifications in *AAS* 58, 14 June 1966: 445; 15 November 1966: 1186). This applied to books in general and not only those on apparitions. However, it is quoted in many devotional works on apparitions that have not been formally approved, as a way of justifying a publication when it could be perceived as resistant to Church decisions. Of course, the Church was not giving an open licence to publish anything as 'one must nevertheless remember the value of the moral law which absolutely prohibits endangering faith and good morals' (*AAS* 58, 15 November 1966). It was simply removing the need for a would-be author to gain episcopal permission (the *Imprimatur*) to avoid formal ecclesiastical censure. In the past, authors of controversial material had to seek a supportive bishop (e.g. Mélanie Calvat gaining the *Imprimatur* for her revelations from the Bishop of Lecce in 1879). The liberalization of Catholic publication that followed Vatican II applied, first of all, to those already established apparitions whose cults were non-canonical and popular (such as Kerizinen and Amsterdam), but also to new cases of which Garabandal was the most internationally famous. Thus Garabandal literature multiplied and the story spread around the Catholic world. Garabandal centres were established in various countries and cities, promoting the messages and organizing pilgrimages; they continue to do so more than fifty years later, despite the failure to achieve recognition in the diocese of Santander. The promotion of Garabandal in the United States was aided by the fact that three of the four visionaries moved there, having married Americans.

The factor that holds together conservative and liberal thinking on Vatican II is the office of the papacy. Catholic conservatism has been staunchly ultramontane since the mid-nineteenth century, but Vatican II and its changes came into being through John XXIII, were completed and developed by Paul VI, and maintained by successive popes thereafter. To be for the absolute authority of the pope and disobedient to the reforms brought in by Vatican II is therefore a contradiction. For this reason, it is very difficult for apparition cults to become schismatic. The only possible recourse for outright rebellion is to argue that the papacy itself has become corrupt, as conservative French Catholics suggested when Leo XIII made diplomatic overtures towards the Third Republic in the 1890s. In the United States in the 1970s, the movement that supported the Marian apparitions of Veronica Lueken, in Bayside, New York (see Laycock 2015), claimed that the true Paul VI had been taken prisoner by an impostor. A similar story was adopted at the apparition shrine El Palmar de Troya near Seville in Spain. While Garabandal avoided schism despite official disapproval, Palmar de Troya did not. This resulted in a new pope being declared in Palmar: the visionary Clemente Domínguez assumed the title 'Gregory XVII' in 1978 (Laurentin and Sbalchiero 2007: 1257–62).

The Palmar de Troya visionary movement began as a series of apparitions to four girls in 1968, with many echoes of Garabandal such as the expectation of the great sign and miraculous communion. Father Luna of Zaragoza was a supporter of both apparition sites and he wrote devotional books on Palmar (1973; 1976), the second attempting to distinguish what he regarded as the 'true' original Palmar from the 'false' schismatic one and criticizing the cardinal archbishop of Seville for not doing so, as the archbishop had referred to the whole phenomenon as 'collective hysteria'. The original visionaries were supplanted by a wave of adults entering the scene and claiming new experiences; Clemente was one of several male adult visionaries. However, where children's visions are taken over by adults who attend the site and whose messages are more complex and sensational, it is usually disastrous for the attempt to gain Church approval. The shift from child to adult visionary was resisted at Beauraing, where Tilman Côme was successfully distanced from the children, but at more recent sites such as Oliveto Citra and places in Ireland (see Chapters 14 and 15 within this volume), it has been problematic. Unless the devotees succeed in identifying a group of 'true visionaries' whose messages are able to be managed and packaged as fully complying with orthodoxy, the apparitions are unlikely to become official, especially so during the years around Vatican II.

The Palmar movement, with its retention of the Tridentine Rite of the Mass, was initially connected to traditionalist Archbishop Marcel Lefebvre, a Frenchman who set up the anti-conciliar Fraternity of St Pius X in Switzerland in 1969. However, after Palmar bishops were consecrated non-canonically by a renegade Vietnamese archbishop, the leaders were excommunicated in 1976. The movement still exists and there is now a third pope in the series, but the 'Christian Palmerian Catholic Church of the Carmelites of the Holy Face' is plagued by dissension; it has lost all connection with the Roman Catholic tradition and is merely a travesty of its more conservative elements.

SAN DAMIANO AND THE 'MADONNA OF THE ROSES'

San Damiano's public apparitions continued a strong national tradition of post-war visions in Italy (some of which are referred to in Chapter 11). Carroll (1992: 55–7) presents two Italian cases near in time to San Damiano, both in the province of Foggia at Orta Nova and Stornarella. The visions to Marietta d'Agostino at Orta Nova, which had begun during the First World War, were not approved but nevertheless a parish church was constructed in the 1970s with the same dedication, *Madonna di Altomare*, as the title of the vision given by the seer. This is, as Carroll observes, implicit approval; he argues that the fact that Marietta's visions had ceased in the 1960s swung the decision in her favour. This was not the case with Domenico Masselli of Stornarella, whose visions began in 1959 and whose followers built an oratory that was not accepted by the diocese. Church approval, not by formally recognizing the apparitions, but by endorsing the building of a church or chapel is relatively common: in Sicily, for instance, there was the case of Cefalà Diana in 1967, where a church was built with the blessing of the archbishop of Palermo.

The seer at San Damiano was fifty-five-year-old Rosa Quattrini, whose visions extended from 1964 to 1981 (they are described in Zimdars-Swartz 1991: 92–123, who draws on the documents by Maisonneuve and de Belsunce 1983; see also Laurentin and Sbalchiero 2007: 852–9, where the entry is written by Maisonneuve and Laurentin). Rosa (known popularly as 'Mama Rosa') recalled earlier miracles that presaged the visions. She was one of four sisters, the only one who had married and not taken up a religious vocation. She had had difficulties in childbearing: three children were born healthy but all by Caesarean section, which resulted in poor health for Rosa. This had become critical in 1961 and she had been hospitalized with eventration (weakening of the diaphragm) and stomach wounds. Virtually bedridden on her return home, according to her account she was visited by a mysterious and beautiful young woman collecting for the sanctuary of Padre Pio at San Giovanni Rotundo (Padre Pio, the most famous Italian mystic of his day, died in 1968 and was canonized in 2002). The woman grasped her hands and she experienced a healing. This account was substantiated by her aunt, despite the latter's initial scepticism (Zimdars-Swartz 1991: 96). Told by the woman to visit Padre Pio at San Giovanni Rotundo, Rosa made the journey in 1962. There she saw the woman again, who this time announced herself to be 'the Mother of Consolation and the Afflicted'. Rosa also recalled that Padre Pio encouraged her to undertake a mission to the sick, which she did for two years until on another visit he told her that this task would be superseded by a great event.

On 16 October 1964, Rosa heard a woman's voice during the Angelus. She was led to a vineyard, where she saw a cloud descend and then disappear to reveal the Virgin Mary, dressed in blue and white, who appeared to her above a plum tree. This time Mary appeared as a heavenly being. Rosa was told that she needed to help Jesus carry the Cross, as he could bear it alone no longer. People should pray a great deal and, if they did not, there would be chastisements. Like many other visionaries, Rosa asked the Virgin for a sign so that others would believe; this was apparently fulfilled by the immediate and unexpected blossoming of the plum tree and a nearby pear tree, above which Mary had ascended. Rosa also experienced a shower of rose petals, and it is the rose that is most associated with San Damiano. The Virgin announced herself to be the 'Madonna of the Roses' and Rosa later set out to create a 'City of Roses', a shrine at the place of apparitions that would include charitable foundations for orphans, the elderly, and the sick. The apparitions continued on the first Fridays of the month.

There are several familiar apparition themes that present themselves in the San Damiano story: a clear schedule for the series of visions, attributed to the Virgin herself; initial scepticism and concern about embarrassment from members of Rosa's family; the cautious support of the parish priest, interested in the affair; the digging of a well at the request of the Madonna (which needed an engineer, unlike Lourdes, where Bernadette's scrabbling was sufficient); and pilgrimage developing very quickly in response to reports of the apparitions. Rosa received messages throughout the period 1964–81; the sheer number of messages led the archbishop of Chambéry to remark that 'they are so abundant and of such great banality' (Bontems cit. Zimdars-Swartz 1991: 120) and the bishop of Albi to contrast them unfavourably to the succinct nature of the Virgin's statements at Lourdes, which could be written on one sheet of paper (Coffy cit. Zimdars-Swartz 1991: 122). More positively, however, Maisonneuve and Laurentin, in supporting the case, find a thread through the messages:

> She invites all of her children to an interior conversion, to a life of prayer and love. She announces great trials for the world, which moves further and further from its Creator and a new era for humanity in which God wishes to reveal his glory. She calls the Church to a purer evangelical life (Laurentin and Sbalchiero 2007: 854, my translation).

In addition, the Madonna, as elsewhere, summoned pilgrims to the apparition site, a 'Paradise' on Earth, and requested prayer, particularly the rosary.

However, the progress of the shrine was not at all smooth and, like Garabandal, San Damiano received ecclesiastical disapproval and prohibition that did not relent until the more tolerant mood towards non-approved apparition shrines in the Church under John Paul II took effect in the 1990s. The diocesan reaction to San Damiano in Piacenza was very similar to that in Santander. The support of the local priest, in this case, Dom Elgardo Pellacini, an advisor to Padre Pio prayer groups, was overturned within a year by a much more sceptical response from the diocese. On 7 September 1965, Bishop Umberto Malchiodi issued a denial that there was any foundation for believing the apparitions to be genuine supernatural manifestations, and also a request that Catholics should not go to San Damiano on pilgrimage. These were followed up by further pronouncements on 15 August 1966, 2 February 1968, and 1 November 1970, the last by a new bishop, Enrico Manfredi. The language of the statements became progressively more authoritative and censorious, with Rosa being banned from experiencing her apparitions publicly, the parish priest prevented from participating, pilgrimage to and promotion of the site both prohibited, and disobedient priests under warnings of losing their licence to officiate in Piacenza. As at Garabandal, these strictures were supported by the Congregation for the Doctrine of the Faith from 1968 (the 1970 decree is given in O'Connor 1975: 1021–2). Reminders and updates of these censures continued throughout the 1970s and 1980s (1976, 1977, 1980, 1986); only in 1995 did Bishop Monari allow priests on pilgrimage, in consultation with the parish, to celebrate Mass and arrange retreats at the site (Laurentin and Sbalchiero 2007: 858).

Rosa's messages were traditional and simple, but her mission was afflicted by difficulty and controversy (Zimdars-Swartz 1991: 109–13). The first attempt to set up the 'City of Roses', under the local group, *Comitato Madonna di San Damiano*, faltered after the 1965 statement of the bishop; the situation was then complicated by the involvement of many foreign pilgrims, especially those from Switzerland and France. Rosa was caught up in a cause that she does not seem to have welcomed. The Swiss devotees helped to publicize the fame of the shrine internationally, but this brought San Damiano into the orbit of the Lefebvre movement against Vatican II. Rosa's lack of cooperation with Lefebvre's plan to celebrate Latin Mass in San Damiano distanced her and the shrine from this movement. However, certain comments attributed to her continued to associate San Damiano with the anti-conciliar cause, such as the claim that receiving communion in the hand was a sacrilege despite it being formally declared acceptable by Paul VI in 1969, reintroducing early Christian customs (communion placed directly into the mouth by the priest has become something of a symbol of conservative Catholicism and communion in the hand has been denounced as sacrilegious at other apparition sites, such as Achill in Ireland). The French and Swiss-French interest in San Damiano led to the bishops from pilgrims' home dioceses becoming involved in the Church campaign to limit the influence of San Damiano. Support for the bishops of Piacenza came from the bishop of Lausanne, Geneva, and Fribourg in 1970, the archbishop of Chambéry in 1973, and the bishop of Albi in 1983. The last two accepted that San Damiano may have represented an understandable response to the reforms of Vatican II and the ensuing radical departure from traditional expressions of the liturgy (Zimdars-Swartz 1991: 120–2). However, the continued pilgrimage and devotion in the face of local diocesan prohibition was the factor that concerned these bishops.

Billet (1973: 43–5) refers to some supposedly miraculous phenomena that convinced pilgrims of the reality of the apparitions at San Damiano. These include the smelling of pleasant perfumes that did not appear to have any source and the existence of photographs that seemed to the devotees to indicate a supernatural presence of light. Billet is sceptical of such signs, concluding that much of this is wishful thinking and illusion, and doubting that a 'physical phenomenon . . . could provide an indisputable argument for the supernatural character of the facts in question' (1973: 45). However, claims of miraculous photographs (also known in apparitions in Egypt in the 1960s) continued and intensified after San Damiano. Laurentin regards most of them as vague marks of little significance but accepts there are some which defy explanation (Laurentin and Sbalchiero 2007: 732). Lisa Bitel describes this phenomenon in the United States some thirty-six years after Billet. She emphasizes the devotees' process of interpretation of the images:

The messages of photos are not obvious to outsiders or fixed, despite the established iconography that has become part of the worldwide culture of Marian apparitions. Witnesses have established a set of shared motifs: a ball of light indicates a divine presence; a shining cross signifies Jesus' Crucifixion and Resurrection; a triangular shape is the veiled Virgin, sometimes holding her holy baby or embracing another figure; a rectangle with rounded top and bottom represents the Gate of Heaven. Other blurs of light symbolize angels, doves, or the face of Jesus (Bitel 2009: 85–6).

Apart from photographs, it has not been uncommon for pilgrims to claim that their rosaries have been transformed from cheap metals into gold, a kind of heavenly alchemy. Light and gold are two popular symbols of the presence of the Virgin Mary. San Damiano, like Garabandal, stands at the beginning of the post-conciliar period during which mass movements have used modern means of communication to promote shrines and this has included the circulation of stories and miraculous images used in convincing others to become believers.

San Damiano was associated with currents of thought that opposed Vatican II because of its timing and the persuasion of some of its followers. However, San Damiano is not primarily a reaction to the council any more than Garabandal; its themes are traditional and express, as in all ages, the anxiety of people of faith as they seek to understand God's perspective on world events and social change. As Zimdars-Swartz puts it: 'The devotees of San Damiano . . . have understood the site as offering purification and protection of both body and soul and a refuge from apocalyptic dangers' (Zimdars-Swartz 1991: 123). Since 1974, San Damiano has been maintained by the group *Ospizio delle Rose*. Rosa was accused of fraud in the years leading up to her death but was exonerated posthumously in the Italian courts. *Ospizio* inherited from her estate in 1982, after Pope John Paul II refused the bequest, and set up some of the charitable works desired by Rosa. Zimdars-Swartz notes that the *Ospizio* 'now promotes a Marian devotion that is international and post-Vatican II in character' (1991: 113). This will have been necessary to encourage the bishop to allow aspects of the cult in the 1990s.

The social and historical context for San Damiano resembles that of Garabandal. After relative underdevelopment in the 1950s, Italy experienced an 'economic miracle' in the first half of the 1960s (Ginsborg 1990: 210–53). Economic expansion meant urbanization as people moved to the cities for employment, and the country experienced growing consumerism with American influence and the coming of mass media, advertising, and new technologies. For Catholic culture in countries such as Italy, Spain, and Germany, this presented a dilemma, with the improving standards of living compromised by various challenges. Ginsborg, writing on Italy, lists these as the influence of television, leisure and mobility, building speculation and destructive changes to the landscape, greater freedom in terms of gender roles, the family,

sexual mores (although in Italy, this progressed slowly), and, most importantly, a decline in religion (Ginsborg 1990: 240–7). A fall in churchgoing in
Italy from 69 to 40 per cent occurred between 1956 and 1968, much of which
was nominal with a very small number closely following Church teaching. San
Damiano could be said to represent the cry of old Italy, rural and Catholic, in
the midst of modernization. This is the most obvious causal factor in provoking the reaction of a visionary cult rather than Vatican II. In this most Marian
of countries with its manifold apparition events, the call to Catholic life needed
ever new and more sensational forms as secularization took hold.

Garabandal and San Damiano were villages facing profound social changes
and a breakdown of the integral Catholic world in which they were situated.
Just as French villagers in the 1870s had seen irreversible development in rural
life in the context of new political regimes, and apparitions of Mary marked
this transition, so the 1960s brought with them the next great step for Catholic
Europe as societies became, to a far greater extent than before, media-driven
and globally aware. The post-war period in which Spain and Italy feared
communism from within was over, although there was still concern about
the military strength of the Soviet Union and nuclear proliferation. However,
there was one overriding challenge that presented a more immediate threat
to Catholic life: consumer culture and better living standards provoking
sweeping secularization that drifted from the cities into the countryside. So
Garabandal and San Damiano drew on older narratives to provide for a new
generation the scenario of Mary's appeal for prayer and belief, her support and
presence, and her warning of future global catastrophe brought on by sin and
God's judgement. These messages have seemed to devotees to be so urgent
that Garabandal and San Damiano, like Amsterdam before them, have attracted a global following but, unlike Amsterdam, they still live in the 'not yet'
space of growing Church tolerance without formal approval.

13

Medjugorje

The Queen of Peace and a Civil War

HISTORY, POLITICS, AND CONFLICT

The election of John Paul II in 1978, the first non-Italian pope for several centuries and a cardinal archbishop from Poland, intensified the struggle between the Vatican and Soviet-dominated Eastern Europe. John Paul II was avowedly Marian; he had been archbishop of Kraków, not far from Auschwitz and the great Polish Marian shrine of Jasna Góra at Częstochowa. All of this signalled to Marian pilgrims that his papacy had a special place in the apocalyptic nature of modern global history and Mary's role in it. The ideas already present in Fátima (the triumph of the Immaculate Heart and the conversion of Russia), developed at Ezkioga and Garabandal (the imminence of apocalyptic disaster and miracles), came to a head in the apparitions in the 1980s. There was one wild prophecy from Garabandal that, after John XXIII, there would be only three more popes before the end of the age. This excited speculation among Marian devotees in the 1980s, although its impact is fading as, in 2013, Pope Francis became the fifth pope in this series. Yet it is Medjugorje, above all other apparition events, that expresses the apocalyptic expectation associated with the fall of communism and the changes in Eastern Europe towards the end of the twentieth century.

Medjugorje presents a problem for research, as no thorough academic and objective treatment has been published in English. Just a few years ago, one might have referred to the work of Dutch anthropologist Mart Bax, but he has since been discredited, having been found guilty of fabricating data (see Jolić 2013). Therefore, his work cannot be included here, as it has no foundation. Zimdars-Swartz included Medjugorje in her work (1991: 233–44), but her research was undertaken in the 1980s and every one of the sources she cites for Medjugorje is a devotional publication in favour of the apparitions. In Apolito's book on devotion to Mary on the Internet (2005), Medjugorje is covered at some length, although his focus is the apparition cult more widely and not this case in particular. There are a few academic articles available on specific issues such as pilgrimage and nationalism. The travel book by American journalist Brian Hall (1994), who includes several pages on Medjugorje, is useful for an understanding of the situation in the summer of 1991; as a neutral observer, his account, like Walter Starkie's on Ezkioga, gives a helpful description of local people and their attitudes. In French, there is the anthropological study by Elisabeth Claverie of the National Centre for Scientific Research (CNRS) (2003), who focuses on the belief system of pilgrims and devotees; she accompanied a pilgrimage herself. Yet much of Claverie's account of the history is based on the work of Ivo Sivrić (1988), an opponent of the apparition cult of Medjugorje. Meanwhile, there are several other works antagonistic to Medjugorje that are no more objective than those in favour: they include the book by E. Michael Jones (1998), a right-wing Catholic journalist who has published anti-Semitic material. He presents a conspiracy theory rather than a thorough analysis.

In the same way as pilgrims in other Catholic nations in Europe, Croats traditionally visit shrines originating in Marian miracles: for example, Marija Bistrica, Sinj, and Ilaca. Medjugorje's history as a shrine began with visions in June 1981. This Croat Catholic tobacco-growing village in rural Herzegovina is the site of possibly the most complex and controversial Marian apparition case of the twentieth century, due to the ecclesiastical, cultural, and political context in which it originated. In fact, the visions began in the nearby hamlet of Bijakovići, part of the Medjugorje parish; Hall (1994: 194) notes the rivalry—rather overlooked in the devotional literature—between Bijakovići and Medjugorje. At its outset, the phenomenon seemed to fall into the classic apparition type: a group of six children, aged between nine and sixteen, claimed to see the Madonna on a hillside, thus attracting many pilgrims. The fact that they had read a book on Lourdes led both visionaries and observers to suppose that it would last a few months, as at Lourdes, Fátima, Beauraing, and Banneux. Yet in the passing years, regular apparitions continue to be experienced by all six visionaries, all of whom are married, the eldest now fifty years old, which suggests that it is the type of apparition whereby adults report visions over many years, as at Kerizinen, Amsterdam, and Montichiari or, even more so, Gimigliano and Balestrino, where the visions started in childhood, too. Even then, it contrasts with those cases because of the origins in a group phenomenon and the apparitions occurring wherever in the world the visionaries travel. It has also become far more famous than those other cases, with Italy the country from where many of its pilgrims have travelled.

When the visions began, Bosnia-Herzegovina was constituted a republic of communist Yugoslavia. Yugoslavia was a federation of various Slav peoples, but it had only been a political entity since the end of the First World War. Enmity between the various nations has been exacerbated by religious difference: Croats are Catholic; Serbs are Orthodox; Bosnians include these two but also Muslims. After the German invasion during the Second World War the fragile union fragmented, leading to a terrible sequence of ethnic atrocities; the Croat *Ustaše* state, allowed to operate as a puppet of the Nazis, was fascist and openly violent. Its borders incorporated Medjugorje; Bijakovići is close to the site of a Croat massacre of Serb families in 1941, which involved men from Medjugorje and Bijakovići. The fortieth anniversary of this mass murder occurred within two months of the outset of the apparitions (Claverie 2003: 211–12). The Serbs came from a village known as Prebilovci, which disappeared as a result; in 1961, the government placed a memorial there and the bodies were exhumed by Serbs in a televised ceremony in 1990 as national tensions ran high before the secessions from Serb-led Yugoslavia during 1991–2 (Hall 1994: 204–9).

Yugoslavia was reunited after the defeat of Germany in 1945, an uncertain period during which there were many reports of apparitions in the country, both Catholic and Orthodox (Alexander 1979: 64–7; Christian 1984: 252–3). The leader of the Yugoslav partisans, Josip Broz Tito, was elected president and he held the communist state together until his death in 1980. While a Croat by birth, he had participated in the Russian Revolution and therefore remained a strong believer in transnationalist unity under communist rule; consequently, he suppressed Croat or Serb nationalism. Of all the communist leaders in Eastern Europe during the post-war years, he had a reputation as a relatively benign dictator, while presiding over economic growth and maintaining political and military distance from the Soviet bloc. His death seems to have been the trigger for the eventual break-up of Yugoslavia and, therefore, increasing tension and uncertainty forms the background to the apparitions in Medjugorje, which began a year after his death.

Marian apparitions in the twentieth century had so often been concerned about the advent of communism. The fact that now they were reported in a communist country in opposition to the authorities was alluring and sensational. Moreover, Yugoslavia was the easiest communist country to visit, its economy based on Mediterranean tourism, and many pilgrims began to gather at an early stage. Initially, the government had accused Medjugorje of being a rallying point for Croat nationalism (Kraljević 1984: 24) and arrested the Franciscan parish priest, Jozo Zovko, along with some other Franciscans and villagers (Claverie 2003: 201–11). Father Zovko, who had become the visionaries' supporter and mentor, was imprisoned for eighteen months, apparently for referring to the forty years in the wilderness, a biblical image easily applied to the period of communist rule in Yugoslavia. The devotional literature records how mass gatherings were prohibited and the visionaries' families were pressured and harassed (Bubalo 1987: 93; Laurentin and Sbalchiero 2007: 1198). The visionaries were subject to psychological tests, a process used in many cases in the past, for example at Lourdes by the French state, at Mettenbuch by the diocese of Regensburg, and at Heede by the Gestapo.

The fact that the Medjugorje visionaries, like many visionaries before them, were found to be of sound mind (Kraljević 1984: 197) is testimony to the objectivity of the psychiatrists involved. Quite soon, the government, in the face of mass support for Medjugorje from the Croats in Yugoslavia and from Catholics overseas, decided to allow the phenomenon to follow its course and to benefit from tax payable on local hostelry, accepting that there was no evidence that the apparitions were openly nationalist (Ramet 1985: 12–18). Indeed, overt nationalism would not have helped the cause of Medjugorje globally, as pilgrimage was based on the perception that the shrine's focus was on peace, prayer, and the revival of Catholic devotion.

Nevertheless, the fear of partition amongst the various republics of Yugo-slavia and the chaos that it would bring was a reasonable one for the govern-ment of the time. Nationalism grew rapidly in the various republics, with only the Serbs, the majority nation, having any interest in maintaining the federal state. The foundation of separate republics from what had been a sovereign country, Yugoslavia, meant in effect secession from Serbia, the largest repub-lic, the site of the capital city Belgrade, and the dominant nation in the Yugoslav army. Genocidal conflict broke out between 1991 and 1995, leading to the independence of the six Yugoslav republics: Slovenia, Croatia, Serbia, Bosnia-Herzegovina, Macedonia, and (eventually) Montenegro. Of all those, Bosnia-Herzegovina, where Croats and Muslims declared independence in 1992, suffered the greatest number of casualties, due to the fact that it was multiethnic and therefore the most affected by ethnic cleansing and land grabbing. The shrine at Medjugorje was caught up in this conflict and pilgrimage all but ceased for three years. NATO air strikes helped bring about a tripartite peace resolution in 1995, leading to an uneasy cooperation between the three ethnic groups that make up the nation.

THE MEDJUGORJE APPARITIONS

The circumstances surrounding the origin of the phenomena cannot be wholly clarified through the mist of all the claims and counterclaims; it is not easy to discern the intentions of the major actors in the drama which took place in this hillside village. The Medjugorje visionaries include four women and two men: Mirjana Dragicević, Vicka Ivanković, Ivan Dragicević, Marija Pavlović (all aged sixteen when the apparitions began), Ivanka Ivanković (fifteen), and Jakov Čolo (ten). Some devotional accounts claim that there is no relation between visionaries of shared surnames (Craig 1988: 18; Laurentin and Rupčić 1984: 25); the objectivity suggested by a group experience is perhaps com-promised if reported by people who are relatives. Yet Claverie (2003: 371–3) states that the Ivankovićs are cousins, and the Dragicevićs, Marija, and Jakov are also cousins of one another. The first apparition occurred on 24 June 1981 on the hillside of Podbrdo when Mirjana and Ivanka went for a walk; Ivanka, whose mother had died the previous month, was the first to see the figure she thought might be the *Gospa* (Croatian for 'Madonna' or 'Our Lady'). Opponents make much of the fact that the girls admitted that they went for a walk to have a smoke; some have suggested that marijuana was involved. Other teenagers were quickly summoned, although the group of six was not fully constituted until the following day, 25 June, which is kept as the anniversary.

The themes in the messages that these visionaries announced in the early weeks and have repeated over many years centre on a call to return to traditional religiosity—Mass, confession, prayer—as well as an accent on the sorrow of the *Gospa*, weeping at the Cross because of the situation in the world. She cries for peace: hence she was called *Kraljice Mira*, 'Queen of Peace' (a traditional title added to the Loreto Litany by Benedict XV during the First World War). She appears as a beautiful young woman in a long grey garment (gold on feast days) and white veil with a crown of stars, hovering on a cloud, sometimes alone, sometimes with infant and/or angels. These are traditional and universal images inculturated as always in the local environment, as she looks and speaks like a Croatian. However, on the first occasion, the vision was unusual, in that the seers reported that the *Gospa* repeatedly covered and uncovered something in her hands that some of them believed to be her baby. A chaotic first week was followed by the Franciscan parish priest inviting the visionaries into the church building where their apparitions could proceed in a protected environment, and from this point, the visions were not public, occurring in the sacristy with only invited persons present (Laurentin and Sbalchiero 2007: 1200). They took on an orderliness and structure that reflected the support of the Franciscans. This was an important moment in the history of the apparitions, as the change of location signified an ecclesiastical decision to take control, which is paralleled elsewhere, although not always so early in the events. The visionaries remained a group until Christmas 1982, from when they all continued to have visions, but not always together. There were also other young people in the village who reported locutions, hearing messages from the Virgin Mary.

The visionary messages were given further structure in 1984, when a weekly message was revealed by Marija Pavlović; this became monthly in 1987. The weekly messages between 1984 and 1987 allow for an analysis of the major themes of Medjugorje in these early years: in 164 messages, prayer is mentioned eighty-eight times; God sixty-four; love forty-six; Jesus forty-four; people's hearts (i.e. genuine faith) twenty-eight; the messages themselves twenty-seven; Mary's empathy and feelings for people twenty-six; graces or divine gifts twenty-six; the Medjugorje parish which Mary is leading twenty-four; Satan twenty-three; encouragement for people to heed the messages and gratitude for them doing so nineteen; 'living the messages' seventeen; Mary's protection or guidance sixteen; Mary's presence sixteen; the need for sacrifices fifteen; Mary's mediation fourteen; chastisement fourteen; joy fourteen; the family thirteen; blessing (of God, Jesus, or Mary) twelve; hearers of the messages as vessels or communicators of them twelve; Mary's prayer twelve; surrender (to God, Jesus, or Mary) eleven; conversion eleven; sin or sinners eleven; peace ten, and so on (the text of the messages is freely available on the web; see also Rooney and Faricy 1987: 121; O'Carroll 1986: 158).

It is clear from the prominent themes that Medjugorje continues traditional Catholic Marian concepts, but that these are being articulated in a new way. The importance of prayer including the rosary, conversion, heartfelt faith and sacrifice, the sin of the world, Satan's temptations, and the danger of chastisement have all been re-emphasized. There are some new markers of sincere faith: the revival of the early Christian tradition of fasting on Wednesdays and Fridays, for example. Sivrić (1982: 59, 79, 89), a Franciscan originally from the village but opposed to Medjugorje, argues that fasting, open-air confession, and inter-faith tolerance were all traditional features of Croat peasant spirituality, although his book scarcely mentions Marian devotion. Where Medjugorje departed from tradition was in its regular, extended repetition of exhortations to believers that is summed up in the very first weekly message on 1 March 1984; this declares that Mary has chosen the parish and wishes to lead it. The accent is on the progress of the believer in prayer over a prolonged period. Medjugorje is also distinctive in the greeting of the *Gospa* ('Dear children . . .') and her farewell ('Thank you for having responded to my call'); these phrases have been reported with several variations in many post-Medjugorje apparitions.

Supporters of Medjugorje claim that the 'spiritual fruits' are pronounced. There have been millions of pilgrims, many of whom report a revival of faith not only at the shrine but on returning home, an experience explained theoretically in Victor and Edith Turner's idea that pilgrimage is a 'liminoid phenomenon', like rites of passage; it acts as an initiation into a new life of faith (Turner and Turner 1978). Many pilgrims have reported their own visions and there has been a host of claimed miraculous phenomena: the sun spinning, rosaries turning gold, photos bearing ghostly images of the Madonna (see e.g. Hall 1994: 187, 196). Attendance at the Catholic sacraments has been abundant. There have been conversions to Catholicism (for example, the American Lutheran Wayne Weible, who has since written books on Medjugorje), and it is claimed that Orthodox, Muslims, and Protestants have visited Medjugorje (Laurentin and Rupčić 1984: 134). However, Hall (1994: 212) met only Catholics and a few Protestants in 1991. In Medjugorje itself, prayer groups and Bible reading groups have been formed and many young people participate. The Queen of Peace called for inter-faith tolerance and reconciliation amongst the different ethnic and religious groups of Bosnia-Herzegovina, thus drawing from Catholic opponents the charge of 'pluralism' (de la Sainte Trinité May 1984: 14). Nevertheless, Gerry Hughes's visit led him to be sceptical about Medjugorje's claimed ecumenism and peace-seeking (Hughes 1987).

The Marian tradition of 'secrets' given to visionaries has been continued quite dramatically at Medjugorje (among others, Laurentin and Sbalchiero 2007: 1207–8). In the early 1980s, the young seers reported that they were receiving ten secrets each but at different rates and, when the ten secrets had been communicated, then that seer would stop having daily apparitions, although they would still experience visions from time to time. According to the seers, Mirjana was the first to receive the ten secrets in 1982, but even as late as 2015, three of the visionaries have still not received all ten and so the daily apparitions continue. Enough has been divulged about these 'secrets' for devotees to know that they are apocalyptic in character although, as in previous cases, the more terrifying aspects are said to be able to be averted by prayer and other expressions of faith. They concern 'chastisements', as at Ezkioga and Garabandal, and a miraculous sign visible on the hill where the apparitions took place, in a similar way to that at Garabandal. Like Conchita González at Garabandal, Mirjana would inform a priest a few days in advance of the sign so that the accuracy of the prophecy would be confirmed. The expectation and concern over these secret messages prompt Catholic priests and other concerned writers to attempt to quieten over-enthusiasm: 'Like all the secrets, without doubt they will tend to disappoint, because the most successful predictions never concern actual history revealed in advance. They are rather warnings, mixed up with instantaneous flashes of insight, incomprehensible before their realization. Their meaning is not revealed until after their accomplishment' (Laurentin and Sbalchiero 2007: 1208, my translation).

Other remarkable aspects include the claim from the visionaries that these will be the last Marian apparitions; there have, of course, been other cases since 1981 but, as the Medjugorje visions are still continuing in 2015, this cannot be refuted yet. It is possible that they might be the last of their kind because of social and economic change. The typical Marian apparition context—a Catholic village in a remote and rural setting in the midst of political and social turmoil—is familiar from centuries past and also in the modern period, at locations such as La Salette, Pontmain, Marpingen, Fátima, Banneux, and the rest. However, popular Marian apparitions have usually taken place in homogeneous Catholic communities where a whole town or village played its part, but such places are no longer remote in the age of the mobile phone, Internet, and air travel, while secularization is advancing even in Catholic strongholds. At the same time, the fame of the warnings and prophecies of Garabandal and Medjugorje may make it hard for those who come after them should they prove to be false.

The visionaries, in their adult lives, have held meetings all over the world at which they experience an apparition; this has both delighted devotees and elicited scepticism from others. Historian Lisa Bitel, in a somewhat tongue-in-cheek style, describes a visit by Ivan Dragicević to a Los Angeles church: he lives part of the year in Boston, in the USA, travels during the rest of the months holding public visions, and is married to a former Miss Massachusetts (Bitel 2009: 69–74). Whereas visionaries of the past have led comparatively quiet lives after the visions end, being no more than local celebrities, the most famous of them (Bernadette Soubirous and Lúcia Santos) becoming cloistered nuns, the continuing visions and global journeys of the Medjugorje seers have led to their rivalling the shrine itself as the centre of the cult.

CATHOLIC RESPONSES TO MEDJUGORJE

Episcopal Judgement

Medjugorje stands in the Diocese of Mostar-Duvno; the bishop's reaction seems to have paralleled that of the state but in the opposite direction. When the state attempted to suppress the shrine at the beginning, Monseigneur Pavao Žanić stood by the visionaries; while not endorsing the apparitions themselves, a circumspect approach that is normal for a bishop, he defended the seers from the charge of nationalism and argued for their honesty, quoting Acts 5:38–9: in summary, if it is of God, it will prevail (Laurentin 1986: 70–1; Kraljević 1984: 201–2). At this stage, he was the target of criticism from the state, the press, and some elements in the Church for supporting the apparitions (Laurentin 1986: 79). However, towards the end of 1981, an old ecclesiastical disagreement began to play its part. A takeover of Franciscan parishes in Herzegovina by secular diocesan clergy had been put into effect a century earlier, after Austria–Hungary took control of the region in 1878. However, the process had stalled and needed to be reinvigorated by a decree of Pope Paul VI in 1975. Some Franciscans, at the instigation of the parishioners who had come to rely on them, rebelled against the policy and came into conflict with the local diocese, the bishop, and the Franciscan province: this problem had become more intense in the communist period (Laurentin and Sbalchiero 2007: 1200). The rebel Franciscans became bolder in using the international mass movement taking place at Medjugorje in making their case against the take-over of parishes. As Žanić was a key figure in the process of diocesan reorganization, he came to regard the apparitions as their invention to challenge his authority in the diocese; this was confirmed in his view when a message apparently from the *Gospa* seemed to support the rebel Franciscans. The replacement for Zovko as parish priest, Tomislav Vlasić, was a particular target for his accusations; at this time, Vlasić's later notoriety as a philanderer had not yet surfaced.

The Franciscans used the success of the pilgrimage shrine at Medjugorje in their argument, but insisted that the apparitions had occurred spontaneously at the initiative of the *Gospa*; the bishop, on the other hand, regarded the emergence of the apparitions as hallucinations that had been manipulated to fuel support for the Franciscan cause. Žanić therefore attempted to prohibit parish support for the apparitions at Medjugorje and prevent the promulgation of its cult; he replaced and silenced Vlasić and then his successor, Slavko Barbarić (Laurentin and Sblachiero 2007: 1201). A diocesan commission, formed in 1982 and reconstituted in 1984, declared its negative findings in 1985 that the supernatural had not been established. However, Žanić was unable to hold back the tide of Catholic opinion as Medjugorje had become a global phenomenon by this time. Supporters disregarded Žanić's episcopal authority and felt that he was overlooking a divine initiative because of a personal agenda. The decision in 1985 was therefore ignored; the Vatican did not come to Žanić's aid but remained silent, leading to much speculation about the pope's private support for Medjugorje.

In all likelihood, Pope John Paul II did regard Medjugorje with some favour, albeit behind the scenes. Medjugorje was a convenient aid to the Vatican's foreign policy in the 1980s, i.e. supporting the United States and attempting to undermine the communist bloc in Eastern Europe. It is quite possible that John Paul II prevented suppression of Medjugorje, despite the opposition of the local bishop and the fact that Cardinal Ratzinger had learned of the sexual misdemeanours of Vlasić. This view is given some support by the fact that the celebrated theologian Hans Urs von Balthasar (popular with John Paul II, who raised him to cardinal) also joined the argument, condemning Bishop Žanić for his uncompromising style when making accusations against Medjugorje's supporters.

The Congregation for the Doctrine of the Faith took the matter out of the hands of the local bishop and passed the decision on to the Yugoslav National Conference of Bishops, which undertook a new enquiry, making a declaration on the case on 10 April 1991. This softened somewhat the decisions made in the diocese. The bishops agreed with Žanić that the Church could not confirm that the apparitions were genuine manifestations of the supernatural, although this was not wholly excluded, and they would leave that decision to a future study. Nevertheless they understood what Medjugorje meant to the faithful from across the world with so many travelling there on pilgrimage (Laurentin and Sbalchiero 2007: 1210). It was therefore important to ensure that these pilgrims received appropriate pastoral support and guidance. The Vatican then clarified that pilgrimages could not be organized by bishops and priests, but they could accompany them. Finally, in 2010, a new international Vatican commission on Medjugorje was established by Pope Benedict XVI. Its report has been received by Pope Francis, and the Catholic world eagerly awaits the findings and the papal decision that will follow.

Žanić's successor in 1993, Ratko Perić, proved to be as hostile to the apparitions as his predecessor had been (Laurentin and Sbalchiero 2007: 1210–11). He has published two books on the Virgin Mary in which he has stated his opposition. In his personal opinion, not only is the supernatural not established at Medjugorje (the decision of the commissions), but the non-supernatural has been established, an even more negative judgement. Meanwhile, there has been some resolution of the disagreement between the diocese of Mostar-Duvno and the Franciscans brokered by the Vatican Congregation of Evangelization, which has resulted in the transferring of parishes (not including Medjugorje) to the secular clergy.

Clerical Support

It is unlikely that Medjugorje could have become the worldwide phenomenon that it is, given that the local bishop was strongly opposed, without the open support of many Catholic clergy. Medjugorje websites list a considerable number of cardinals and bishops who have visited the shrine. First and foremost among the priestly supporters is the Mariologian René Laurentin, historian of nineteenth-century French shrines such as the Rue du Bac, Lourdes, and Pontmain, who does not hide his excitement that he has had the opportunity to see a large-scale event unfold in his lifetime and not just read about it in archives. Laurentin collaborated with the Croatian Franciscan Ljudevit Rupčić, one-time prisoner of the communist state, in publishing *Is the Virgin Mary Appearing in Medjugorje?: An Urgent Message for the World given in a Marxist Country* (1984). This work, with its strongly implied 'yes' to the question of the title, brought Medjugorje to the attention of many Catholics worldwide. Laurentin then worked with a doctor, Henri Joyeux, in publishing the results of a series of unprecedented tests on the visionaries while in ecstasy, entitled *Scientific and Medical Studies on the Apparitions at Medjugorje* (1987). These tests included placing electrodes on the visionaries and measuring heartbeat, blood pressure, hearing, and brain patterns. According to the authors, these ruled out pathology, epilepsy, sleep, hallucination, and catalepsy. Yet science, it was admitted, could not establish the supernatural status of an apparition. 'We would be quite willing to define [the ecstasies] as a state of active, intense prayer, partially disconnected from the outside world, a state of contemplation with a separate person whom they alone can see, hear and touch' (Laurentin and Joyeux 1987: 75). The book also considered fasting, cures, 'luminous phenomena', and the possibility of a diabolical origin. The book is ultimately a theological work in favour of the apparitions, employing testing using technological equipment in an attempt to rule out reductionist explanations of the phenomena.

Laurentin also published a series of short books updating supporters of Medjugorje (the *Dernières Nouvelles*, '*Latest News*'). In these, he tried to reach some kind of resolution to the difference of opinion between himself and Bishop Žanić. Zimdars-Swartz (1991: 243) also suggests that he presented the story of Medjugorje in a way that diminished its more sensational aspects, thus making it more palatable to a wider Catholic audience; she calls this a 'mellowed apocalypticism' in which the content of the messages is not necessarily to be understood literally, but where the urgency of the call to prayer and Christian love is central.

Various bishops have also supported Medjugorje. Archbishop Franić of Split was the most prominent, being a senior Croatian cleric; he opposed Žanić and supported the apparitions at the Yugoslav episcopal conference of 1985 (O'Carroll 1986: 149, 203). Bishop Pavel Hnilica, a Slovakian Jesuit consecrated secretly during the communist period, visited Medjugorje on several occasions. He was said to have the ear of Pope John Paul II and reported that the pope was privately interested in Medjugorje, seeing it as a continuation of Fátima in the battle with communism; however, Hnilica's reputation does not really help the cause of the apparitions, as he has been tainted with the scandal of the Vatican banking crisis of the 1980s. Archbishop Kuharić of Zagreb, president of the Yugoslav episcopal commission that made a judgement on Medjugorje in 1991, remained objective as was appropriate to his position, but he presided over a decision that encouraged the continuation of non-official pilgrimage; he described Medjugorje as a 'Marian sanctuary', much to the chagrin of Bishop Perić (Laurentin and Sbalchiero 2007: 1210). Finally, Cardinal Schönborn, archbishop of Vienna, was reported to have made a private pilgrimage at New Year in 2010 without informing the local bishop, causing the latter frustration (in *America*, 18 January 2010).

Priests Against Medjugorje

Medjugorje also has its opponents within the clergy from further afield than the diocese of Mostar-Duvno, and some have been outspoken in publishing their arguments. It is clear, however, that they have a predisposition to dislike Medjugorje in the same way as the devotees are inclined to accept it. Ivo Sivrić, a Franciscan native of Medjugorje, was not accepting of Marian apparitions in general, seeing them as expressions of the need for a loving Mother, and remained scornful even of Fátima. His knowledge of the region and language (demonstrated in a publication on the regional culture: Sivrić 1982) gave him an advantage in attempting to discredit the Medjugorje case and he claimed to have access to tape recordings and interviews suppressed by the devotees (Sivrić 1988: 35). He insists that the visionaries had been given a book on Lourdes before their own apparitions and not afterwards as they claimed

(Sivrić 1988: 169). His book, *La Face Cachée de Medjugorje* ('The Hidden Face of Medjugorje') was written in collaboration with a Canadian layman, Benoit Bélanger, who was interested in geomagnetic reasons for the many strange phenomena of light reported at Medjugorje. Sivrić argues that, at the origin of the Medjugorje apparitions before the Franciscans took charge, there is plenty of evidence of folk beliefs that are not orthodox in the Catholic doctrinal system (Sivrić 1988: 61).

Michel de la Sainte Trinité had quite different reasons for opposing Medjugorje; unlike Sivrić, he was a staunch supporter of Fátima and a member of the *Contre-Réforme Catholique*, a group founded by Abbé Georges de Nantes in opposition to Vatican II. Sivrić and de la Sainte Trinité show how rationalists and traditionalists within the Catholic clergy may come to an agreement in their opposition to the claims made at Medjugorje. For de la Sainte Trinité, Medjugorje is an apparition that threatens to transplant Fátima and justify the reforms of Vatican II and, for these reasons, it is a fabrication of the Devil. Therefore, he sets out to show that it was unbecoming of the Virgin Mary and gives examples of rough and familiar language used by the seers while in trance, and strange laughing attributed to Mary that show her to be the Devil dressed as an angel of light (de la Sainte Trinité 1984: 6, 14). De la Sainte Trinité is right to see Medjugorje as the post-conciliar apparition par excellence, which for him is a disqualifying factor but, for many others, proof of its authenticity. Medjugorje messages include a call to Bible reading, prayer groups, and ecumenism that accord with the reforms of Vatican II. Many are Christocentric in content and the integration between apparitions and sacramental liturgy in the early days (the daily apparition at 6:40 pm was followed by Mass) reinforced this (Claverie 2003: 357). De la Sainte Trinité referred to Medjugorje as 'a great charismatic project' (1984: 3) with some justification, and the charismatic movement in Catholicism is clearly rooted in the post-Vatican II period.

The Catholic charismatic movement came into being in 1967; it was championed by Cardinal Suenens of Malines/Mechelen-Brussels, a prominent figure at Vatican II strongly associated with both ecumenism and the Marian cult. It understands Marian apparitions as *charismata* and it is well disposed to ecumenism and the spiritual leadership (if not ordination) of women. Apolito suggests that, in the United States, the birthplace of Pentecostalism, concentration on immediate experience and the individual makes charismatic Christianity popular, and that charismatics are often involved in Marian visions in America (2005: 28–30). Medjugorje has a special appeal to Catholic charismatics and its origins have charismatic connections too. Craig (1988: 82) relates the well-known story of how Franciscan priest Tomislav Vlasić attended a charismatic renewal conference in May 1981, one month before the visions. There he met the famous charismatic nun and healer, Sister Brierge McKenna, who had a vision of a twin-towered church with Vlasić surrounded by huge crowds; a charismatic priest, Emilio Tardif, prophesied that God would send his Mother to Vlasić. Vlasić replaced the arrested Jozo Zovko as parish priest of Medjugorje in August 1981. Hall (1994: 200–1) reports Jozo Zovko 'slaying in the Spirit' in 1991, serving in a nearby parish.

Despite the Catholic opposition to Medjugorje, like all other apparitions it belongs to its time, a period after Vatican II when Marian devotions were in decline in local parishes, but the accession of the first Polish pope gave a fresh impetus to large-scale Marian shrines and pilgrimages. The Eastern European provenance ensured that Medjugorje would be seen by most as extending and updating Fátima's anti-communist message, not subverting it as de la Sainte Trinité thought. In all these respects, Medjugorje was destined to succeed in global Catholicism and its only detractor with any influence was the local bishop, whose involvement in a local ecclesiastical disagreement gave him second thoughts, but the parochial nature of that question was unlikely to derail the global driving forces behind Medjugorje.

MEDJUGORJE AND THE CROATIAN STATE

Far more serious than ecclesiastical politics was another regional problem, by no means as internationally insignificant, which gave rise to renewed calls for Medjugorje to be seen as a great conspiracy. That problem was the question of the break-up of Yugoslavia into nationalist factions and the association of Medjugorje with Croat independence. It is difficult to deny some connection, given that the foundation date of the new Croat state was chosen as 25 June 1991, exactly ten years after the beginning of the cult of Medjugorje; subsequently, the Croatian president, Franjo Tjudman, visited the shrine. Croatia was internationally recognized along with Slovenia and established as a separate nation during the remainder of 1991, despite terrible conflict in that part of its territory bordering Serbia. In turn, the Muslims and Croats of Bosnia-Herzegovina outnumbered the Serbs in a referendum and so that state declared its independence and was recognized by the European Community and the USA in April 1992. The problem of Bosnia-Herzegovina was that very many Croats and Serbs lived within its borders along with the Bosniak Muslims and the call to nationalism included claims to the Bosnian territories in which Croats and Serbs lived, with the purpose of these being annexed by Croatia or Serbia. In order to establish areas as homogeneous and monoethnic, communities began 'ethnic cleansing', a term describing either the eviction or murder of ethnic minorities in a region. This had already begun in Croatia but became far more widespread in Bosnia-Herzegovina. There, the Croat–Muslim alliance broke down and the Croats of Bosnia-Herzegovina tried to force the breakaway of a region known to them as 'Herzeg-Bosna', which could be attached to Croatia.

This area had a nominal capital in Mostar, just a few kilometres from Medjugorje, and it included the village within its notional borders.

There can be no doubt that Medjugorje was caught up in the Croat nationalist cause and the attempts to rid the region of Muslims and Serbs. Medjugorje literature referred to Muslims as 'fundamentalists' and reported without critique a Medjugorje Franciscan, Slavko Barbarić, applauding his countrymen convicted of war crimes (*Mir* 5, June 2000). Claverie (2003: 237–9, 364) points out that Barbarić's book *Mother, Lead us to Peace!* (1995) includes the clear implication that Medjugorje is in Croatia, as have some Medjugorje websites since. However, the inclusion of the Medjugorje region in Croatia is a nationalist dream and not political reality. The extent of anti-Muslim feeling in Medjugorje was demonstrated when the village appeared on international television on 24 August 1993, when a food convoy bound for starving Muslims in Mostar was obstructed there. Hall (1994: 188, 199) relates how all the consumerist activities targeting pilgrims in Medjugorje were blamed on Muslims, which was clearly inaccurate, and he gives several other examples of Croat nationalism in Medjugorje and Bijakovići, many of whose men were involved in fighting against Muslims in Mostar (Hall 1994: 332–3). Neither could Medjugorje avoid the taint of wartime corruption: an English businessman used the fame of Medjugorje to collect money, purportedly for war orphans, but this was channelled into the Croat military. Joseph Wiinikka-Lydon makes these three pertinent points about the connection of Medjugorje to Croat nationalism, amongst others:

> The Medjugorje phenomenon's sacred resources, in addition to its financial resources and effects, were used by violent Croat nationalist groups to support their ambitions during the war... Medjugorje came to hold a central place in the Croat nationalist imagination before, during, and even after the war... Indeed, the Virgin of Medjugorje was seen as the protectress of the Croats in both Croatia and Herceg-Bosna. (Wiinikka-Lydon 2010: 3–4)

At the heart of this problem surrounding the Marian symbol was the understanding of the Queen of Peace whereby peace is achieved through violence (Wiinikka-Lydon 2010: 11–14). However, this is clearly in opposition to the moral ideals of interfaith tolerance and harmony expressed in the early days of the apparitions.

It surprised people when the visionaries stated that their prophecies of future chastisements were not related to the Bosnian conflict on their home soil, the worst civil war on the European continent since the 1930s, but were instead global in scope. Medjugorje was claimed to have miraculously escaped bombing (a more mundane explanation is the presence of UN and Red Cross garrisons because of the convenience of accommodation built for pilgrims); however, it did not avoid the general blindness to the repercussions of the actions of one's own people that customarily accompanies civil war and nationalistic aspirations. Nevertheless, despite all this, not even Medjugorje's most outspoken critics regard Croat nationalism as the *cause* of the visions. As we have seen, Sivrić saw them as emerging in the folk culture of the region and de la Sainte Trinité understands the phenomenon solely in terms of the general Catholic argument over Vatican II. Jones (1998: 358) regarded it as a case of teenagers seeing ghosts because of their proximity to a site of wartime atrocity and the ensuing phenomenon being taken up in the cause of the Franciscans resisting the bishop. Other negative factors—the inability of Medjugorje and its 'Queen of Peace' to remain above the excesses of inter-community hatred and the growing wealth of the visionaries—are seen by him as later developments on what was a shaky foundation.

Skrbiš (2005) shows how nationalism allies itself to religious themes around the divine election of a nation or people (in this case, Croatia), but he does not regard the apparitions and nationalism as existing in a cause-and-effect relationship; rather, they are separate phenomena that can become conflated: 'The apparitional phenomenon is constantly caught up in the antagonistic tension between the universalistic Christian appeal of the Virgin's messages and the possibility of its particularist/local appropriations, such as in national-ism' (Skrbiš 2005: 458). Claverie (2003: 26–9) distinguishes between Medjugorje and 'Medjugorje', the former a village with an ethnic identity and socio-political context, the latter a site at the centre of an international cult, multiethnic and diverse. The poles of this tension identified by Skrbiš and Claverie include the global, universal dimension, appealing to Catholics of all nations, visiting the shrine as pilgrims, and eagerly awaiting its messages and prophecies. This is the image presented by the visionaries themselves as they avoid connections between the apparitions and the regional political situation. Then there is the local and national dimension, which has been characterized by ecclesiastical, political, and military conflict. Writers denouncing Medjugorje expect its devotees to be swayed when they discover the more unpleasant features of this second part of the story, but the characteristic response of the believer is to point out how Satan would wish to destroy something that is fruitful and of God, and so the negative aspects can be ascribed to him. Medjugorje tried to play its part in the reconstruction after the civil war in the setting up of special accommodation for orphans (Claverie 2003: 27). Probably, as for other shrines, the local history of the origins is something that will be forgotten and outlived, and the drama of global apocalyptic will prevail, irrespective of the apocalyptic-like horrors that were witnessed in the region itself.

THE MEDJUGORJE CULT

The apparitions have transformed Medjugorje. The village became a town in the late 1980s due to the building of hotels and other pilgrim facilities

(Claverie 2003: 30). New chapels have appeared, some built by pilgrims attached to the charismatic movement. The region was accustomed to sending its men as 'guest workers' to Germany before the 1980s, but these returned to help with the building work. Like Blackbourn's nineteenth-century examples (1993: 30–1), the fame of Medjugorje's shrine has moved it from being a marginal rural community to enjoying status as a regional centre. In the same way as shrines such as Lourdes and Fátima, the setting for the visions has passed from local to international. Yet Claverie (2003: 46) distinguishes Medjugorje from these two earlier shrines because, due to the prolongation of apparitions over the years, it is seen by the pilgrims as a place where the Virgin continues to be especially present. Apolito (2005: 38–41) charts the global growth of Medjugorje: an average of one million pilgrims a year during the 1980s, numbers which resumed after the civil war in 1995. Websites on Medjugorje represent thirty different languages (Apolito 2005: 3–4).

Apolito also notes how the Medjugorje cult was originally Croat, but then the scope broadened so that the majority of supporters were Italian and then American. The Franciscans in America, at for example Steubenville, supported their colleagues in Bosnia-Herzegovina by coordinating publicity about Medjugorje, and many other associations have been involved in this work (Apolito 2005: 36, 43). In the United States, belief in divine miracles flourished from the late 1980s into the 1990s; interest in apocalyptic prophecies grew in Protestant and Catholic circles in America during the Reagan years (Apolito 2005: 46–8). Medjugorje can be identified as the key catalyst in the increase in reports of apparitions in the United States from 1986 on (see, for example, Garvey 1998); Apolito compares this 'epidemic' to other explosions of apparitions, but more global in scope than in 1930s Belgium, for example (Apolito 2005: 22–3, 35–6, 44–5). American apparition sites where visionaries originally went to Medjugorje and returned to experience their own apparitions include Scottsdale, Emmitsburg, Lubbock, and Conyers. The energetic activity of the Marian cult in America has led to the voicing of strong reservations: William A. Reck, an American Medjugorje devotee and promoter and a member of the Riehle Foundation, a Catholic Marian publisher, wrote *Dear Marian Movement: Let God be God* (1996). There he criticizes coreligionists for their sensationalism, false prophecy, questionable fundraising, and lack of knowledge of the Catholic tradition. While Jones (1998), in contrast to Reck, is committed to the unmasking of Medjugorje as a whole because he claims that it leads to 'ruined lives', many of his examples are American and so confirm Reck's anxiety that they are bringing Medjugorje into disrepute. Whether or not his claims can be substantiated, he does at least demonstrate the enormous influence of Medjugorje in the United States. To add to these doubts about the soundness of the Marian cult in the United States, there are also many experiences that lend themselves to ridicule and scepticism when 'miraculous' shapes of Mary are reported in tortillas or on window panes.

The Medjugorje cult's rise in the 1980s means that post-1980s technology is used for its promulgation, an era of the widening influence of television further afield than Western Europe and English-speaking countries, the birth of the Internet, and the greater accessibility of travel opportunities. Ironically, reaction to the pervasiveness of modern technology often uses television, video, and the web to promote its values. This is the case in Medjugorje, where the *Gospa* told the visionaries to 'turn off your television sets' but television became a major medium for spreading the messages (Apolito 2005: 10). Apolito wonders whether the daily schedule of apparitions in Medjugorje, unlike any before, owes something to the model of daily television viewing (Apolito 2005: 11).

So Medjugorje, because of its development in an age of air travel and the Internet, promises to be the best known and most followed apparition in history. The lack of a formal pronouncement from the Vatican adds to the intrigue of the case in the way that the 'third secret' of Fátima used to do. The controversial nature of Medjugorje's ecclesiastical history may not help its cause, nor will scandal involving Father Vlasić, Marija Pavlović, and a German woman said to have been healed at Medjugorje, all members of a religious community including both men and women in Italy that broke down amid allegations of sexual liaison (Caldwell 2008). There are also problems in the association with visionaries such as the Greek Orthodox painter, tennis player, and mystic Vassula Rydén, who is influential in Catholicism: she travels around the world like the Medjugorje seers; she is divorced and remarried; she has been censured by the Vatican and by the Greek Orthodox Church for heterodoxy in her messages; and she disregards boundaries between the Catholic, Orthodox, and Protestant traditions (Apolito 2005: 173–4). Rydén is supported by pro-Medjugorje priests René Laurentin, Michael O'Carroll, and Archbishop Frane Franić (there is a long list of bishops, Catholic and Orthodox, whom Rydén's website claims to be in support of her mission: <http://www.tlig.org/en/testimonies/churchpos/> accessed 31 May 2015). She is part of an extensive global cult of visionary Catholicism that stands in some tension with the Catholic hierarchy, and this situation is unlikely to be resolved under Pope Francis, whose emphasis is on reminding the Church of its pastoral heritage.

Yet it is not clear that a negative judgement on Medjugorje would cut off the supply of pilgrims and devotees, such is the extent of popularity of the site, its visionaries, and messages. Very many Marian apparitions worldwide since the 1980s seem to have some reference to them or have been inspired by them. After Lourdes and Fátima, Medjugorje has become the third great Catholic Marian apparition case in the modern era to create a template for all successors. The best examples of its influence in Europe are in Ireland and Italy (explored in Chapters 14 and 15). However, Medjugorje has gone beyond Lourdes and Fátima in its intensity of regular apparitions over a long period and in its urgent and terrifying apocalyptic predictions (which clearly draw on Ezkioga and Garabandal, among others). Neither has Medjugorje any precedent in the extent of its worldwide influence and its controversy.

There was another case of a Marian apparition in Catholic Europe with a similar basis in the aspiration of a nation to secede from a communist neighbour, at Hrushiw in Ukraine. The initial visionary was eleven-year-old Maria Kizyn whose first vision in 1987 occurred on the first anniversary of the nearby Chernobyl nuclear reactor disaster, which therefore framed the social context of the phenomenon at its outset. Other visionaries emerged, including Josyp Terelya, a Soviet gulag survivor exiled to Canada later that year; he supported the apparitions and took them in a nationalist direction with the Virgin Mary promising the independence of Ukraine (which occurred in 1991). They have not had the impact of the Medjugorje case, although the shrine is important in Ukraine and a web search reveals international knowledge and interest in the case.

14

Grottoes, Statues, and Visions in Ireland

FROM MOVING STATUES TO APPARITIONS

As the fame of Medjugorje grew and reinvigorated the world of Marian apparitions, 1985 witnessed a new chapter in Marian devotion in Ireland. On St Valentine's Day, 14 February, in Asdee (County Kerry), children reported seeing a moving statue of the Virgin and Child in the parish church; by the autumn there were reports of moving statues from every part of the Republic of Ireland, the majority in the southern counties, although many pilgrims arrived from the north. The statues were often at Lourdes-style grottoes, such as at Ballinspittle (County Cork), the site of the most widely publicized case from 22 July 1985. Some people claimed that the face of Mary on the statues changed into that of Jesus or Padre Pio, who had a large following in Ireland. The moving statues of Ireland were reported in the international media; the fame of Ballinspittle provoked Protestant campaigners from Dublin into smashing the face of the statue, calling the events 'idolatry'. The second phase of the 1985 Marian phenomena in Ireland involved apparitions at shrines with statues; the best-known sites were Inchigeela (County Cork), Melleray (County Waterford), and Carns (County Sligo). Initially, the visionaries were children, usually aged ten to sixteen. Eventually, however, they gave way in prominence to adults with longer and more complex messages. These included Christina Gallagher, whose first experience was at Carns, and Mary Casey at Inchigeela.

Ireland in 1985 saw an outbreak of Marian phenomena much like those at Lourdes in 1858, Belgium during 1933, and across Europe in the post-war period. Ireland is no stranger to Marian visions; after Knock in 1879, there were several twentieth-century cases, the most famous at Kerrytown (County Donegal) in 1939. Many of the shrines that gained public attention during 1985 had claimed previous visions going back over the years, none of which had gained the attention of the national media. However, the 1985 explosion generated a rush of reports that led to fame and a certain notoriety in the media of Ireland and several other English-speaking countries regarding the moving statues and visions. This suggests that certain social triggers were present that explain the outbreak of and mass interest in these phenomena. They provoked a national debate in which a range of voices competed for the right to interpret the visions and what they meant for the future of Catholicism in Ireland.

While it cannot be demonstrated that international interest in Medjugorje triggered the original children's experiences of moving statues, it certainly provided a framework for the visions that followed them; many of the messages are based clearly on the Medjugorje 'formula': peace, prayer, the Mass, conversion, and a future chastisement that can only be averted by an intensification of these practices. Visionary teenager Colleen McGuinness of Carns had visited Medjugorje before her own experiences, and peace was the major theme at Inchigeela, where the vision referred to itself as the 'Queen of Peace'. Allen (2000: 347–56) emphasizes the important role of a visionary's elder sister, Mary O'Sullivan, in the process of interpreting the messages at Inchigeela: a highly educated woman interested in Medjugorje, she wrote the booklet describing the apparitions (O'Sullivan 1989).

The Inchigeela apparitions began while the moving statue of Ballinspittle in the same county was being featured regularly in the media. Rose O'Sullivan and Marie Vaughan (aged eleven and ten respectively) visited a Lourdes grotto in Inchigeela on 5 August 1985. The girls reported an apparition of the Virgin Mary, who on the following day spoke the single word, 'Peace'. More substantial messages began on 8 August: 'Bring more children to pray, tell the families to get together to pray the rosary'. Prayer was necessary if catastrophe was to be avoided: 'My Father is very sad in heaven and my Son is very sad'. Certain themes figure repeatedly in the Irish cases of the mid-1980s: the importance of prayer, the imminence of danger, the power of Satan, the special role for Ireland in God's plan, and entreaties for peace. In June 1986, the emphasis on peace at Inchigeela continued with the message, 'I am the Queen of Peace'. The desire for peace in Bosnia-Herzegovina translated easily into Ireland because of the conflict in Northern Ireland (the 'Anglo-Irish agreement' was signed in November 1985). Many pilgrims to apparition shrines in the Republic came from Northern Ireland. June 1986 also saw the arrival at Inchigeela of an adult visionary, Mary Casey, whose longer messages had clear connections with the Medjugorje tradition. In August 1986, another child visionary, Kelley Noonan, appeared on the scene. There were many more visionaries at the two grottoes of Inchigeela among the crowds that gathered, but Mary Casey became the leading visionary. The apparitions ceased in March 1987 apart from isolated visions reported by pilgrims to Inchigeela and in the group that gathered around Fiona Bowen, who went on to found a shrine in County Limerick (Allen 2000: 356–63).

The Melleray visions began a few days after Inchigeela, on 16 August 1985 (the promotional account giving details is that of Deevy 1990). The site centred on another Lourdes grotto near the famous Cistercian monastery of Melleray, a grotto built a few years earlier at the instigation of one of the monks, Father Celestine. At first, the statues moved as they had elsewhere, but on 18 August, Tom Cliffe and Barry Buckley (twelve and eleven respectively) began to report talking apparitions to large crowds. The themes of prayer, catastrophe, and the danger from the Devil resembled those at Inchigeela, but were articulated quite differently. The boys saw biblical visions, such as the Flood and the Passion, which heightened the apocalyptic mood of the messages; apparitions of Christ and Satan occurred along with those of Mary. The world had ten years to mend its ways: prayer and the Mass were central to this endeavour. The Church was in peril: 'If the world does not improve the Devil will take over the Church.' Ireland was important: 'I love the Irish people . . . I am praying with the people to God, to forgive the Irish people . . . I want the Irish people to spread my message to the world . . . God is pleased with Ireland. Ireland will be saved' (Deevy 1990). The Melleray case was much shorter and more intense than the visions of Inchigeela; Melleray's grotto, like Inchigeela's, has a stream that was considered especially blessed by Mary and became the source of holy water. In the same way as Inchigeela, a committee was set up to ensure that only the messages and visionaries they considered authentic remained in the published story of the apparitions. Zimdars-Swartz (1989) has documented the work of this committee as an example of the way in which educated Catholics edit the many sensational messages that emerge during an apparition event.

The apparitions at Carns followed the others on 2 September 1985 (the promotional booklet is by Curry 1987). Like those at Melleray, the main phase of the visionary period lasted for a limited period, about nine days. The visionaries comprised four girls in their early teens: Patricia, Colleen, and Mary McGuinness (two sisters and a cousin), and Mary Hanley. The messages were limited to 'Faith and Hope', although visions of Mary, stars, St Bernadette, Christ, the Sacred Heart, and the Cross appeared in the clouds in the night sky. No shrine existed at Carns before these visions, but one was constructed at the edge of a farmer's field. Carns' most famous visionary is Christina Gallagher, although she is not associated specifically with the site: all but the first of her visionary experiences have occurred elsewhere. On visiting the site during September 1985, however, she reported a powerful experience of the Passion of Christ.

SOCIAL INTERPRETATIONS OF THE VISIONARY PHENOMENA

What were the triggers for the moving statues and apparitions? There were many attempts to explain them. One popular notion among the sceptical was that they represented a hysterical response to bad weather and a consequent poor harvest (in, for example, the *Sligo Champion*, which published reports on Carns). People in Ireland in 1985 were extremely concerned about the threat of an impending rural crisis; a bad harvest in Ireland triggers painful cultural memories of the nineteenth-century famines. At Melleray, one question to the apparition concerned the harvest and the answer was that people should pray for an improvement in the weather. The bad weather theory went on to speculate that it also caused summer boredom, leading to increased pilgrimage whenever there was a report of a moving statue. This could not have been a key factor in the origin of the widespread moving statues as they began in February, and so it could only explain the intensifying of the phenomenon in July. Yet the national context does show a heightened anxiety over the rural economy and its social structure at this time. Rural and agricultural life had been an intrinsic part of the national identity of the Republic, but government policy in 1984 had prioritized urban development over previous trends (Hoggart, Buller, and Black 1995: 39, 162). The hallmarks of modernization in Europe, industrialization and urbanization, had come relatively late to Ireland, and the 1980s were generally regarded as an era of rapid social change (as debated in Fahey 1994; Hornsby-Smith 1994). Many problems encountered in the Irish Republic were similar to those in Britain during the same period: unemployment, uncertainty over job tenure, greater power for multinational companies, drug abuse, and high crime rates. This was coupled with an apparent breakdown in the traditional rural social fabric, with many young people migrating to the cities (Hoggart, Buller, and Black 1995: 48, 188–9; Corish 1996).

A second and associated reason for public anxiety can be located in the national moral crisis. The mores of the Catholic Church and what Tom Inglis (1987) calls its 'moral monopoly' had been challenged since the 1960s and the 1980s saw a deepening of the process. The alliance between Church and Irish state, a legacy of the common struggle against British colonialism, was beginning to weaken during this period. The abortion and divorce referenda, in 1983 and 1986 respectively, were won by the conservative lobby, but only after a bitter battle and a low poll turnout (Inglis 1987: 80–9). Contraceptives had been available in clinics from 1979, and in 1985 they began to be sold over the counter after a liberalization of the law (Ardagh 1995: 178–86). The falling birth rate and higher incidence of births outside marriage supported the notion that views on sex and marriage were changing (Corish 1996: 149). Surveys suggested that the Church's views on sexual morality and family life were no longer held in generally high esteem and that people looked to the Church for 'spiritual' rather than moral needs (Whelan and Fahey 1996: 110–11). Church attendance figures, although very high, were at their lowest among young urban dwellers and the unemployed, suggesting problems for the Church in the future (Hornsby-Smith and Whelan 1994). The number of surveys of church-going practice undertaken in the post-1960 period betrays an anxiety in Ireland about the vitality and long-term durability of the Catholic tradition.

The modernizing lobby, with its centre in Dublin and voice in much of the Irish national media, promoted a pro-European nationalism favoured by the majority of the nation (Hoggart, Buller, and Black 1995: 14). Between Ireland's entry into the European Community in 1973 and the recession of 2008, the country prospered economically and also accepted modernizing laws in accordance with the EC's policies on human rights, for example on equal opportunity in jobs and wages, which had an important influence on gender roles in Ireland and contradicted traditional Catholic perspectives on the complementary roles of the sexes (Ardagh 1995: 201–6). The liberal non-ecclesiastical establishment in Ireland largely held a position respectful of national cultural and spiritual heritage, yet which was also clearly European in outlook with the accent on human rights and social action.

The accession of the charismatic John Paul II as pope in 1978 had fostered hopes of a dramatic resurgence of Catholicism and his visit to Ireland in 1979, the centenary of the Knock apparition, drew millions to open-air Masses. Nevertheless, in 1990, the Channel 4 television documentary *The Whole World in His Hands* questioned whether the visit of eleven years earlier had represented a wake for Irish Catholicism rather than its renewal. By 1985, it would have been increasingly apparent in Ireland that the pope's visit had not reversed the trend of social and religious change that was painful for the Church. The period of John Paul II's papacy was one in which the battle for the survival of what was perceived to be traditional Catholic culture often inspired mass pilgrimages at Marian shrines; in Ireland, this centred primarily on Knock. None of the new apparition shrines came anywhere near to rivalling Knock; their appeal remained relatively small-scale and they were all but abandoned by the clergy except where priests quietly and privately accepted the role of spiritual advisors to the visionaries. Those priests who supported the cults openly, such as Father Gerard McGinnity, were soon ostracized. The clergy as a whole angered the visionaries by their indifference or opposition.

The moving statues and visions gave rise to much public debate in Ireland over the Catholic heritage of the nation and its future. The visionaries and their devotees, like many elsewhere in Europe mentioned in this book, fall into an older European pattern of claims to a divine mandate, which legitimizes a 'traditional' Catholic identity in the face of secularizing and liberal movements. When the moving statues became apparitions with messages in August 1985, the references to a nation in danger were not slow in coming; the visionary cults conceived an Ireland which was in danger of losing its heritage. The children's messages contained references to the Devil trying to take over the world or the Church, and the anger and sadness of God. There was a moral warning at Inchigeela against the youth using their bodies as instruments of pleasure. However, the messages tackling issues such as abortion and divorce came with the adult visionaries.

CLERICAL PERSPECTIVES

The Catholic priestly hierarchy, although they might have shared some of the moral and doctrinal presuppositions of the visionaries, form a separate interest group in the apparition debate. Elsewhere in the modern period, Catholic bishops have had a two-pronged strategy towards Marian apparitions. They select a few cases that conform to certain rules of orthodoxy and Church discipline, and promote them into mainstream Catholic devotional practice. In doing so, they harness popular religion in the interests of maintaining the Catholic community and its belief system amid the rapid social changes of modernity. However, they have regarded the great majority of cases as an embarrassment to the Church's reputation in the struggle for credibility. The visionaries, unless they can be relied on and managed like those at Lourdes and Fátima, can easily become an alternative source of authority, even if deferring to the hierarchy in matters of doctrine and morality. The Irish hierarchy's enactment of the first part of this strategy has been to maintain the national shrine status of Knock (even Knock took over fifty years to achieve official recognition). Other cases have therefore been ignored or condemned by Irish bishops, in line with the second part of the strategy.

The Irish bishops promulgated a conservative Catholic agenda with some consistency in the twentieth century (Ardagh 1995: 157–78), but they did not allow an enthusiastic lay visionary movement to act as a mouthpiece for it. Thus Bishop Murphy of Cork, faced with large numbers at Ballinspittle and Inchigeela in his diocese, refused to sanction the reports of the miraculous. He was initially cautious but not unsupportive: 'Direct supernatural intervention is a very rare happening in life . . . I understand that crowds are gathering there [Ballinspittle] in a great spirit of prayer. This is certainly a praiseworthy thing' (30 July 1985, statement issued by the Diocesan Office, Cork). But, within a year, he was a firm opponent of the continuing visions:

> The very multiplication of alleged apparitions in recent times is in itself a strong indication that they lack credibility. God does not display his power in such ways. To portray Our Lady as giving an endless stream of messages, some of which border on the absurd, is another indication of unreliability. (Cork Diocese: 19 August 1986)

He interpreted the moving statues and visions as compensation for the loss of traditional devotions consequent on the reforms of Vatican II. Other bishops have followed a similar pastoral policy. The dioceses of Killala (for Carns) and Waterford (for Melleray) adopted a policy of playing down the apparitions, although an annual Mass was eventually allowed at Carns. Bishop Brendan Comiskey of Ferns recorded his scepticism in writing (Comiskey 1989). The hierarchical view, therefore, holds to a conservative understanding of Catholic teaching, stressing the traditional moral order. Yet they reject the alternative voice of the visionaries who wish to articulate this same view in a more apocalyptic way, stressing personal mystical experience and urgency over the slow-moving priestly authority and cyclical liturgy of the Church institution.

Some commentaries on the moving statues and visions offered alternative theories. Peadar Kirby, echoing points already made in his book *Is Irish Catholicism Dying?* (1984), felt that the institutional Church, in its anxiety to stress the conservative moral position of the Vatican, was missing the opportunity to tackle the increasing social malaise of the nation: poverty, unemployment, and economic injustice. This was provoking people to seek spiritual fulfilment outside the institution, but in an inappropriate way:

> Few could honestly describe the moving statues or right to life campaign as wholesome features of contemporary Irish life...however adequate [they] may have been to the traditional closed and predominantly rural society of twenty years ago, the sacramental and devotional rhythms of traditional Irish Catholicism offer few resources to help Irish people develop a spirituality adequate to the challenges and needs of today's more urban, youthful, and consumerist society. (Kirby 1986: 174)

Joseph O'Leary was a priest who did not rate the moving statues and visionary phenomena, seeing them as unreflective, superstitious, idolatrous, and conservative, but at the same time conceded that they contained an important message. Therefore, he argued that they had *implicit* value, representing a people's Church, non-institutionalized pilgrimage, visionary imagination, simple faith, and a spiritual heritage resisting the secularization of Irish culture (O'Leary 1986).

Some years later, Andrew Greeley, an American Catholic priest and writer, articulated the liberal view in Irish Catholicism that the Church needed to abandon its focus on sexual morality and emphasize instead spirituality (Greeley 1994: 137–8, 142). This reasserted the Church's role as source and symbol of a national spiritual heritage without accepting the conservative agenda. In a similar vein, Michael Drumm (1996) suggested that the interest in outdoor statues, shrines, and grottoes represented in part a rediscovery of the Celtic spirituality of pre-famine Ireland: not so puritan on sexual matters, but with a love of the outdoors, worshipping God in nature, harvest festivals, and sacred places. The liberal priests, like the conservatives, were seeking an Irish Catholic national identity against secularizing trends. However, in contrast, they argued for a forward-looking Irish Catholicism with its almost unique opportunity to combine social reform, national identity, and a spiritual tradition based on gospel values. For them, the moving statues and apparitions were ephemeral phenomena, symptoms of a need to rediscover an underlying spiritual heritage rather than the beginning of a mass movement. The visions of 1985 feature in the liberal argument as an elusive one-off event pointing the Church back to its Celtic spiritual resources. These views have to contend with the fact that with the subsidence of the popular phenomena of 1985–7, the shrines were often left in the hands of traditionalists with moral and religious agendas not in agreement with the liberal approaches.

THE MEDIA VIEWPOINT

Television, radio, and newspapers, national and local, played their part in the promotion of the Marian fervour of 1985. Tom Inglis traced the decline of the Church's 'moral monopoly' in the Republic of Ireland to the advent of television in the 1960s, when hitherto taboo topics began to be discussed: 'It was the media, and in particular television, that brought a constant advocacy for an individualist, consumerist, sexualized, urban lifestyle that broke the unquestioning "respect for the cloth", and has forced the Church into giving a public account of itself' (Inglis 1987: 94). The media was often experienced by conservative Catholicism as antagonistic (Ardagh 1995: 163); the visionary Mary Casey, probably inspired by Medjugorje's message to this effect, said that her experiences had led her to discard the family television set. In the 1980s and 1990s, the media exposed many uncomfortable facts that put the Church and its teaching in a bad light. The visions of 1985 came in the wake of the contraception and abortion debates which had culminated in widespread publicity surrounding two tragedies: the death of two illegitimate babies in County Kerry under suspicious circumstances (McCafferty 1985: 53–8; Allen 2000: 332–40), and also the death of a fifteen-year-old mother and her baby in County Longford while trying to give birth in secret (Ardagh 1995: 181–2; Allen 2000: 330–2). In the 1990s, this exposure continued with several stories of sexual misdemeanour and, more seriously, child abuse by priests and members of religious orders, leading to the criticism of the Church in the Irish government's commission of inquiry into child abuse, which reported in 2009.

The media encouraged the interest in moving statues in 1985, as the phenomena made a good story and provoked a national debate on the role of religion in the nation's culture. Some journalists agreed with the press secretary of the government information services in his view that 'three quarters of the country is laughing heartily' at the events in Ballinspittle. It is true that the moving statues were the butt of jokes in Ireland, on the chat shows and in the papers (Ryan and Kirakowski 1985: 69); nevertheless, many of the reports were sensitive when recounting people's experiences and refrained from prejudging the events. Despite this, the media interest proved uncomfortable for the ecclesiastical establishment. Some journalists were sceptical and aired anticlerical views and, while some seemed to be moved, it was by the sheer mass of people at the shrines rather than any conversion experience. Others called for the Church to initiate a scientific examination. For example, the *Cork Examiner* (25 September 1985) asked whether the Church was avoiding a scientific observation of Ballinspittle because it wanted to encourage the devotion that resulted from the moving statue. Instead, it was University College Cork which responded to the call for an investigation by sending a team of psychologists to Ballinspittle, who concluded that the events represented not a hallucination but a 'visual effect' (Ryan and Kirakowski 1985: 45–56). The sceptical Church hierarchy were probably happy with this answer. Nevertheless, in some cases journalists seized on the opportunity to attack the Church, for example Eamonn McCann: 'There are many thousands of people in Ireland who desperately want to believe in supernatural signs. Times are, indeed, perplexing. Many things which Irish Catholics have been taught by the Church to believe under pain of mortal sin have been shown to be nonsense' (McCann 1985: 35). He listed teaching on contraception, divorce, and abortion in this category.

AFTER THE 1980S

In the years that followed the heyday of the shrines in the mid-1980s, two divergent views were held by local people on the subject of the visions. On the one hand, there was a general sense of relief that things had quietened down. Many people regarded the phenomena as curiosities or even embarrassments from the past. This was the attitude of many clergy, both parish priests in the locality of the shrines and officials in dioceses. On the other hand, there were people for whom the apparitions still had considerable importance, and they maintained the shrines and promoted their messages. They felt that the Irish people in general had not listened to the warnings of the Madonna, and they found evidence in the accelerated decline in church attendance and Catholic practice throughout the 1990s (see Corish 1996; Kenny 2000: 295–309). Thus, at Melleray, the view of shrine-keepers interviewed in July 1997 was that the visionary warning—ten years for people to improve their moral and prayer lives—had been unheeded, the opportunity had been lost, and serious consequences may follow. Further liberalization by government via referendum— divorce was legalized in 1995 (and same-sex marriage at the time of writing in

2015)—along with continued decline in allegiance to the Church in the 1990s, provoked the visionary Christina Gallagher to issue intensified calls for a renewal of conservative Catholicism. Most shrines displayed notices calling on people to support the traditional Church line on abortion, divorce, family life, and contraception. The holy well at Ballinacoola near Ferns, County Wexford, is a good example. A schoolgirl, Joanne Farrell, had visions there in the late 1980s. In 1999, the well was surrounded by placards, such as one that read: 'No power on earth, Church or State, has a mandate to change the laws of God under any circumstances: abortion, euthanasia, divorce . . .'.

The shrine devotees continued to circulate reports of healings and arranged gatherings at the shrines for regular devotional practices, the rosary and the Divine Mercy prayers of St Faustina being the most common forms; Padre Pio has also been a favourite saint, invoked in intercessory prayer. In 1997, Father Halloran, at that time a priest in the parish in which Carns is situated, said that older devotions such as the rosary, processions, and Marian hymns were important at the shrines because they no longer took place in the local parishes. This, of course, represented a sign of the weakening of the popularity of such devotions: one had to travel to special places to participate in them. There were still occasional reports of new miracles (e.g. a claimed bleeding statue in County Wexford that attracted the attention of British television in the early 1990s).

After the enthusiastic pilgrimages of the mid-1980s, other visionaries emerged including the Considine sisters, Judy and Sally Ann. From 1988, they reported visions in their hometown of Mayfield in Cork, then at Grantstown, County Wexford, and later Tipperary; their visions are summarized in the leaflet *Our Blessed Mother Speaks to Her Children* (see also Allen 2000: 312–15). The apparition phenomenon also spread to Northern Ireland from where pilgrims normally travelled to the shrines in the Republic. At Bessbrook, a village divided into Protestant and Catholic halves in County Armagh, two adult visionaries, Beulah Lynch and Mark Treanor, reported visions in 1987 and 1988. The content of their messages (to be found in the leaflet *Messages Conveyed by Our Lady during Apparitions at the Grotto in Bessbrook Chapel during the Summer of 1987*) was similar to earlier cases and echoed Medjugorje. The parish at Bessbrook was given the opportunity by the diocesan authorities to investigate the case and concluded a negative verdict on the apparitions; nevertheless, pilgrims continued to arrive for some years. This was partly due to the influence of Father Gerard McGinnity, a former Maynooth lecturer, who had become a fervent supporter of apparitions since visiting Medjugorje in the early 1980s. McGinnity championed the messages from a variety of locations in Ireland and acted as a commentator and theologian. He did not share the Church's caution and reserve, nor its concern to discern the worth of the visions on an individual basis, but seemed to accept most if not all of the cases that came to his attention (as demonstrated in his talk on cassette tape, *Marian Times in Ireland*). Thus McGinnity was asked to stay away from Bessbrook, and did so, but not before raising its profile.

McGinnity's major and most controversial contribution to the visionary movement, however, was his role as 'spiritual director' to Christina Gallagher of County Mayo. Gallagher became the most famous of Ireland's post-1985 visionaries (her messages are promoted in Vincent 1992; Petrisko 1995; McGinnity and Gallagher 1996; a leaflet, *Our Lady Queen of Peace House of Prayer: Four Testimonies*, 2001, is available at her shrine). She was a pilgrim to Carns in the early days, having had her first extraordinary experience there in 1985, a vision of Christ suffering on the Cross. Her apparitions of Mary began in earnest in 1988 in Dublin, and have inspired international interest, particularly in the United States and the Philippines. She was able to raise money to found, in 1993, the 'Our Lady Queen of Peace House of Prayer' on Achill Island, a place of remoteness, mountains, and beauty with holiday facilities, therefore a good choice for a pilgrimage site. Like her counterparts elsewhere, Christina's visionary messages continue to convince people of divine displeasure in the face of which the threat of future catastrophe could only be alleviated by prayer and devotional practices along with a strict morality.

There are several charismatic faculties claimed for Christina Gallagher. She is a visionary, but also a stigmatist: photographs are available showing the marks and blood on her head, hands, and feet. In addition, she claims a vocation of suffering (in the tradition discussed in Chapter 5 within this volume), i.e. suffering for the sins of others and sharing in Christ's passion. Furthermore, she is supposed to have the gifts of healing and 'infused knowledge' or 'knowing souls', being able to read the lives, hearts, and memories of those who consult her, especially priests. Gallagher reports seeing and hearing many supernatural figures in her visions: angels, saints, Jesus, and the words of God the Father. Yet she follows the typical modern pattern in claiming that Mary is the central person in the visions and author of most of the messages. Gallagher's Mary is a Medjugorje-style Madonna in an Irish context. Like others (Mary Casey and the Considine sisters), many of her visionary phrases ('my/dear children', 'Queen of Peace') are echoes of Medjugorje, and the messages of all these adult seers refer explicitly to Medjugorje at some point. There are calls to traditional Catholic practices (Mass, confession, fasting, prayer, especially the rosary), to a peaceful heart, and to the conversion of 'sinners'. There is also a concern for priests, for an alleged loss of strong faith and moral fibre among them, and recommendations as to the role that visionaries might play in supporting them spiritually. The pope is held in special concern; while he is above the suspicion that Christina has of the fidelity of the priesthood, he will nevertheless suffer the consequences of the general decline in Catholic faith. Satan is particularly strong at the present time, which is a time of darkness and evil. Thus God will be forced to punish humankind and the messages are full of apocalyptic warnings and indications that natural disasters are part of a build-up to a God-given catastrophe in the near future (with many references to the Book of Revelation): 'The time of God's justice has now begun, and this can be seen from the countless calamities and disasters, involving millions of people, across the globe. Strangely many of these seemed to go almost unreported' (*Four Testimonies*, p. 16). These are familiar themes. The Irish messages, however, are unique in their mention of Mary's concern for their mother country and its special place in her plan (which, for Gallagher, it might not fulfil unless the Irish return to prayer); Gallagher's list of Mary's concerns includes issues that dominated Irish debate in the late twentieth century such as sexual libertarianism, abortion, and in-vitro fertilization.

Gallagher's fame began in 1990 when she was featured on Irish television in a programme on the bleeding statue of Akita, Japan. The Akita story, like many twentieth-century visions, also includes the central theme of a coming chastisement. Another link to previous apparitions is Gallagher's revelation of a new medal, known as the 'Matrix Medal'. It is similar to its famous French predecessor, the Miraculous Medal, but its hearts of Mary and Jesus bleed, and the image of Mary is not the familiar standing figure from whom rays of grace sweep down upon the earth, but a Mary kneeling and pleading before the Cross for her wayward children (another Medjugorje image). Thus Gallagher's medal, while functioning as a healing and protective talisman like those before it, illustrates her emphasis on urgency in the face of a coming chastisement. Another link to previous apparitions is Gallagher's claim to have had a vision of hell, recalling Lúcia dos Santos, and to have received a miraculous host given by an angel and visible to onlookers, repeating the experience of Conchita González.

The House of Prayer (<http://www.christinagallagher.org>, accessed 31 May 2015) has a chapel, bookshop, café, and outdoor gathering area which accommodates a couple of hundred or so pilgrims thronging at weekends when Gallagher and McGinnity are present; the visionary blesses the crowd and receives people with particular problems and illnesses (visit, 2001). They mostly come from Ireland, north and south, but there are also some from England, Europe, and the United States (their presence is very helpful to Achill's bed-and-breakfast trade). There are, of course, many home and overseas outlets for books, medals, images, and information by newsletter or Internet, and so the supporters probably number several thousand.

This work began with episcopal blessing: the archbishop of Tuam, Joseph Cassidy, formally opened the house on 16 July 1993 (Feast of Our Lady of Carmel). However, a new archbishop, Michael Neary, and a commission of enquiry constituted in 1996 changed the mood from cautious encouragement to a greater reserve and distance. It followed the usual pattern in its search for positive criteria: orthodoxy of messages and practices; good character and behaviour of visionaries and significant supporters; 'spiritual fruits' (usually, strength of prayer and devotion of a large number of pilgrims); and evidence that the phenomena may be supernatural in origin. The decisions of the committee were made known in a statement on 16 December 1997. The orthodoxy of Christina Gallagher and her collaborators was not questioned, and the spiritual fruits acknowledged. However, the archbishop noted that: 'No evidence has been presented which might prove beyond reasonable doubt the occurrence of supernatural phenomena of whatever kind in this situation other than faith' (statement issued by the archbishop of Tuam, available from the Diocesan Office and also published in the *Irish Catholic*, 8 January 1998). This non-committal statement is not necessarily negative and this middle way between approval and disapproval has been chosen before, most notably by the National Conference of Yugoslav Bishops considering Medjugorje.

Yet Neary followed this by concern that the House of Prayer be more fully integrated into the life of the local parish. Its work had, in his view, 'drifted' from the original understanding between Archbishop Cassidy and Christina Gallagher (it had been intended as a place of 'adoration of the Blessed Sacrament, the recitation of the Rosary and the provision and maintenance of a place of spiritual retreat for priests'). Therefore the house was reined in more tightly under the jurisdiction of the diocese and incorporated more clearly into the parish structure. Only the priests of the local parish could celebrate the sacraments at the house's chapel and occasional others with the express permission of the archbishop. The use of funds was also implicitly questioned by being put under a tighter diocesan control and accounts would have to be regularly submitted. The house would be re-established as a 'private association', thus distancing it from the work of the archdiocese.

Ireland has established traditional shrines that attract visitors from home and abroad (Knock, Croagh Patrick, Lough Derg). Yet in the 1980s, the national context, with its many parallels in other European Catholic countries and the influence of Medjugorje, inspired a rush of new shrines, some at pre-existing grottoes. Gallagher's Our Lady Queen of Peace House of Prayer on Achill is the most visited survivor of these shrines in Ireland perhaps along with the grottoes at Inchigeela and Melleray. It has become a place of international interest, but only for those attracted by the popular formula of apocalyptic visions that warn of chastisements and promise miracles. These are common around the globe and such revelations are compelling because they provide divine encouragement (peace and reconciliation with God as the reward for prayer and moral correctness) at the same time as declaring divine displeasure (chastisement and disaster if the world continues to sin). These basic themes are set in an enticing package of secrets, special devotions, and sacred places. With modern global communications and the opportunity for air travel, this formula is renewed and repeated in many different locations where there is a Catholic population.

15

The 1980s

Italy, Spain, France, and England

ITALY IN THE 1980s

In Italy, apparitions continued throughout the twentieth century. One of the most well-known cases of Marian phenomena involved an Italian priest, Stefan Gobbi, whose locutions of Mary began in Fátima in 1972, and continued until 1992 (he died in 2011). He founded the Marian Movement of Priests in Como and published the messages for a wide and eventually global readership, claiming that Mary was encouraging priests to pray constantly, to remain faithful to Rome, to avoid modern temptations such as television, and to consecrate themselves to the Immaculate Heart. Laurentin and Sbalchiero (2007: 1131) state that the movement worldwide included 400 bishops, more than 10,000 priests, and many thousands of the laity. While reports of apparitions in Italy tended to decline towards the end of the century, website lists show a temporary increase in the 1980s. Italy is also the country that generated the most support for Medjugorje in the 1980s, being a near neighbour of Yugoslavia by road or ferry. Therefore, Italy in the 1980s continued to be a Marian apparition 'hot spot'.

The socio-political turmoil that often underlay the context of apparitions earlier in the twentieth century is seemingly absent in the Italy of the 1980s. The state of Italy in that decade resembled that of many other Western European nations: decline in agricultural employment and heavy industry but growth among the urban middle classes; increasing wealth (more so in the north) but also the presence of a large underclass dependent on benefits; a trend towards the nuclear family and away from the extended family; women more likely to be in employment than staying in the home (again, not so evident in the south); growth in educational achievement and large reductions in illiteracy; social association based on volunteering, clubs, and self-help rather than collective political action (Ginsborg 1990: 406–18). Italy after the economic boom of the 1960s gradually adopted an American model of traditional family values allied to democracy and consumer capitalism (Ginsborg 1990: 424–5). So what in all this might cause some controversy amongst the Catholic community, given the Church's own favouring of American foreign policy in the Cold War in the 1980s after the accession of Pope John Paul II? The answer must be the same as elsewhere in Western Europe, dominated as it was by the American economy after the Second World War. The American model, despite the prominence of 'family values', promotes a liberalism that allows for alternative lifestyles and choices in areas of life such as the role of women, sexuality, and faith. In Italy, church attendance was between 60 and 70 per cent in the 1950s, but dropped to a steady 35 per cent after 1970 (Ginsborg 1990: 434), a figure better than many other European nations but of concern to a nation such as Italy that regarded itself as the home of Catholicism. This in itself provides the context for apparitions in otherwise relatively stable times and places.

Like those in Ireland, the two most famous Italian apparitions of the 1980s both began in 1985 and were influenced by Medjugorje. In Schio, a town on the edge of the Dolomites north of Vicenza, the seer Renate Baron was an engineer, town councillor, and Marian devotee. He had rescued a statue of Our Lady of the Rosary from a corner of a sacristy when aged nineteen; while kneeling before this same statue in the church of San Martino in Aste on the outskirts of Schio on 25 March 1985, now aged fifty-one, he experienced his first apparition as the statue came to life (according to the promotional account in Association Opera dell' Amore n.d.). He was later to describe how the Child remained a statue while the Madonna moved and spoke; the Child only came alive at a later date when Eucharistic Hosts were placed in the church in a new tabernacle. The Madonna described herself as the *Regina dell' Amore* ('Queen of Love'). Her messages followed similar themes to those at Medjugorje: return to God (conversion), the Eucharist, love of neighbour, prayer and fasting, and consecration to Mary (Association Opera dell' Amore n.d.: 28–33). Laurentin and Sbalchiero (2007: 1318) mention some apocalyptic messages. Along with the apparitions, there were stories of miraculous perfume and a weeping statue of the infant Jesus, which increased interest in the shrine.

The apparitions led Baron to found the *Association Opera dell' Amore* ('Association for Works of Love') and the Cenacle, a community of men devoted to prayer based in a villa near the church of San Martino. Financial support allowed Baron and his supporters to buy a large area of land near San Martino, which is now the site of a Way of the Cross winding up a hillside, a new church, and gardens that include chapels, statues, and plaques. All this exists despite the lack of approval from the local diocese in Vicenza which, after the arrival of a new bishop in 1988, laid prohibitions on the cult (Laurentin and Sbalchiero 2007: 1317–18). Nevertheless, pilgrims arrive from several countries. The association states that it is recognized by local government, has successfully refuted accusations of financial mismanagement, and that several members are involved in missions in Brazil, Kenya, and Russia (Association Opera dell' Amore n.d.: 49–61). Renato Baron's death in 2004 did not result in the cessation of activity or the waning of interest in the shrine at Aste. The esteem in which he is held is rare for a lay male visionary in twentieth-century Europe.

The case of Oliveto Citra in Campania, near Salerno, is well documented in an anthropological study by Paolo Apolito (1998). The apparitions began on 24 May 1985, when a group of boys aged between eight and twelve claimed to have seen the Madonna near the ruined castle in the village, after they heard the crying of a baby. They summoned a young woman, Antia Rio, who continued to have visions afterwards in her house (Apolito 1998: 14–15; Laurentin and Sbalchiero 2007: 1251–2). The phenomenon then took on a collective aspect, with many seers and messages, ranging from those stressing peace and joy to others which had an apocalyptic edge. The priest was favourable, the bishop uncommitted, although he allowed the building of a small monument to mark the initial site of apparitions. Yet the episcopal commission of enquiry did not approve the visions. Laurentin (1991: 95) suggests that there were 'many apparitions, perhaps too many' at Oliveto Citra for the Church to be comfortable, although he applauds the role of the priest in cultivating the positive and orthodox elements of the phenomenon. Many pilgrims arrived in Oliveto Citra; Apolito records the way in which the clergy acted as instruments for the growth of popularity of the apparitions, even while the local diocese was maintaining reserve. The Vatican press agency as well as the secular press spread the news of Oliveto Citra in 1985; some priests (for example, the Jesuit Robert Faricy in *Maria in Mezzo a Noi: Le Apparizioni a Oliveto Citra*, 1986) wrote about the case, thus bringing it to wider attention and others encouraged interest and pilgrimage (Apolito 1998: 33–4).

Apolito, undertaking research on the site quite early in the events, presents an analysis of the human activity which, in his view, created the apparition as a public phenomenon in terms of dialogue, discussion, claim, and promulgation: 'The apparition, described by protagonists, witnesses, curious bystanders, and even critics as a visual event, was revealed in the analysis as predominantly an event of words' (Apolito 1998: 8). This discourse constituted the apparition's objectivity. This is not a simple case of children reporting a vision and others witnessing trance states: Oliveto Citra was unable to produce a central seer or group of seers with a compelling presence. The fragmentary nature of the apparition events was given coherence by the discussion amongst the community leaders, even where they were critical, as they gathered the various accounts together into a single narrative:

> The phenomenon would not have taken hold if all had depended on the credibility of the children. Even when the children were, at first, taken seriously, few

people believed in the apparition of the Madonna... in spite of their claim to have withheld judgement, the main community leaders contributed decisively to the transformation of the visions from a subjective experience to objective events. (Apolito 1998: 8–9)

The parish priest was decisive in limiting the reputation of the seers because of their unreliability, thereby placing the importance of the visionary event as a whole above any particular visionary; he took control by deciding what in the visions could be accepted from an orthodox point of view and what could not. Thus the edited narrative took on an authority separate from those who had originally reported it. The interest in the visions by leaders also attracted pilgrims, whose piety was then interpreted as a sign of the authenticity of the visions (Apolito 1998: 9). In this way, Apolito argues for the circularity of the apparition phenomenon, a theory that can be posited for other cases; the process of investigation and authoritative control, rather than the visions themselves, created a description of an event which was then convincing to believers.

Medjugorje was inevitably in the background of most apparition events occurring in Italy in the mid-1980s, as was the cult of Padre Pio. The Medjugorje messages were distributed amongst Oliveto's pilgrims and Medjugorje supporters also travelled to Oliveto Citra. As at Medjugorje, Oliveto's visionaries announced that the Virgin's birthday, traditionally celebrated on 8 September, was actually 5 August. However, Medjugorje's Franciscan-inspired sacramental spirituality provided the exemplar for a modern apparition shrine, and this cast some doubts on the activities of some pilgrims at Oliveto Citra, particularly those who were thought to have come from Naples, the 'Neapolitans' (Apolito 1998: 31–2). The expressive devotion of this region, drawing from the shrine of Madonna dell' Arco near Naples, involved physical actions such as fainting, fitting, and exorcism. While this boosted the excitement in Oliveto Citra in the early days, comparisons with the quietness and peace of Medjugorje were made, and eventually the 'Neapolitan' style was discouraged, causing a reduction in pilgrims from the Naples region.

Apolito distinguishes between the social-anthropological aspect of the pilgrimage at Oliveto Citra and previous studies of peasant or folk religion (1998: 32–3). The committee included liberal professionals and a doctor, and among the various seers were a student, a 'bourgeois' housewife, and a white-collar worker. Therefore, unlike the folk religion studied in the 1950s and 1960s, Apolito points out that this was not a 'lower'-class phenomenon and that the role of the clergy and middle classes demonstrates this (Apolito 1998: 33). Apolito associates this with the 'international Catholic visionary culture' of recent times (1998: 33), but in fact most famous European Marian apparitions in the nineteenth and twentieth centuries enjoyed clerical and professional class support. At Lourdes, the origins of the phenomenon in peasant culture were soon superseded by the interest of the middle and upper classes and there was priestly support throughout, although this took time to spread from the lowest clerical rank (the curate) to the highest in the diocese (bishop). Across the range of Marian apparitions, Catholic societies, publications, and personalities are crucial to the fame and prestige of the case, whether or not the Church decides in favour.

Apolito's account is particularly interesting when he picks out features unsettling for most believers and hence edited out of the official account. Whereas the presence of the Devil is not unexpected at Marian sites where good and evil are in conflict, there are very many reports of apparitions of the Devil amongst Apolito's observations, and it is not always clear—unlike the narrative of doctrinal theology—that the Madonna will triumph over him (Apolito 1998: 166–76). There are also references to healing plants and the souls in purgatory, part of the folklore of the region, which did not reach the published materials (Apolito 1998: 62–3, 118, 239). Rather, Apolito sees the editing process at Oliveto Citra and in other modern apparitions as downplaying the cultural past in favour of a millenarian rupture in history that will bring discontinuity with the past and a new age through apocalyptic chastisement (Apolito 1998: 240).

Laurentin lists several other cases in Italy that began in the 1980s (Laurentin 1991: 100–5, 142–4, 177–89). Table 15.1 gives a sense of the scope and type of these cases, and the number which have some reference to Medjugorje as a template.

In the 1990s, there was another Medjugorje-inspired phenomenon at Civitavecchia, on the west coast near Rome (Laurentin and Sbalchiero 2007: 1077–8). There, a Medjugorje statue brought to Italy in 1994 appeared to weep tears of blood. The bishop of Civitavecchia-Tarquinia, Girolamo Grillo, took charge of the statue and placed it in his private chapel. An enquiry followed, and apparently the results confirmed human blood and ruled out both fraud and natural explanations. The statue was returned to the parish near Civitavecchia. However, not all the clergy were convinced, and the Congregation for the Doctrine of the Faith took the matter out of the hands of Monsignor Grillo, as he was now regarded as a chief witness. No pronouncement came from the Vatican, but the bishop declared his belief in the prodigy.

RECENT CASES NOT DERIVED FROM MEDJUGORJE

To conclude the main chapters of the book, there are a few prominent 1980s cases that do not derive from Medjugorje. They illustrate other streams in the Marian apparition tradition while being placed, like Medjugorje, in a 1980s

Table 15.1. Apparitions in 1980s Italy (as catalogued by Laurentin 1991 and Laurentin and Sbalchiero 2007)

Place	Dates	Brief details (age of visionary given for first apparition)	Laurentin and Sbalchiero reference (2007)*
Belluno	October 1985	Francesca Payer, 13; Medjugorje references ('Queen of Peace', 5 August as birthday of Mary)	1051, 1080–1
Belpasso, Catania (Sicily)	May 1986– May 1988	Rosario Toscano, 15; Medjugorje references ('Queen of Peace', secrets); chapel built with episcopal blessing	1051–3
Bisceglie, Puglia	June 1985	Roberto dell' Olio, 7	1059
Borgo Meduna, Pordenone	March 1987– March 1990	Rossana Salvadore, 11; love, prayer, conversion: as at Medjugorje the apparitions ceased except for one annually	1284–7
Casavatore, Naples	December 1985	Primary-school-aged children including Loredana Troncini, 10	1074
Crosia, Consenza-Bisignano	May 1987– April 1988	Vincenzo Fullone, 14 and Anna Blasi, 12; chapel restored with episcopal blessing, Medjugorje references (ten secrets, sun dances)	1084–5
Gargallo di Carpi, near Modena	December 1984–93	Gianni Varini and others, adults; small monument erected on farmland; episcopal rejection; Medjugorje reference ('Mother of Peace')	1127
Matera, Andria	October 1987–95	Locutions to Nicolina Taddonio, adult	1195
Pescara	1987–8	Maria Antonina Fioritti, adult, member of Medjugorje group; great sign foretold for 28 February 1988 leading to a large disappointed crowd (estimated 120,000)	1268
Sofferetti, Calabria	July 1985–92	Group of adults; Medgugorje references (conversion, secrets, Mary on cloud)	1330

(*where this contradicts the 1991 publication, the 2007 information is preferred)

context of conservative Catholic reaction to liberalism, immorality, and irreligion which, in the apparition narrative, will lead to divine punishment.

El Escorial, Spain

In Spain, Garabandal remained the dominant place of interest for apparition devotees after the 1960s, especially following the schism at Palmar de Troya. Spain emerged from the Franco regime in 1975 to a revived monarchy under which liberal democracy was instituted during a time of economic problems that lasted until the mid-1980s. The Church was concerned that a post-Franco era would bring a return to the Second Republic situation in which the Church was marginalized. The 1978 constitution therefore sought to reassure the Church that it was still integral to Spanish society, yet there was concern among the bishops about the advent of moral liberalism (Callahan 2012: 565–73): 'For the hierarchy of the 1980s and early 1990s, evident slippage in religious practice and the advance of sexual permissiveness signified a national moral crisis of disturbing proportions' (Callahan 2012: 575). Reflecting this, one notable case of visions emerged in the 1980s at El Escorial, the home of the royal palace near Madrid. El Escorial's visions predate Medjugorje, originating on 13 November 1980 to Luz Amparo Cuevas, a forty-nine-year-old mother of seven (Laurentin and Sbalchiero 2007: 1110–13). The event began in the traditional way: crowds gathered and the Church stated its cautious reserve, asking priests not to encourage the pilgrims. Mary is known at the shrine in El Escorial as Our Lady of Sorrows. Amparo seems to have had a troubled life: her mother died when she was six months old; she had had to make a living as a child merchant; and in 1980, her husband was unemployed, making it difficult to care for her children.

Amparo's Virgin asked for the building of a chapel and demanded conversion, prayer, and daily rosary. The world was on the precipice of disaster; thus Amparo continued the familiar themes of the twentieth century, present at Spanish shrines such as Ezkioga and Garabandal. Indeed, there are echoes of Fátima and Garabandal, such as the conversion of Russia and the danger of priests and bishops leading Catholics astray. To suffer for the sins of the world, Amparo received the stigmata. The visions appeared to be fruitful for her family: her eldest child became a doctor and her husband underwent a conversion experience, while Amparo continued to receive long messages on the first Saturday of each month. Eventually, there was some movement from the Church: in 1993, Cardinal Suquía Goicoechea of Madrid visited Amparo and celebrated Mass in her home in recognition of the fruits of her apparitions. In 1994, he recognized the association that she had inspired, whose three branches worked for the poor, for families, and for vocations, and appointing a chaplain. Despite some opposition from the town council, the chapel requested by Amparo was erected in 2000 and the shrine, known as Prado Nuevo ('New Meadow'), features an ash tree and spring. Amparo also inspired the opening of a seminary for priests dedicated to serving the abandoned elderly.

Amparo continued to experience visions until her death in 2012. She continued the tradition of other adult women visionaries as a victim soul. She has had more success with the official Church than Jeanne-Louise Ramonet; she persuaded the local diocese to give some recognition to the cult, like Ida Peerdeman, but not the apparitions, as with Bärbl Reuss. Just as Antonie Rädler achieved at Wigratzbad, Amparo's shrine, despite the relatively short period of its existence, has gained a seminary. Most importantly, the area has a new, popular, and active shrine that attracts international interest.

La Talaudière, France

France was known as the country of Marian miracles in the nineteenth century, but not in the twentieth. The apparitions at L'Île-Bouchard in the Centre in 1947 did achieve a measure of episcopal approval and an annual pilgrimage, but they certainly do not rival the shrines in Portugal, Belgium, Spain, and Bosnia-Herzegovina. In the 1980s, one apparition did come to the public's attention, at La Talaudière near St Étienne between October 1981 and May 1982, but all that remains some twenty-two years later is a shrine and chapel in the back garden of a local house, which still belongs to the visionary's family. There is little sign of pilgrimage. If anything, the case serves to reinforce the fact that France's nineteenth-century shrines remain dominant and that the age of great new visions in France is at an end. La Talaudière came too early to be a Medjugorje copy (although the problems caused by people staring at the sun at Medjugorje were repeated at La Talaudière). It stands rather as a pale replica of the apparitions at Lourdes and the images in the garden shrine are of Our Lady of Lourdes. The little shrine rather contrasts with its surrounding neighbourhood, an erstwhile mining community and industrially developed suburb on the outskirts of St Étienne.

Yves Chiron (2007: 322–3) includes La Talaudière among a group of visions that he refers to as 'false apparitions' or illusions. He cites as reasons the problems that the family were experiencing at the time of the apparitions: the death of children and the blinding of the father, a former miner, in an accident that led to him becoming an alcoholic. The visionary, the fourteen-year-old daughter Blandine Piégay, experienced frequent illness. The messages asked for prayer and repentance and prophesied future wars. The local bishop declined to open an enquiry, but published a notice prohibiting the cult and any collecting of funds, while declining to make a statement about the visions out of respect for the fragile health of the persons involved (see also Laurentin and Sbalchiero 2007: 1169).

La Talaudière is an example of a shrine made famous by press-generated interest, but the context and the personalities involved ensured that there was no lasting pilgrimage. Now it stands as an example of the way in which aspirations to build shrines can become localized. It is reminiscent of the vestiges of many cases in Belgium that attracted public attention for brief periods during the 1930s and are now largely neglected.

Surbiton, England

Despite a sizeable Catholic population, England is not renowned as a country of apparitions. Generally, apparitions thrive in homogeneous Catholic communities rather than those mixed with other denominations and faiths. In England the word 'apparition' is associated mostly with ghosts rather than with the Virgin Mary. Nevertheless, there are some isolated examples. While Sudbury in Suffolk is the site of a well-known Marian shrine, it was in neighbouring Middleton in Essex where visions were reported in the early 1930s (Halliday 2003). Several people, including the Anglican rector, Clive Luget, saw a ball of light travelling through the village on 11 December 1932. This may have been inspired by the apparitions at Beauraing, which were occurring during December 1932. Later, seven-year-old Francis Thornber had visions of the parish church as it had existed in medieval times and received some secret messages. People did come to Middleton as pilgrims; children and some adults, including clairvoyants and spiritualists, reported visions, but the parish church did not achieve the status of a shrine as interest declined. Luget seems to have been an eccentric figure, an Anglo-Catholic who turned more and more to the Latin Mass and who was eventually sidelined and retired. Other reports in England are notable for their sparseness and lack of impact. Lists include claims of miraculously blooming roses (Stockport, 1947) and a weeping statue (Newcastle, 1954).

While the 1980s saw social turmoil in England's cities and in its mining communities, with high levels of unemployment and cuts in social funding, this was not the context for the apparitions in Surbiton that began in 1983. As elsewhere in Catholic Europe in the 1980s, moral liberalism stands as the major contextual factor. Surbiton is a London suburb better known for the stereotypical stockbroker commuter than for Catholic visions, but there a forty-three-year-old mother of three, Patricia de Menezes, reported a vision of a child crucified (Laurentin and Sbalchiero 2007: 1177–8). This harrowing image became the motif for a campaign against abortion based on Patricia's visions, which include Marian apparitions. She founded the Community of Divine Innocence, which is still active (http://divine-innocence.org, accessed 31 May 2015); aborted babies were to be seen as martyrs. However, the Archdiocese of Southwark has issued a rebuttal of the visionary and her organization, having referred to the Congregation for the Doctrine of the Faith in Rome in 2007 for the following summary:

> There are four main areas of concern in the writings of Mrs Patricia De Menezes:
> 1. The exaggerated claims made for the Community of Divine Innocence.
> 2. The inappropriate words and phrases attributed to Jesus.
> 3. The questionable demand made concerning the status of aborted children.
> 4. The intemperate language used in the 'Inspirations' when attacking Church authority (<http://www.rcsouthwark.co.uk/statement_cdi_2.html>, accessed 31 May 2015).

This is a classic statement of the disagreement between official and popular religion. Visionaries claim that Christ or Mary is giving them sanction to found a shrine and a community of devotees, that their messages are innovative and crucial for the future life of the Church, and that the Church is in error when it refuses to listen to them. The Church, on the other hand, so often finds in these messages overstatement, misunderstanding of doctrine and tradition, or egocentricity.

Surbiton, like other cases, represents a reaction to liberalism; its distinctive feature is a focus on the availability of abortion, the issue that has become a byword in modern Catholicism for the moral degeneration of modernized societies. Indeed, the Soviet Union was the first European country to legalize it in 1920 and Nazi Germany allowed it in certain cases as part of its eugenics programme, providing more evidence for Catholics of its absolute depravity.

Generally, 1980s apparitions took place amidst growing conservative Catholic concern about the hegemony of liberal society, particularly with regard to the family, sexuality, and abortion. It drew on the prevailing tradition in which there was anticipation of divine judgement and punishment and a belief that an affluent society was the cause of human sin that could not be sustained into the future. Interestingly, the obvious scientific counterpart to this theology, that the demand on environmental resources can not be maintained, does not seem to have entered into the apparition tradition, except in the case of a marginal American visionary, Annie Kirkwood. In Ireland, Italy, and Spain there was increasing anxiety about the strength and role of the Church; its marginalization in recent history has not been under the direct assault of anticlerical republicanism, but is due to increasing pluralism, consumerism, and lifestyle choice of free-market capitalist societies. Another important aspect of liberal democracy, the free press, gave these apparition cults publicity but not gravity; visions, moving or bleeding statues, and stigmata make good stories, but often that is all they remain.

16

Conclusion

The last two centuries have seen rapid social change in Europe; all European countries have faced advancing secularization, either gradually through social developments or forcibly and rapidly through new forms of political power. In Catholicism, apparition cults express anxiety about developments that appear to be detrimental to traditional faith practice and lifestyle. European Catholics live either in countries that have been predominantly Catholic, or in regions that have been predominantly Catholic, such as western and southern Germany, or in nominally Protestant or Orthodox countries where Catholicism is a large minority. Marian apparitions are most influential in the first two of these. While European Catholics hold a wide range of views, and there are many liberals and radicals among them as well as conservatives, the Catholic subcommunities in which apparition cults have arisen are generally those that have resisted political, social, and moral change.

The most direct form of uncomfortable change is that in which Catholics experience persecution through legislative decisions about the status of Catholic organizations, or the role of Catholic teaching in schools, or when the public markers of national Catholic identity are suppressed, although in the twentieth century the direct violent anticlerical confrontations of the French Revolution have not been repeated on any appreciable scale. The Portuguese Republic of 1910–26, the Spanish Republic of 1931–6, the Third Reich in the mid-1930s, and the communist domination of Eastern Europe, either in the Soviet Union (especially Lithuania and Ukraine) or elsewhere after Soviet invasion in 1945, are all clear examples of the Catholic Church in conflict with government. This is not to say that all was harmonious between the priesthood and pro-Catholic governments, such as those under Salazar in Portugal, Franco in Spain, or governments led by Christian Democrats in Germany or Italy in the post-Second World War era. However, apparitions have been particularly prevalent in contexts where the Catholic Church regarded itself as being in a struggle for existence. Thus, the Portuguese Republic formed the context for Fátima, the Spanish Republic for Ezkioga, and Nazi persecution for many cases in Germany, whereas, in communist Eastern Europe, the suppression of Catholic gatherings and media meant that visions were reported but did not lead to large-scale pilgrimages. Thus it is no surprise that Medjugorje, arising towards the end of the communist era in the most west-facing of Eastern European societies, is the only prominent example.

Communism's innate hostility to Catholicism meant that, in the twentieth century, the countries where it was perceived as a substantial threat provided the most fertile soil for apparitions. The Fátima message became one of concern about Soviet Russia when communists were gaining ground in Spain where the visionary lived in a convent. Catholic Belgium in the 1930s perceived itself to face four perils: the growth of secularization, the increasing popularity of socialism, economic depression, and fear of the resurgence of Germany. Therefore, its apparition epidemic in 1933 can be understood in social historical terms. After the Second World War, many apparitions echoed the Fátima message because they originated in countries where communism had a real chance of power, primarily France and Italy. In post-war Germany, one third of the original country was under communism while West Germany was the country proximate to the Iron Curtain and would have been the first to succumb to Soviet invasion. It was also a country in post-war turmoil; hence Germany too saw many apparitions and cults in the period 1946–52. There was also the real threat of a new war, particularly acute in the late 1940s and early 1960s. In France, Jeanne-Louise Ramonet of Kerizinen worried about Russian invasion. In the Netherlands, Ida Peerdeman's visions display concern over the possibility of global conflict involving many nations.

The other great trial for traditional Catholicism arises from the social and moral change in liberal democracies. This has become the most enduring of the threatening contexts in which apparitions spring forth to issue their warnings and reassurances. America may have helped to liberate Western Europe from Nazism and communism, but it also spread its own doctrines of liberalism and consumerism. From the 1950s, visionaries across Europe began to articulate concerns about the effects of these. Garabandal and San Damiano have been interpreted as instances of Catholic resistance to Vatican II, but they are better read as responses to socio-economic change and the many upheavals it brings. Vatican II itself belongs to the context of liberalization and global awareness in the 1950s and 1960s, the catastrophic events of the first half of the century persuading churches and faiths to work together for justice and peace in an uncertain world where atheism or religious indifference was gaining ground in all societies. This general unease about the direction of humanity is the background for visions such as those at Medjugorje, which soon left behind its communist context; although this had caused international interest at first, it was never a concern of the messages of the *Gospa*. After Medjugorje, the many apparitions of the 1980s drew on its inspiration and continued its theme of the need for peace and faith in a divided world, following the example of Pope John Paul II. Visions were particularly prevalent in Ireland and Italy, countries with a strong Catholic heritage experiencing a decline in the power of the Church. However, after the 1980s, the desire for wholly new apparition cases seems to have waned in Europe, and the already existing cases have satisfied the desire for the miraculous, especially as many visionaries, such as those from Medjugorje, continue to claim apparitions that have lasted decades. In the 1990s, the United States became the country with most apparition reports, many of which follow the Medjugorje template.

Throughout the second half of the century, air travel facilitated pilgrims in reaching remote places. The wider availability of the camera opened the door to a whole new domain of the miraculous, as pilgrims found unexpected shapes and colours that they interpreted as indicating a supernatural presence. The Church liberalized Catholic communication after Vatican II, all of which helped visionary cults spread their message and gain new followers. Yet it was during the 1990s, due to the introduction of the Internet, that a revolution in the means of communication occurred. As a result, apparition news and messages are instantaneously available today; people can post their views on blogs and personal websites. The web community, as Apolito (2005) has shown, creates new modes of authority and power bases that subvert hierarchies and canonical ways of deciding on visions.

The twentieth century has also seen a shift in the locus of vision, the sign of Marian presence, from place to person. The idea that apparitions occur to charismatic people is not new; many famous saints such as Bridget of Sweden, Catherine of Siena, and Teresa of Avila experienced visions. However, for the general Catholic populace, it has been the *shrine* that is all important. Long after the time of the visionary, the resulting shrine still stands and the apparition story is just one aspect of the complex of sacred spaces and symbols that constitute the shrine as a holy site. Before the age of modern travel, the network of local and regional shrines was crucial in providing opportunities for people to visit a sacred space within reach of their homes; a new age arrived when thousands of Lourdes pilgrims used the railway to travel to the shrine over great distances. Bernadette of Lourdes and Lúcia of Fátima understood their role as secondary to the foundation of the shrine and the movement of pilgrims and devotees attached to it. However, Lúcia also contributed to the change from place to person by claiming later visions away from Fátima and putting the emphasis on secrets that only she could reveal. While most apparitions in the twentieth century continued the traditional importance of the location of visions, so that people travelled to shrines to enjoy the presence of Mary that they symbolize, Medjugorje's visionaries have initiated a different approach. While their home parish remains important and central, they experience visions wherever they go in the world and so pilgrims do not need necessarily to travel to Bosnia-Herzegovina. As a third alternative to places and people, sometimes statues transported from shrines, especially Fátima, have provided a secondary locus of presence, bringing the shrine to the believer rather than the other way round.

It is a standard principle in the Marian apparition cult that visionaries are ordinary people, not particularly worthy of the honour, chosen for divine reasons that may remain inscrutable. Yet those visionaries who succeed in focusing an apparition event on themselves, away from the cacophony of alternative visionaries usually present when apparitions occur, could hardly be described as ordinary. They are charismatic individuals, able to hold the attention of growing crowds, able to articulate a spiritual message in the face of unending questions, able to meet the challenge of scrutiny by both Church and state, able to retain their status over years of adulation, scepticism, and supervision by interested parties. Of course, the messages arise through a whole process of community interaction. Yet some visionaries achieve the fame and reputation that gives them independence as an authority in their own right, so that they articulate spiritual ideas that have influenced millions of Catholics, including all ranks of the clergy; hence they deserve the epithet 'popular theologian'. These have almost all been women in the modern period and, up to and including the twentieth century, the most prominent female contributor to the development of the Catholic devotional tradition has been the visionary. Her archetype, the Virgin Mary, is the supernatural figure most seen in popularized Catholic visions.

The evolving form of apparitions contrasts with comparative stability in the content of messages, which have precedents both in the Bible and in the Catholic tradition through the centuries. Mary is a mother figure who appears to people in order to console and reassure her children, and to remind them of the divine providence which is offered to humanity, but also to warn the world that global disaster is imminent when the divine gift is rebuffed through sin and indifference. There is a choice: deviation leading to punishment or joyous acceptance of the divine blessing; the current trajectory is the former of these. Like a Hebrew prophet, Mary brings not only good news, but also relays the threat of terrifying apocalyptic events in which God's judgement meets human sin head on. Even at Lourdes, the shrine known for quiet prayer and lack of apocalyptic fervour, the visionary stressed 'penitence'. Mary's presence, which is seen as a great blessing attracting pilgrims to the visionary sites, is therefore double-edged. In order to provide a future testimony to this presence, the vision asks for a shrine to be built, a small chapel at first which may, with the gathering crowds, be subsumed into an extensive sanctuary with basilicas, pilgrim hotels, and an array of shops and restaurants. It could be said that the relative comfort of the shrine facilities and the ease of travel there belie the underlying message: despite the emphasis on penance, modern pilgrims and devotees do not dress in sackcloth, follow the instructions of St Paul to do little else other than preach the Gospel and wait for the *parousia*, or retreat into the desert like the Essenes or St Antony. In other words, pilgrims use and enjoy the fruits of the modern world while condemning its dominant ideologies and lack of religious practice.

The term 'alternative history' has been used to emphasize the point that the narrative of sin and divine judgement, conveyed through the prophetic role of the Virgin Mary, is not simply a remnant of medieval theology, even though it may represent a continuation of that tradition. It is sincerely held by a considerably large number of modern people, living in the modern world in the same way as their contemporaries and holding a particular world view. Of course, this narrative is a metanarrative, an articulation of meaning and purpose that transcends the available data and remains parallel to social-historical analyses of cause, effect, and context. Where the Marian prophetic tradition occasionally follows other forms of apocalyptic—such as that of the Jehovah's Witnesses—in arguing that its claims of the imminence of divine judgement are evidenced by natural and social disasters currently occurring, it is at its weakest. If such events presage the Day of Wrath, one can point to even more terrible times in the past and ask why these did not climax in the great chastisement before now. Visionary prophecy is at its strongest when it eschews the attempt to find historical evidence, but stays with the medium of revelation as the sole source for its claims. This also allows the faith community to unify popular and intellectual theologies under a spectrum of interpretation, from the more literal understanding of the inevitability of divine chastisement (i.e. it will happen at such-and-such a date which will be revealed soon) to an eschatological one where the apocalypse occurs outside history (and expectations of a specific date are sublimated into a symbolic understanding).

The apparition and its shrine are the locus of supernatural presence, which is primarily that of the Virgin Mary; yet her presence signifies that Christ, the Holy Spirit, saints, angels (and the Devil too) are understood to exercise particular influence there. Catholicism, of course, stands at the opposite end of the Christian spectrum to radical Protestantism. While Catholics do not disagree with the Quaker mantra that God is everywhere, they also believe that there is clear relief between sacred and profane. The sacred is especially present in saints, liturgical acts, and also at shrines. Catholics hold the importance of pilgrimage in common with other religions and believe that the shrine provides a source of grace and a transformative energy that aids the pilgrim when returning home. In Catholicism, the maternal figure of Mary enjoys an association greater than any other with holy sites, places regarded as having been established by divine initiative.

Generally, the Church prefers the honouring and marking of the bare presence of the Virgin Mary to the messages of urgency that accompany the visions. For this reason, the twenty-first century will see a continuation of the balancing act between official Catholicism—which emphasizes scripture, tradition, and reason—and popular Catholicism—which has an expectancy that the contemporary world is the special time chosen by God for the unfolding of apocalyptic events. Several shrines across Europe have been accepted as diocesan sanctuaries while the Church remains uncommitted to the founding apparitions that gave rise to them. Future pronouncements about twentieth-century apparitions, such as Medjugorje, will probably reflect this spirit of compromise and achieve a circumscribed accommodation of popular devotion into the Catholic canon.

Bibliography

Albera, Dionigi and Couroucli, Maria (eds). 2012. *Sharing Sacred Spaces in the Mediterranean: Christians, Muslims and Jews at Shrines and Sanctuaries.* Bloomington and Indianapolis: Indiana University Press.

Alexander, Stella. 1979. *Church and State in Yugoslavia since 1945.* Cambridge: Cambridge University Press.

Allen, Michael. 2000. *Ritual, Power and Gender: Explorations in the Ethnography of Vanuatu, Nepal and Ireland.* Manohar: Sydney Studies in Society and Culture.

Alonso, Joaquin-Maria. 1967. *Historia da Literatura sobre Fátima.* Fátima: Edições Santuario.

Alonso, Joaquin-Maria. 1973. 'Histoire "Ancienne" et Histoire "Nouvelle" de Fatima', in *Vraies et Fausses Apparitions dans l'Église,* edited by Joaquin-Maria Alonso et al. Paris: Lethielleux.

Alonso, Joaquin-Maria. 1979. *The Secret of Fatima: Fact and Legend.* Cambridge: Ravensgate.

Alonso, Joaquin-Maria et al. (eds). 1973. *Vraies et Fausses Apparitions dans l'Église.* Paris: Lethielleux.

Apolito, Paolo. 1998. *Apparitions of the Virgin Mary at Oliveto Citra: Local Visions and Cosmic Drama.* University Park: Pennsylvania State University Press.

Apolito, Paolo. 2005. *The Internet and the Madonna: Religious Visionary Experience on the Web.* Chicago: University of Chicago Press.

Aquinas, Thomas. 1922. *Summa Theologiae Volume II.2 (CLXXI–CLXXXIX).* London: Burns, Oates, and Washbourne.

Ardagh, John. 1995. *Ireland and the Irish: Portrait of a Changing Society.* London: Penguin.

Art, Jan. 2012. 'The Cult of the Virgin Mary, or the Feminization of the Male Element in the Roman Catholic Church? A Psycho-Historical Hypothesis', in *Beyond the Feminization Thesis: Gender and Christianity in Modern Europe,* edited by Patrick Pasture, Jan Art, and Thomas Buerman. Leuven; Leuven University Press.

Association Opera dell' Amore. n.d. *The Apparitions of Our Lady in Schio.* Schio: Association Opera dell' Amore.

Astley, Jeff. 2002. *Ordinary Theology: Looking, Listening and Learning in Theology.* Aldershot: Ashgate.

Badone, Ellen (ed.). 1990. *Religious Orthodoxy and Popular Faith in European Society.* Princeton: Princeton University Press.

Badone, Ellen. 2007. 'Echoes from Kerizinen: Pilgrimage, Narrative, and the Construction of Sacred History at a Marian Shrine in Northwestern France'. *Journal of the Royal Anthropological Institute* 13: 453–70.

Barthas, Casimir and da Fonseca, Gonzaga. 1947. *Our Lady of Light.* Dublin: Clonmore and Reynolds.

Beattie, Tina. 2007. 'Mary in Patristic Theology', in *Mary: the Complete Resource,* edited by Sarah J. Boss. London and New York: Continuum.

Becarud, Jean. 1969. 'Spain', in *The Catholic Church Today: Western Europe*, edited by M. A. Fitzsimons. South Bend: University of Notre Dame.

Bennett, Jeffrey S. 2012. *When the Sun Danced: Myth, Miracles and Modernity in Early Twentieth-Century Portugal*. Charlottesville and London: University of Virginia Press.

Bertone, Tarcisio and Ratzinger, Joseph. 2000. *The Message of Fatima*. Vatican City: Congregation for the Doctrine of the Faith <http://www.vatican.va/roman_curia/con gregations/cfaith/documents/rc_con_cfaith_doc_20000626_message-fatima_en.html>, accessed 31 May 2015.

Bertone, Tarcisio and de Carli, Giuseppe. 2008. *The Last Secret of Fatima*. New York: Doubleday.

Beyer, Jean. 1959. 'Le Procès Canonique de Banneux Notre-Dame', in *Notre-Dame de Banneux Volume II*, edited by Louis-Jozef Kerkhofs. Liège: Dessain.

Billet, Bernard. 1973. 'Les Faits des Apparitions non reconnues par l'Église', in *Vraies et Fausses Apparitions dans l'Église*, edited by Joaquin-Maria Alonso et al. Paris: Lethielleux.

Bitel, Lisa. 2009. 'Looking the Wrong Way: Authenticity and Proof of Religious Vision'. *Visual Resources* 25 Nos. 1–2: 69–92.

Blackbourn, David. 1993. *Marpingen: Apparitions of the Virgin Mary in Bismarckian Germany*. Oxford: Clarendon.

Bode, Franz-Josef. 2000. Statement of 25 March. Heede <http://www.sankt-petrus-heede.de/cms/html/gebetsstaette/dokumente.html> accessed 31 May 2015.

Boss, Sarah J. 2000. *Empress and Handmaid: On Nature and Gender in the Cult of the Virgin Mary*. London and New York: Cassell.

Boss, Sarah J. 2004. 'The Immaculate Heart of Mary: Visions for the World', in *The Church and Mary* (Studies in Church History 39), edited by R. N. Swanson. Woodbridge: Boydell and Brewer.

Boss, Sarah J. 2007. 'Marian Consecration in the Contemporary Church', in *Mary: the Complete Resource*, edited by Sarah J. Boss. London and New York: Continuum.

Bossard, Alphonse and Chenot, Albert. 1981. 'L'Interprétation du Message de 1933 au Concile', in *Apparitions et Message de Beauraing: 1932–1982. Cahiers Marials* 130. Paris: Missionaires Monfortains de France.

Bouflet, Joachim. 2003. *Quand la Gestapo traquait les Apparitions*. Chambray-lès-Tours: CLD.

Bouflet, Joachim and Boutry, Philippe. 1997. *Un Signe dans le Ciel: Les Apparitions de la Vierge*. Paris: Bernard Grasset.

Bouritius, G. J. F. 1979. 'Popular and Official Religion in Christianity: Three Cases in Nineteenth-century Europe', in *Official and Popular Religion: Analysis of a Theme for Religious Studies*, edited by Hendrik Vrijhof and Jacques Waardenburg. The Hague: Mouton.

Bourke, Vernon J. 1945. *Augustine's Quest of Wisdom: Life and Philosophy of the Bishop of Hippo*. Milwaukee: Bruce.

Braun, Karl. 1998. Statement of 1 May. Heroldsbach <http://www.gebetsstaette-heroldsbach.de/htm/gruendung.htm> accessed 31 May 2015.

Brettell, Caroline B. 1990. 'The Priest and His People: the Contractual Basis for Religious Practice in Rural Portugal', in *Religious Orthodoxy and Popular Faith in European Society,* edited by Ellen Badone. Princeton: Princeton University Press.

Brinkmann, Johannes (ed.). 1999. *Mary in Heede: Queen of the Universe.* Meersburg: WETO-Verlag.

Brown, Lyn and Gilligan, Carol. 1992. *Meeting at the Crossroads: Women's Psychology and Girls' Development.* Cambridge, MA and London: Harvard University Press.

Bubalo, Janko. 1987. *A Thousand Encounters with the Blessed Virgin Mary in Medjugorje.* Chicago: Friends of Medjugorje.

Burnon, Pierre. 1933. *Le Vrai Visage de Tilman Côme.* Genval: Robin.

Burton, Richard E. 2004. *Holy Tears, Holy Blood: Women, Catholicism, and the Culture of Suffering in France, 1840–1970.* Ithaca and London: Cornell University Press.

Caldwell, Simon. 2008. 'Sex, Lies and Apparitions'. *The Spectator,* 4 October: 18–19.

Callahan, William J. 2012. *The Catholic Church in Spain 1875–1998.* Washington DC: Catholic University of America.

Campbell, Steuart. 1989. 'Fatima's Dusty Veil'. *New Humanist* 104: 22–3.

Carroll, Michael P. 1983. 'Visions of the Virgin Mary: The Effects of Family Structures on Marian Apparitions'. *Journal for the Scientific Study of Religion* 22/3: 205–21.

Carroll, Michael P. 1985. 'The Virgin Mary at La Salette and Lourdes: Whom did the Children see?'. *Journal for the Scientific Study of Religion* 24/1: 56–74.

Carroll, Michael P. 1986. *The Cult of the Virgin Mary: Psychological Origins.* Princeton: Princeton University Press.

Carroll, Michael P. 1992. *Madonnas that Maim: Popular Catholicism in Italy since the Fifteenth Century.* Baltimore and London: Johns Hopkins University Press.

Charue, André-Marie. 1946. *Beauraing: Documents Episcopeaux.* Remy: Diocèse de Namur.

Chiron, Yves. 2007. *Enquête sur les Apparitions de la Vierge.* Paris: Perrin/Mame.

Christian, William A. 1984. 'Religious Apparitions and the Cold War in Southern Europe', in *Religion, Power and Protest in Local Communities: The Northern Shore of the Mediterranean,* edited by Eric Wolf. Berlin: Mouton.

Christian, William A. 1989. *Person and God in a Spanish Valley,* rev. ed. Princeton: Princeton University Press.

Christian, William A. 1996. *Visionaries: The Spanish Republic and the Reign of Christ.* Berkeley: University of California Press.

Claverie, Élisabeth. 2003. *Les Guerres de la Vierge: Une Anthropologie des Apparitions.* Paris: Gallimard.

Coles, Robert. 1992. *The Spiritual Life of Children.* London: Harper Collins.

Comiskey, Brendan. 1989. 'A Contemplative not a Chatterbox'. *Irish Catholic,* 14 September.

Community of Divine Innocence website <http://divine-innocence.org> accessed 31 May 2015.

Corish, Marguerite. 1996. 'Aspects of the Secularisation of Irish Society 1958–1966', in *Faith and Culture in the Irish* Context, edited by Eoin Cassidy. Dublin: Veritas.

Craig, Mary. 1988. *Spark from Heaven: The Mystery of the Madonna of Medjugorje.* London: Hodder and Stoughton.

Curry, M. 1987. *'Faith and Hope': Our Lady's Message, Carns.* Culleens: Our Lady's Shrine.

Dammertz, Viktor Josef. 2000. Statement of 20 March. Augsburg <http://www.bistum-augsburg.de/index.php/bistum/Hauptabteilung-VI/Glaube-und-Lehre/Glaubenslehre/Glaubensfragen/Marienfried-Ereignisse-von-1946> accessed 31 May 2015.

Deevy, William. 1990. *Our Blessed Lady is Speaking to You. Are you Listening? Her Messages from Melleray Grotto*, 2nd ed. Melleray: Grotto Committee.

De Greeff, Etienne. 1933. 'Notes sur les Faits de Bearaing', in *Les Faits Mystérieux de Beauraing: Études, Documents, Réponses*, edited by Bruno de Jésus-Marie et al. Paris: Desclée de Brouwer.

De Jésus-Marie, Bruno. 1933. *Les Faits Mystérieux de Beauraing: Études, Documents, Réponses*. Paris: Desclée de Brouwer.

Delfosse, Jean. 1969. 'Belgium', in *The Catholic Church Today: Western Europe*, edited by M. A. Fitzsimons. Notre Dame: University of Notre Dame Press.

De la Sainte Trinité. 1984. *Apparitions à Medjugorje?* St Parres-les-Vaudes: Contre-Réforme Catholique.

De Marchi, John. 1986a. *Fatima from the Beginning*, 6th ed. Fátima: Missões Consolata.

De Marchi, John. 1986b. *Temoignages sur les Apparitions de Fatima*, 5th ed. Fátima: Missões Consolata.

De Montfort, Louis-Marie. 1957. *Treatise on the True Devotion to the Blessed Virgin*. Romsey: Fathers of the Company of Mary.

Derselle, C. 1933. *Et si c'était le Diable?* Brussels: L'Édition Universelle.

Dhanis, Edouard. 1944. 'Bij de verschijningen en de voorzeggingen van Fatima'. *Streven Jaargang* 11: 129–49, 193–215.

Dhanis, Edouard. 1952. 'À propos de "Fatima et la Critique"'. *Nouvelle Theologique* 64: 580–606.

Diocese of Southwark website <http://www.rcsouthwark.co.uk/statement_cdi_2.html> accessed 31 May 2015.

Drumm, Michael. 1996. 'Irish Catholics: A People formed by Ritual', in *Faith and Culture in the Irish* Context, edited by Eoin Cassidy. Dublin: Veritas.

Duffner, I. 2003. *The Art of Divine Love or Berthe Petit: Belgian Mystic and Apostle of the Devotion to the Sorrowful and Immaculate Heart of Mary*. Tanjore: Don Bosco.

Endean, Philip. 2007. 'How to Think about Mary's Privileges: A Post-Conciliar Exposition', in *Mary: The Complete Resource*, edited by Sarah J. Boss. London and New York: Continuum.

Ernst, Robert. 1988. *Die Seherin aus dem Ruhrgebiet*, new ed. Stein am Rhein: Christians-Verlag.

Evans, Martin and Godin, Emmanuel. 2014. *France since 1815*, 2nd ed. Abingdon and New York: Routledge.

Fahey, Tony. 1994. 'Catholicism and Industrial Society in Ireland', in *The Development of Industrial Society in Ireland*, edited by J. Goldthorpe and C. Whelan. Oxford: Oxford University Press.

Fernandes, Joaquim and d'Armada, Fina. 2007. *Celestial Secrets: The Hidden History of the Fatima Incident*. San Antonio and New York: Anomalist.

Flannery, Austin (ed.). 1996. *Vatican Council II: Constitutions, Decrees, Declarations*. Northport: Costello and Dublin: Dominican.

Frain, John. 2009. *The Cross and the Third Reich*. Oxford: Family Publications.

Gallagher, Christina website <http://www.christinagallagher.org> accessed 31 May 2015.

Garvey, Mark. 1998. *Searching for Mary: An Exploration of Marian Apparitions across the U.S.* New York: Penguin/Plume.

Gebara, Ivone and Bingemer, Maria Clara. 1989. *Mary, Mother of God, Mother of the Poor.* Tunbridge Wells: Burns and Oates.

Gebetstätte Wigratzbad. 2010. *Pilger in Wigratzbad.* Altötting: Kirche Heute Verlag.

Genicot, Leopold. 1973. *Histoire de la Wallonie.* Toulouse: Universitaires.

Ghiaie di Bonate website <http://www.madonnadelleghiaie.it/> accessed 31 May 2015.

Gilligan, Carol. 1991. 'Women's Psychological Development: Implications for Psychotherapy', in *Women, Girls and Psychotherapy*, edited by Carol Gilligan, Annie Rogers, and Deborah Tolman. New York: Haworth/Harrington Park.

Gilligan, Carol. 2011. *Joining the Resistance.* Cambridge and Malden: Polity.

Gilsdorf, Richard. 1990. 'Garabandal saved my Priestly Life'. *Garabandal* 23/3: 21–5.

Ginsborg, Paul. 1990. *A History of Contemporary Italy: Society and Politics 1943–1988.* London: Penguin.

Graef, Hilda. 1950. *The Case of Therese Neumann.* Cork: Mercier.

Greeley, Andrew. 1994. 'Are the Irish really losing the Faith?'. *Doctrine and Life* 3: 137–42.

Green, Celia and McCreery, Charles. 1989. *Apparitions.* Oxford: Institute of Psychophysical Research.

Griech-Polelle, Beth. 2002. *Bishop von Galen: German Catholicism and National Socialism.* New Haven: Yale University Press.

Griffiths, Richard. 1966. *The Reactionary Revolution: The Catholic Revival in French Literature 1870–1914.* London: Constable.

Guerrini, Fabrizio. 2008. 'Quella bambina che vedeva la Madonna'. *La Provincia Pavese*, 6 April 2008, <http://ricerca.gelocal.it/laprovinciapavese/archivio/laprovinciapavese/2008/04/06/PT3PO_PQ301.html> accessed 31 May 2015.

Guiot, Alain. 2010. *Les Apparitions de la Vierge Marie à Gilles Bouhours.* Paris: Lanore.

Hall, Brian. 1994. *The Impossible Country: A Journey through the Last Days of Yugoslavia.* Boston: David R. Godine.

Halliday, Robert. 2003. 'Father Clive Luget and the Visions of Middleton'. *Ecclesiology Today* 31: 23–9.

Harris, Ruth. 1999. *Lourdes: Body and Spirit in the Secular Age.* London: Penguin.

Hart, Tobin. 2003. *The Secret Spiritual World of Children.* Novato: New World Library.

Harvey, Graham (ed.). 2002. *Shamanism: A Reader.* London and New York: Routledge.

Hastings, Adrian (ed.). 1991. *Modern Catholicism: Vatican II and After.* London: SPCK.

Hastings, Derek. 2010. *Catholicism and the Roots of Nazism: Religious Identity and National Socialism.* Oxford: Oxford University Press.

Hay, David and Nye, Rebecca. 1998. *The Spirit of the Child.* London: Harper Collins/Fount.

Hermkens, Anna-Karina. 2009. 'Mary's Journeys through the Warscape of Bougainville', in *Moved by Mary: The Power of Pilgrimage in the Modern World*, edited by Anna-Karina Hermkens, Willy Jansen, and Catrien Notermans. Farnham: Ashgate.

Hierzenberger, Gottfried and Nedomansky, Otto. 1996. *Erscheinungen und Botschaften der Gottesmutter Maria: Vollständige Dokumentation durch zwei Jahrtausende.* Augsburg: Bechtermünz.

Hoggart, Keith, Buller, Henry, and Black, Richard. 1995. *Rural Europe: Identity and Change*. London: Edward Arnold.

Hornsby-Smith, Michael. 1994. 'Social and Religious Transformation in Ireland: A Case of Secularisation?', in *The Development of Industrial Society in Ireland*, edited by J. H. Goldthorpe and C. T. Whelan. Oxford: Oxford University Press.

Hornsby-Smith, Michael and Whelan, Christopher. 1994. 'Religious and Moral Values', in *Values and Social Change in Ireland*, edited by Christopher Whelan. Dublin: Gill and Macmillan.

Hughes, Gerald. 1987. 'Walking to Jerusalem 5: A Taste of Peace'. *The Tablet* 20 June: 655–6.

Hyde, Brendan. 2008. *Children and Spirituality: Search for Meaning and Connectedness*. London and Philadelphia: Jessica Kingsley.

Hynes, Eugene. 2008. *Knock: The Virgin's Apparition in Nineteenth-Century Ireland*. Cork: Cork University Press.

Inglis, Tom. 1987. *Moral Monopoly: The Catholic Church in Modern Irish Society*. Dublin: Gill and Macmillan/St Martin's.

Jacobs, Frans. n.d. *La Visionnaire d'Onkerzele: Leonie Van den Dyck (1875–1949)*. Malines: Frans Jacobs.

John of the Cross. 1994. *The Collected Works*. Washington DC: Institute of Carmelite Studies.

Jolić, Robert. 2013. 'Fabrications on Medjugorje: on Mart Bax' Research'. *Studia Ethnologica Croatia* 25: 309–28.

Jones, Michael E. 1998. *The Medjugorje Deception: Queen of Peace, Ethnic Cleansing, Ruined Lives*. South Bend: Fidelity.

Joset, Camille-Jean. 1981–4. *Dossiers de Beauraing*, 5 vols. Namur: Recherches Universitaires.

Jung, Carl. 1954. *Answer to Job*. London: Routledge and Kegan Paul.

Kaufman, Suzanne. 2005. *Consuming Visions: Mass Culture and the Lourdes Shrine*. Ithaca and London: Cornell University Press.

Kenny, Mary. 2000. *Goodbye to Catholic Ireland*. Dublin: New Island.

Kerkhofs, Louis-Jozef (ed.). 1953–9. *Notre-Dame de Banneux*, 3 vols. Liège: Dessain.

Kirby, Peadar. 1986. 'On Moving Statues: a People's Cry for Spirituality'. *Doctrine and Life* 4: 172–7.

Kowalska, Maria Faustina. 2012. *Divine Mercy in My Soul: Diary of Saint Maria Faustina Kowalska*. Stockbridge, MA: Marian.

Kraljević, Svetozar. 1984. *The Apparitions of Our Lady of Medjugorje*. Chicago: Franciscan Herald Press.

Kselman, Thomas. 1983. *Miracles and Prophecies in Nineteenth-Century France*. New Brunswick: Rutgers University Press.

Künzli, Josef. 1974. *Les Apparitions de Marienfried*. Jestetten: Miriam.

Künzli, Josef (ed.). 1996. *The Messages of the Lady of All Nations*. Goleta: Queenship.

Lambertini, Prospero. 1852. *Heroic Virtue: A Portion of the Treatise of Benedict XIV on the Beatification and Canonization of the Servants of God*, 3 vols. London: Thomas Richardson and Sons.

Laurentin, René. 1965. *Mary's Place in the Church*. London: Burns and Oates.

Laurentin, René. 1983. *The Life of Catherine Labouré*. Collins: Sisters of Charity of St Vincent de Paul/Vincentian Fathers.

Laurentin, René. 1986. *Medjugorje: Récit et Chronologie des Apparitions*. Paris: OEIL.

Laurentin, René. 1991. *The Apparitions of the Blessed Virgin Mary Today*, new ed. Dublin: Veritas.

Laurentin, René and Durand, Albert. 1970. *Pontmain: Histoire Authentique*, 3 vols. Paris: Lethielleux.

Laurentin, René and Joyeux, Henri. 1987. *Scientific and Medical Studies on the Apparitions at Medjugorje*. Dublin: Veritas.

Laurentin, René and Rupčić, Ljudevit. 1984. *Is the Virgin Mary Appearing at Medjugorje?* Washington DC: The Word Among Us Press.

Laurentin, René and Sbalchiero, Patrick (eds). 2007. *Dictionnaire des 'Apparitions' de la Vierge Marie: Inventaire des Origines à nos Jours, Methodologie, Bilan Interdisciplinaire, Prospective*. Paris: Fayard.

Laycock, Jospeh P. 2015. *The Seer of Bayside: Veronica Lueken and the Struggle to Define Catholicism*. Oxford: Oxford University Press.

Les Amis de Kerizinen. n.d. *Kerizinen: Messages of Christ and the Blessed Virgin 1938–1965*. Plounevez-Lochrist: Les Amis de Kerizinen.

Lewy, Guenter. 2000. *The Catholic Church and Nazi Germany*, new ed. Boston MA: Da Capo.

Leonard, Paul. 1990. 'The Plot (to Silence Our Lady) Thickens'. *Fatima Crusader* 31–2: 4–8.

Lipkes, Jeff. 2007. *Rehearsals: The German Army in Belgium, August 1914*. Leuven: Leuven University Press.

Luna, Luis. 1973. *La Mère de Dieu m'a Souri*. Paris: Nouvelles Éditions Latines.

Luna, Luis. 1976. *Le Vrai et le Faux Palmar*. Marquain: Jules Hovine.

Maisonneuve, Roland and de Belsunce, Michel. 1983. *San Damiano, Histoire et Documents*. Paris: Téqui.

Maistriaux, Fernand. 1932. *Que se passe-t-il à Beauraing?* Louvain: Rex.

Manuel, Paul Christopher. 2003. 'The Marian Apparitions in Fátima as Political Reality: Religion and Politics in Twentieth-Century Portugal'. *Center for European Studies Working Paper* 88: 1–21.

Margry, Peter J. 2009a. 'Paradoxes of Marian Apparitional Contestation: Networks, Ideology, Gender, and the Lady of All Nations', in *Moved by Mary: The Power of Pilgrimage in the Modern World*, edited by Anna-Karina Hermkens, Willy Jansen, and Catrien Notermans. Farnham: Ashgate.

Margry, Peter J. 2009b. 'Marian Interventions in the Wars of Ideology: The Elastic Politics of the Roman Catholic Church on Modern Apparitions'. *History and Anthropology* 20: 243–63.

Mariaux, Walter. 1942. *The Persecution of the Catholic Church in the Third Reich*. London: Burns and Oates.

Martindale, C. C. 1950. *The Message of Fatima*. London: Burns, Oates and Washbourne.

Martins, António. 1984. *Novos Documentos de Fátima*. Porto: Livraria Apostolado da Imprensa.

Matheson, Peter. 1981. *The Third Reich and the Christian Churches*. Edinburgh: T. and T. Clark.

Matter, Ann E. 2001. 'Apparitions of the Virgin Mary in the Late Twentieth Century: Apocalyptic, Representation, Politics'. *Religion* 31: 125–53.

McCafferty, Neil. 1985. 'Virgin on the Rocks', in *Seeing is Believing: Moving Statues in Ireland*, edited by Colm Tóibín. Dublin: Pilgrim.

McCann, Eamonn. 1985. 'A Most Impressive Scene to Behold', in *Seeing is Believing: Moving Statues in Ireland*, edited by Colm Tóibín. Dublin: Pilgrim.

McDonough, Frank. 2001. *Opposition and Resistance in Nazi Germany*. Cambridge: Cambridge University Press.

McGinnity, Gerard and Gallagher, Christina. 1996. *Out of the Ecstasy and onto the Cross: Biography of Christina Gallagher*. Achill: Our Lady Queen of Peace House of Prayer.

Miracle Hunter, web-based information on Marian apparitions <http://www.miraclehunter.com/marian_apparitions> accessed 31 May 2015.

Miravalle, Mark (ed.). 1995. *Mary Coredemptrix Mediatrix Advocate, Theological Foundations: Towards a Papal Definition?* Santa Barbara: Queenship.

Morcillo, Aurora G. 2008. *True Catholic Womanhood: Gender Ideology in Franco's Spain*. DeKalb: Northern Illinois University Press.

Morgan, David. 2009. 'Aura and the Inversion of Marian Pilgrimage: Fatima and her Statues', in *Moved by Mary: The Power of Pilgrimage in the Modern World*, edited by Anna-Karina Hermkens, Willy Jansen, and Catrien Notermans. Farnham: Ashgate.

Noel, Gerard. 2008. *Pius XII: The Hound of Hitler*. London and New York: Continuum.

Nolan, Mary and Nolan, Sidney. 1989. *Christian Pilgrimage in Modern Western Europe*. Chapel Hill: University of North Carolina Press.

Nye, Rebecca. 2009. *Children's Spirituality: What it is and Why it matters*. London: Church House.

O'Carroll, Michael. 1986. *Medjugorje: Facts, Documents, Theology*. Dublin: Veritas.

O'Connor, James. 1975. *Canon Law Digest*, Vol. 7. Mundelein: St Mary of the Lake Seminary.

O'Leary, Joseph. 1986. 'Thoughts after Ballinspittle'. *The Furrow* 37/5: 285–94.

Orsi, Robert A. 2009. 'Abundant History: Marian Apparitions as Alternative Modernity', in *Moved by Mary: The Power of Pilgrimage in the Modern World*, edited by Anna-Karina Hermkens, Willy Jansen, and Catrien Notermans. Farnham: Ashgate.

O'Sullivan, Mary. 1989. *Inchigeela: A Call to Prayer*. Inchigeela: Inchigeela Queen of Peace Group.

O'Sullivan, Michael E. 2009. 'West German Miracles, Catholic Mystics, Church Hierarchy, and Postwar Popular Culture'. *Zeithistorische Forschungen/Studies in Contemporary History* 6, <http://www.zeithistorische-forschungen.de/16126041-OSullivan-1-2009> accessed 31 May 2015.

O'Sullivan, Michael E. 2012. 'A Feminized Church? German Catholic Women, Piety, and Domesticity 1918–1938', in *Beyond the Feminization Thesis: Gender and Christianity in Modern Europe*, edited by Patrick Pasture, Jan Art, and Thomas Buerman. Leuven: Leuven University Press.

Paroisse de L'Île-Bouchard. 1988. *Les Faits Mystérieux de L'Île-Bouchard*. L'Île-Bouchard: Paroisse de L'Île-Bouchard.

Pasture, Patrick. 2012. 'Beyond the Feminization Thesis. Gendering the History of Christianity in the Nineteenth and Twentieth Centuries', in *Beyond the Feminization Thesis: Gender and Christianity in Modern Europe*, edited by Patrick Pasture, Jan Art, and Thomas Buerman. Leuven: Leuven University Press.

Paz, José. 2001. 'Perspectives on Religious Freedom in Spain'. *Brigham Young University Law Review* 2001/2: 669–710.

Pelletier, Joseph. 1970. *God Speaks at Garabandal.* Worcester MA: Assumption.

Pelletier, Joseph. 1971. *Our Lady Comes to Garabandal.* Worcester MA: Assumption.

Pérez, Ramon. 1981. *Garabandal: the Village Speaks.* Lindenhurst: Workers of Our Lady of Mount Carmel.

Petrisko, Thomas. 1995. *The Sorrow, the Sacrifice and the Triumph: The Apparitions, Visions and Prophecies of Christina Gallagher.* Achill: Our Lady Queen of Peace House of Prayer.

Phillips, Anne. 2013. 'God Talk/Girl Talk: A Study of Girls' Lives and Faith in Early Adolescence, with Reflections on those of their Biblical Fore-sisters', in *The Faith Lives of Women and Girls,* edited by Nicola Slee, Fran Porter, and Anne Phillips. Farnham and Burlington: Ashgate.

Pilgerverein Heroldsbach. 2009. *Rosenkönigin von Heroldsbach.* Passau: Kunstverlag Peda.

Poggi, Gianfranco. 1972. 'The Church in Italian Politics, 1945–50', in *The Rebirth of Italy 1943–1950,* edited by S. J. Woolf. London: Longman.

Pope, Barbara. 1985. 'Immaculate and Powerful: the Marian Revival in the 19th Century', in *Immaculate and Powerful: The Female in Sacred Image and Social Reality,* edited by Clarissa Buchanan, Constance Buchanan, and Margaret Miles. Boston MA: Beacon.

Porte, Cheryl A. 2005. *Pontmain, Prophecy, and Protest.* New York: Peter Lang.

Poulain, Auguste. 1950. *The Graces of Interior Prayer: A Treatise on Mystical Theology,* 5th ed. London: Routledge and Kegan Paul.

Preston, Paul. 1994. *The Coming of the Spanish Civil War: Reform, Reaction and Revolution in the Second Republic.* London and New York: Routledge.

Rahner, Karl. 1963. *Visions and Prophecies (Questiones Disputatae 8–10).* New York: Herder and Herder.

Rahner, Karl. 1974. *Mary, Mother of the Lord.* Wheathampstead: Anthony Clarke.

Ramet, Pedro. 1985. 'The Miracle at Medjugorje—a Functionalist Perspective'. *The South Slav Journal* 8, Nos. 1–2: 12–20.

Ratzinger, Joseph and Bovone, Alberto. 1990. *Donum Veritatis.* Vatican City: Congregation for the Doctrine of the Faith, <http://www.vatican.va/roman_curia/congregations/cfaith/documents/rc_con_cfaith_doc_19900524_theologian-vocation_en.html> accessed 31 May 2015.

Ratzinger, Joseph and Messori, Vittorio. 1985. *The Ratzinger Report.* Leominster: Fowler Wright.

Reck, William. 1996. *Dear Marian Movement: Let God be God.* Milford: Riehle Foundation.

Rhodes, Anthony. 1989. 'The Pope of the First World War: Benedict XIV (1914–1922)'. *The Month* June: 248–52.

Rooney, Lucy and Faricy, Robert. 1987. *Medjugorje Journal: Mary speaks to the World.* Great Wakering: McCrimmons.

Rutten, René. 1985. *Histoire Critique des Apparitions de Banneux.* Namur: Mouvement Eucharistique et Missionaire.

Ryan, Tim and Kirakowski, Jurek. 1985. *Ballinspittle: Moving Statues and Faith.* Cork: Mercier.

Rydén, Vassula website <http://www.tlig.org/en/testimonies/churchpos/> accessed 31 May 2015.

Sandhurst, B. G. 1953. *We Saw Her*. London: Longmans, Green and Co.

Santos, Lúcia. 1973. *Fatima in Lucia's own Words*. Fatima: Postulation Centre.

Sarrach, Alfons. 1997. *Die Madonna und die Deutschen*, 2nd ed. Jestetten: Miriam-Verlag.

Scheer, Monique. 2006. *Rosenkrantz und Kriegsvisionen: Marienerscheinungskulte im 20. Jahrhundert*. Tübingen: Tübinger Vereinigung für Volkskunde.

Schellink, Gustaaf. 1994. *Het Wonderbaare Leven van Leonie Van Den Dijck*. Onkerzele: Komiteit voor de zaak Leonie Van Den Dijck.

Schillebeeckx, Edward. 1964. *Mary, Mother of the Redemption*. London: Sheed and Ward.

Schillebeeckx, Edward and Halkes, Catharina. 1993. *Mary Yesterday, Today, Tomorrow*. London: SCM.

Schimberg, Albert Paul. 1947. *The Story of Therese Neumann*. Milwaukee: Bruce.

Schneider, Kathy. 2013. 'Defending Catholic Education: Secular Front Organizations during the Second Republic of Spain, 1931–1936'. *Church History* 82/4: 848–76.

Schönstatt International. 2010. *Schoenstatt: A Place of Grace*. Amtzell: Walther Schmid.

Schüssler Fiorenza, Elisabeth. 1994. *Jesus, Miriam's Child, Sophia's Prophet: Critical Issues in Feminist Christology*. London: SCM.

Schwebel, Lisa J. 2004. *Apparitions, Healings and Weeping Madonnas: Christianity and the Paranormal*. Mahwah: Paulist.

Šeper, Franciscus and Hamer, Hieronymus. 1978. *Normae Congregationis*. Vatican City: Congregation for the Doctrine of the Faith, <http://www.vatican.va/roman_curia//congregations/cfaith/documents/rc_con_cfaith_doc_19780225_norme-apparizioni_lt.html> accessed 31 May 2015.

Servais, Fernand. 1933. *La Verité sur les Faits Extraordinaires de Beauraing*. Brussels: Union des Oeuvres de Presse Catholique.

Shoemaker, Stephen J. 2007. 'Marian Liturgies and Devotion in Early Christianity', in *Mary: the Complete Resource*, edited by Sarah J. Boss. London and New York: Continuum.

Sivrić, Ivo. 1982. *The Peasant Culture of Bosnia-Herzegovina*. Chicago: Franciscan Herald Press.

Sivrić, Ivo. 1988. *La Face Cachée de Medjugorge, Volume 1: Observations d'un Theologien*. Saint-François-du-Lac: Psilog.

Skrbiš, Zlatko. 2005. 'The Apparitions of the Virgin Mary of Medjugorje: The Convergence of Croat Nationalism and her Apparitions'. *Nations and Nationalism* 11/3: 443–61.

Socci, Antonio. 2009. *The Fourth Secret of Fatima*. Fitzwilliam: Loreto.

Spretnak, Charlene. 2004. *Missing Mary: The Queen of Heaven and her Re-Emergence in the Modern Church*. New York: Palgrave Macmillan.

Starkie, Walter. 1934. *Spanish Raggle-Taggle: Adventures with a Fiddle in North Spain*. London: John Murray.

Stern, Jean. 1980, 1984, 1991. *La Salette: Documents Authentiques, Dossier Chronologique Intégral*. 3 Vols. Paris: Desclée de Brouwer/du Cerf.

Sudati, Ferdinando. 2004. *Dove Posarono i suoi Piedi: Le Apparizioni Mariane di Casanove Staffora (1947–1956)*, 3rd ed. Barzago: Marna Spiritualità.

Taylor, Thérèse. 2003. *Bernadette of Lourdes: Her Life, Death and Visions*. London: Burns and Oates.

The Lady of All Nations Foundation. 1999. *The Messages of the Lady of All Nations*. Amsterdam: The Lady of All Nations Foundation.

The Lady of All Nations Foundation. 2009. *Day of Prayer in Honor of Mary, the Mother of All Nations*. Amsterdam: The Lady of All Nations Foundation.

The Lady of All Nations Foundation website <http://www.de-vrouwe.info> accessed 31 May 2015.

Theotokos website <http://www.theotokos.org.uk/pages/approved/appariti/trefonta.html> accessed 31 May 2015.

Thurston, Herbert. 1934. *Beauraing and other Apparitions: An Account of some Borderline Cases in the Psychology of Mysticism*. London: Burns, Oates and Washbourne.

Toussaint, Fernand and Joset, Camille-Jean. 1981. *Beauraing: Les Apparitions*. Paris: Desclée de Brouwer.

Turner, Victor and Turner, Edith. 1978. *Image and Pilgrimage in Christian Culture: Anthropological Perspectives*. New York: Columbia University Press.

Turner, Victor and Turner, Edith. 1982. 'Postindustrial Marian Pilgrimage', in *Mother Worship*, edited by James Preston. Chapel Hill: University of North Carolina Press.

University of Dayton, Ohio, web-based information on Marian apparitions <http://campus.udayton.edu/mary/resources/aprtable.html> accessed 31 May 2015.

Van den Steen, Christian. 1996. 'Tilman COME dit Côme Tilman ou l'Aventure Beaurinoise sans Lendemain d'un "Miraculé"-Mystificateur'. *Beauraing et sa Région: Archéologie, Histoire et Folklore* 12: 22–36.

Van Gehuchten, Paul. 1933. 'Un Témoignage sur les Faits de Beauraing', in *Les Faits Mystérieux de Beauraing: Études, Documents, Réponses*, edited by Bruno de Jésus-Marie, Etienne de Greff, A Jansens, and P van Gehuchten. Paris: Desclée de Brouwer.

Van Osselaer, Tine. 2009. 'Christening Masculinity? Catholic Action and Men in Interwar Belgium'. *Gender and History* 21/2: 380–401.

Van Osselaer, Tine. 2010. 'Mystics of a Modern Time? Public Mystical Experiences in Belgium in the 1930s'. *Revue Belge de Philosophe et d'Histoire* 88: 1171–89.

Van Osselaer, Tine. 2012. 'Sensitive but Sane: Male Visionaries and their Emotional Display in Interwar Belgium'. *Low Countries Historical Review* 127/1: 127–49.

Van Osselaer, Tine. 2013. *The Pious Sex: Catholic Constructions of Masculinity and Femininity in Belgium, c.1800–1940*. Leuven: Leuven University Press.

Vernet, Marie-Reginald. 1988. *Le Vierge à Pellevoisin: Mère de Miséricorde et Mère de l'Église*. Paris: Téqui.

Vincent, R. 1992. *Please come back to me and my Son: Our Lady's Appeal through Christina Gallagher to the People of Ireland and all Humanity*. Achill: Our Lady Queen of Peace House of Prayer.

Volpini, Angela. 2003. *La Madonna Accanto a Noi*. Trento: Reverdito Edizioni.

Volpini, Angela website <http://www.angelavolpini.it> accessed 31 May 2015.

Vox Populi Mariae Mediatrici website <http://fifthmariandogma.com> accessed 31 May 2015.

Vrijhof, Hendrik and Waardenburg, Jacques (eds). 1979. *Official and Popular Religion: Analysis of a Theme for Religious Studies*. The Hague: Mouton.

Warner, Marina. 1990. *Alone of All her Sex: The Myth and Cult of the Virgin Mary*. London: Pan/Picador.

Wheeler, Douglas. 1978. *Republican Portugal: A Political History 1910–1926*. Madison: University of Wisconsin Press.

Whelan, Christopher and Fahey, Tony. 1996. 'Religious Change in Ireland 1981–1990', in *Faith and Culture in the Irish Context*, edited by Eoin Cassidy. Dublin: Veritas.

Wiinikka-Lydon, Joseph. 2010. 'The Ambivalence of Medjugorje: The Dynamics of Violence, Peace, and Nationalism at a Catholic Pilgrimage Site during the Bosnian War (1992–1995)'. *Journal of Religion and Society* 12: 1–18.

Wuillaume, L. 1982. 'Histoire de l'Interprétation du Message', in *Banneux, Apparitions et Message, le Cinquantenaire: 1933–1983. Cahiers Marials*. Paris: Missionaires Montfortains de France.

Zimdars-Swartz, Sandra L. 1989. 'Popular Devotion to the Virgin: The Marian Phenomena at Melleray, Republic of Ireland'. *Archives de Sciences Sociales des Religions* 67: 125–44.

Zimdars-Swartz, Sandra L. 1991. *Encountering Mary: From La Salette to Medjugorje*. Princeton: Princeton University Press.

Index

Printed and bound by CPI Group (UK) Ltd, Croydon, CR0 4YY